MW00856144

The Lost Way to the Good

THE LOST WAY
TO THE GOOD

Dionysian Platonism,
Shin Buddhism,
and the
Shared Quest to
Reconnect a Divided World

BY THOMAS PLANT

Angelico Press

First published in the USA
by Angelico Press 2021
Copyright © Thomas Plant 2021

For information, address:
Angelico Press, Ltd.
169 Monitor St.
Brooklyn, NY 11222
www.angelicopress.com

paper: 978-1-62138-790-9
cloth: 978-1-62138-791-6

Book and cover design
by Michael Schrauzer

For Yasuna

CONTENTS

ACKNOWLEDGMENTS

HOW FAR BACK SHOULD I LOOK DOWN THE track, to those who led me onto the old and trusted way which led me to write this book? My thanks could start from infancy. Some of my later childhood mentors are mentioned in the book, so I will leave them there for you to find in due time. The seeds were sown then, but they began to flower in my PhD thesis at Cambridge about a decade ago. This by no means a "book of the thesis," but since there is considerable conceptual overlap with it, particularly in the latter chapters, it may be a good landmark for beginning my thanks. I am grateful, therefore, to Professor Julius Lipner for taking me on as his doctoral student and guiding me, and to Professors Michael Pye and Douglas Hedley for examining and correcting my work. I am also indebted to Professor Hedley for inviting me to be a Fellow of the Cambridge Centre for the Study of Platonism, and to the members of the Centre's reading group whose wisdom has led me deeper into the tradition. Among them, I am especially grateful for my research partner in the project *Metaphysics Across Borders*, Hasan Spiker, for his guidance on the sections of this book pertaining to Islam, and for his prayers and fellowship.

In the Buddhist world, I thank Professor Kemmyo Taira Sato for keeping me involved in dialogue with the True Pure Land tradition at his Three Wheels Temple in London for over a decade, and Michael Conway, Takeshi Kaku, Mark Blum, Mitsuya Dake, Eisho Nasu, Dennis Hirota, and James Dobbins for the time and advice they gave me in Kyoto in conversations which they have by now probably forgotten, but which were very helpful to me. I owe especial thanks to John Paraskevopoulos of the Australian Honganji Buddhist mission, who encouraged me to write this book and meticulously proofread it.

I am grateful too to those who gave me the luxury of the time to write this book, among them the Spalding Trust, whose funding made it possible to reduce my teaching commitments; Mrs Susan Hannam, Head Teacher of Lichfield Cathedral School, who let me do so; and Bishop Zerubbabel Katsuichi Hirota, who made sure that my new employment at Rikkyo University left me time to complete my writing and revisions. Not least, I must thank my wife, Nao, who has tolerated me working through holidays while looking after our young family.

My final thanks are reserved for John Riess at Angelico Press for taking on what may seem to many editors a somewhat niche project by a first-time author, and for recognizing what I hope is its potential to address wide-reaching concerns about religion, tradition, and modernity from the apparently obscure bases of Dionysian Platonism and Shin Buddhism. He and his team have brought the journey to fruition, but not, I hope, to an end. There is travel yet to be done, and I am blessed with the best of fellow pilgrims.

RIKKYO UNIVERSITY, TOKYO
Saturday, 6 November 2021

INTRODUCTION

THE GOOD. *THE* GOOD. EVEN THE TITLE OF THIS book may raise hackles or, at least, an eyebrow. Anyone can accept that there is my good, or your good—but things that are good for me may not be so good for you. "The Good," with a capital G, suggests that there is one Good for you and me and everyone. But maybe you don't much like people telling you what's good for you. Maybe you think we should be free to decide on what is good for ourselves.

I can sympathize. To quote Fr Ted of 1990s Irish comedy fame, "I'm a priest, not a fascist: fascists walk around dressed in black telling people what to do." There are noble reasons to be skeptical of strict definitions of goodness imposed from on high. Suspicion against moral authority of any kind, whether Church, state, or family, is widespread. Given the moral failings of all three of those institutions, this is understandable, though I suspect there is rather more to explain the unprecedented extent of today's suspicion: a certain amount of transference and scapegoating, for a start. Those who hate the old authorities are at least as likely to adopt a hectoring and moralizing tone as the targets of their loud and public ire. So, to be clear, while this book is about absolute goodness — about *the* Good — it is not interested in moralizing. It is certainly not about me telling people what is good. It is not even about God telling people what is good. It is about *discovering* the Good: not imposing anything, but unveiling what is already there.

Already there? An incipient, universal goodness, not relative to what is good for me, or you, but a goodness that exists independently? The word "exist" will need a certain amount of nuancing, but broadly, yes. I know it defies what many North Americans and Western Europeans count as common sense. But that common sense, the common sense of only a minority of the population of the world, has only been so for a minority even of that minority's history.

This could now easily descend into a game of cowboys and Indians. I could line up the goodie philosophers and theologians against the baddies and show why the goodies need to win the fight. But the battle lines are readily reversed. The story of heroic frontiersmen turns into the story of beady-eyed genocidal colonists; the story of howling scalp-hunters into the story of victimized noble savages. The moral and spiritual reasoning that motivates one side becomes suspect and the other worthy of uncritical praise. The nostrum that history is written by the victors places the burden of critical scrutiny on their accounts of affairs, no doubt, but it does not render their accounts entirely untrustworthy or invalid. In reality, the various religious and philosophical traditions of the world have, at some time in their history, been responsible for both good and bad. Christianity has been oppressed and has instigated oppression. Islam, likewise. Dalai Lamas have ordered the destruction of entire villages on a point of Buddhist doctrine, and Zen was used to justify Second World War kamikaze tactics. Atheistic secularism, too, has been used to justify the incarceration, torture, and mass murder of religious people in the Socialist and Communist regimes of the French Revolution, USSR, and China, which continues to "re-educate" Uighur Muslims to this day. Admittedly, I do think those newer regimes are run to a great extent by "baddies," however well-meaning some of them may be, and I hope the reader may forgive me the occasional lapse into invective. But overall, this book is not about goodies and baddies. No amount of point-scoring of one religion against another, or of religion versus secularism, is going to get us back on the path.

That there is a path, though, I am in no doubt. It is just that those of us living in the West and, more broadly, countries under Western influence, have largely lost sight of it. It is a path that once reached from Ireland to Beijing, a way that wound carefully around the contours of reality: but Europeans and North Americans wanted faster, more direct routes. We were not content to discover reality. We had to invent reality for ourselves. We cut our own straight and narrow paths, blew our way through the hillsides with split atoms and surgical steel, lined the roads with soaring concrete towers, thought we could pave our way to paradise in a horizontal Babel of information highways. Satisfied with our new infrastructure, we blew up the bridges and cut ourselves off from the rest of the world. We knew better than them.

A popular account of modern Western superiority goes something like this: Once upon a time, we lived in a Dark Age of medieval superstition, hostile to scientific enquiry, with rigid class systems, gender roles, and dogmatic ideology, all imposed by violence on the basis of unsubstantiated articles of faith. Happily, the dawn of the Enlightenment brought scientific advances that have benefitted humanity, driven away the shadows of superstition, and emancipated women and the poor.

There is some truth to this picture — but not as much as often supposed. The Enlightenment has solved many problems, but it has created more. The particular problem I want to focus on is the privatization of truth and the relegation, on the pretext of reasoned Enlightenment neutrality, of any sense of the common good from the public square.

Ancient and medieval belief in the supernatural Good was not something privately held. It was argued publicly and rationally. Much of the time the nature of reality was disputed with a greater freedom than the popular image of the *Monty Python* Spanish Inquisition might have us suppose, and while the stakes were higher (and hotter) than nowadays, the modern Western academy is hardly in a position to preach to the past about the suppression of unpopular opinions: just ask Jordan Peterson or Germaine Greer. In ancient pagan Greece, the Islamic world, and medieval Christendom, rationally articulated belief in a real, absolute Good actively drove scientific discovery, and this trajectory paved the way to today's technological advances, for both good and ill. The Enlightenment sundering of faith from reason, on the other hand, used empirical, "scientific" methods of observation to justify sexism, racialism, and eugenics to indenture workers and to kill on an unprecedented scale. A misapplication of Darwin's findings would provide the scientific grounding for far more oppressive ideologies than any religion had ever contrived.

There are good reasons to be critical of Enlightenment claims for the objectivity of scientific, empirical reasoning. Its scope is limited by the weakness of our senses, the failures of our powers of observation, and more fundamentally by the bounds of time and space and laws of number within which it must operate. Metaphysical principles are beyond its purview. That said, science is not the "baddie" in this story. I will be critical of our technocratic mindset, but I am not about to don the tie-dyed hemp sackcloth of the eco-warrior and rally us back to the Stone Age. Modern science has been a great boon to humanity, but the same caveats apply to science as to the cowboy. The scientist's perspicacious gaze upon the great vistas of human knowledge has all too often narrowed to the prospector's greedy squint. As someone who relies on an electric-powered machine to sleep at night and looks forward (somewhat tentatively) to a Coronavirus vaccination, I am grateful for Western advances in medicine and biological science. On the other hand, the role of scientific experimentation in the development of the Coronavirus is, to say the least, unclear at time of writing. Its rapid propagation by modern transport technologies is surely undeniable. Evolutionary theory heralded a new age of eugenics and racialism. The splitting of the atom yielded both affordable energy and the most devastating weapons yet contrived, let alone Chernobyl and Fukushima. Motor cars and airplanes have brought the freedom of the sky and the open road, but they have forced mass movement of labor, thereby breaking up families and neighborhoods, and polluting the earth. A naive faith in science and Enlightenment empiricism is no better than a naive faith in anything else.

Nor will I don the black turtleneck of the French *philosophe* and profess that science is only one narrative among others and does not deserve its privileged claim to truth. Postmodernists and, later, advocates of critical theory have challenged the hegemony of Enlightenment assumptions, and in particular the assumption that the West, whether in its religion, its science, or its modern social mores, is superior to the rest of the world. To that extent I am in sympathy. Where I differ from postmodernists, insofar as I understand their famously and deliberately convoluted prose, is that I see their relativism and unremitting skepticism about all traditionally inherited social norms as the product of exactly the same historic errors of Western thought as the excesses of the Enlightenment they profess to despise. The Enlightenment modernists claim that scientific reason has sole access to universal truth and, despite its historical mistakes at vast environmental and social cost, the solution to the world's ills is to press on with more of the same, and to press it onto all people. They see postmodernists as destructive obscurantists with nothing to replace the society they want to overthrow. The postmodernists and their critical theorist heirs see the modernists as oppressive enforcers abusing their arbitrary and illegitimate power to crush all difference, but stress this difference to such a degree that they leave no room for any commonality. For them, all is multiplicity and difference; truth is to be defined solely by the exercise of power, and justice means seizing that power from the oppressor. Yet both modernists and postmodernists are in common thrall to a myth of inexorable progress: one by the reinforcement of social bonds, the other by their dissolution, and both by means of technologically augmented power. They are well-meaning, and in many cases their intentions overlap: it was, after all, a combination of religious and modernist sensibilities rather than postmodernist theory that led to the emancipation of slaves, votes for women, and the widespread decriminalization of homosexuality, for example. Their means to those ends, however, are limited by an obsession with power that is the peculiarly Western result of rejecting any appeal to a real, transcendent Good.

Neither the optimistic absolutism of the modernist faith in empirical reasoning nor the pessimistic skepticism of postmodernists can offer an escape from the social, environmental, psychological, and spiritual maladies of our day. This is not to deny that there is something of value to both the Enlightenment and its critics. What both parties need to consider, though, is the incoherence of articulating their values while simultaneously declaring their own position neutral, beyond cultural limitation, and value-free. At face value, the modernist would seem to be the worse culprit in this regard. Nonetheless, both the modernist and postmodernist decry the exceptionalism of their Christian forebears — the dogmatic, unbending, medieval Church — while they seek at least as forcibly to impose their own, single ideological agenda on the world. Those of more postmodern bent are faced with the incoherence of setting targets for diversity of race or gender while forbidding any diversity of thought; of militating for the downfall of consumer capitalism while promoting a consumerist mindset to sexuality and a proprietary approach to one's own body; of decrying the hegemony of Western medicine while treating sexual differentiation by reproductive organs as a problem in need of surgical or pharmaceutical solutions; of eliminating sexual binaries by binarizing body from mind and nature from culture; of arguing that gender and even sex are distinctions with no more than a socially constructed reality while professing support for women's rights; of denouncing all social constructs yet advocating socialism; of castigating imperialism while militating to erase any cultural resistance to their own ideology. The incoherence, in short, of declaring that the default worldview should be that there is no default worldview. If no worldview is ultimately true, then why should anyone believe theirs?

Either way, belief in any reality beyond the material is relativized and relegated to the status of purely private concern: a matter for consenting adults in the freedom of their own homes, as it were. Again, the intention is not bad. Freedoms of conscience and religion are hard-won and deserve protection. There is, however, a shadow side to the privatization of belief. Saying that anyone can believe what they like can easily segue into saying that what other people believe does not really matter. When you then artificially cordon off a section of supposedly inviolable mores and make them exempt from freedom of expression, you make a two-tier system that demarcates acceptable from unacceptable areas of public discourse. In our age of relativism, "unacceptable" is the euphemism of choice for judgmental and hence forbidden words like "bad," "evil," or "wrong." In the bad — sorry, *unacceptable* — old days (because to modernists and postmodernists alike the past is *always* unacceptable), our Christian ancestors used to think they were the ones with the One True Religion and a

God-given mandate to impose it on the world. Their modern, secularist successors like to think that we are over that now: that we have grown out of telling people what to believe and how to think. Unless, that is, we are talking about sex, or race, or rights, or politics, or science, or medicine, or pollution, or trade, or schooling. Modernists and postmodernists alike are quite happy to assert their superior understanding of these matters and to condemn any heretical deviations. You may believe what you like about the existence of the soul in a fetus, as long as you do not bring it to bear in any debate on those areas, such as medicine, science, law, or political discourse. For modernists, these topics have been quarantined from the public square by a supposed democratic consensus. Postmodernists, on the other hand, are justifiably suspicious of the power dynamics at play in establishing such a consensus, but their zeal to eliminate all traditional power structures ends with them promoting a single party line on almost every social issue. There are certain tenets to which we publicly have to subscribe, and our thoughts on these matters, however rationally we advocate them, are privatized into irrelevance. Any cultural resistance to these mores at home or abroad is to be stifled, either because from the modernist perspective those cultures are "medieval" and hence backward or, for the postmodernist, because they are oppressive. And sometimes they are; but the modernist's lack of self-reflection and the postmodernist's obsession with it limit the capacity for either to see the harm being caused by their own positions and impositions.

Whether it is religion, modernist scientism, or postmodern relativism that Westerners seek to impose on the world, our action amounts to exceptionalism and hubris. In each case we are claiming to have exclusive access to the truth, and that exclusivity is the besetting sin of the Occident. It is not that Western Christianity, Western science, and Western postmodern philosophy are without value. Far from it! The problems start when any one of these forgets that it is in itself only one part of a wider and older intellectual tradition, and attempts parricide. This is how fundamentalism is born, whether that of a paper pope or mitered monster, a green-gloved Goebbels or a Twitter tricoteuse. First, books are burnt and, before long, people.

But the West has not always understood itself to be the unique arbiter of acceptable thought. Peter Frankopan's *Silk Roads* books[1] have helped

---

1 Peter Frankopan, *The Silk Roads: A New History of the World* (New York: Vintage Books, 2017). Peter Frankopan, *The New Silk Roads: The Present and Future of the World*, Large print edition (Rearsby, Leicester: WF Howes Ltd, 2019).

remind readers that Europe has taken history's center stage only for the last few hundred years. Before that, Europe was a side-show. The real power was always in the East, flowing up and down the silk roads linking Europe to China. Until our own age of empire, we were subject to the vicissitudes of those old routes of trade and warfare, taking part in both in our own limited ways. The silk roads gave us a connection, albeit tenuous, to the rest of the known world. And what is true of our older economic and political connectivity to the wider world is also true of our intellectual and spiritual landscape. Parallel to the silk roads ran a string of intellectual silk nodes. For at least the first millennium, really until the late Middle Ages, the West was at the far end of a spool of interwoven philosophical threads that stretched all the way to China. The threads of Christianity, Islam, Zoroastrianism, and Buddhism were knotted together with a vast range of now much smaller schools and sects. Some of these are remembered in Gerard Russell's *Heirs to Forgotten Kingdoms*.[2] The knots were tied along the line in varying configurations. Loose ends would stick out from time to time and lead to their own unconnected destinations. Most of the threads would be tied off in some places, sometimes to be continued later down the line. But there was a continuity among them, even amid their diversity.

Europe's political and economic hegemony coincides with its sundering of that many-knotted thread. It was to Europe's economic gain that we made empiricism the exclusive arbiter of truth and depended more on the scientific method and the technologies that it produced. These innovations allowed Europeans to propagate their ideas, whether by printing press, carbine, or any of the other engines of empire. They led to advances in medicine which the West enjoys today and has contributed to the world, among other great material goods — though one must admit that we have often exported those goods by the violence of empire or the threat of economic sanction for those who refuse to accept our bounty. In any case, this overemphasis on the material has come at spiritual cost: the loss of the sense that the world has any value beyond its utility to us; the loss of recognition of people, plants, and animals as anything more than resources; the loss of wisdom that led us to believe the definition of reality is ultimately subject only to the most powerful will, whether God's or, in his absence, whoever can develop the most advanced weaponry to seize the most resources.

The thread that had bound Europeans to the rest of the world and to

---

2   Gerard Russell, *Heirs to Forgotten Kingdoms* (London: Simon & Schuster, 2015).

one another was, in the broadest sense, Platonism. This allowed the West to join in an endeavor, shared from Ireland to Beijing, of articulating not just physical but *metaphysical* reality. Medieval Christian scholars had seen truth in the works of Muslims and Jews, all of whom were working in recognizably the same Platonic framework. For later Western Christians, especially after the Reformation, the idea that any non-Christian might have access to any truth whatsoever became heretical. Even other Christians could be in the dark, whether the Antichrist was seen in the chair of St Peter or the pulpit of the Protestant tabernacle. Later, it was the atheistic revolutionaries who proclaimed themselves the enlightened ones. In short, whoever we were, we alone had the light. The rest of the world was superstitious and wrong. The West deserved to conquer the world's resources, its people, and even its gods.

The Western Church handed its mantle of exceptionalism over to modern Western secularists who increasingly denied the existence of anything beyond the things we could measure, weigh, seize, own, or kill. Now, Christians like me find our old exceptionalism turned against ourselves. In both the modern and postmodern West, among all world religions, Christianity holds a special place of opprobrium as the skeleton in the closet of our wayward past. There is a rather patronizing sense that while Westerners should have grown out of religious superstition by now, its persistence is understandable among less technologically advanced peoples and so, for now, we should humor their proclivities. We quite like our holiday selfies with saffron-robed Thai monks and our garden-center Buddhas, and we are all for the integration of Muslim immigrants, so we pay less attention to the less pacific historical elements of foreign religions than we do to those of our Western Christian forebears. This distaste for Christianity is amplified by guilt about historic missions in Africa, India, and the Far East. The hospitals, schools, sanitation systems, and agricultural methods which the missionaries imported along with their churches are seen in today's skeptical and power-obsessed age as a sweetening of the pill, cynical instruments of conquest, little victories of heart and mind to soften the ground for the cavalry and the concentration camps. This is part of the truth. But the precise nature of some of the less picturesque practices Christianity displaced, the eagerness with which so many Africans, Indians, and Asians adopted Christianity, and the fact of pre-existent, ancient Christian churches dating to long before the arrival of the colonists, are all omitted from this account. Nor is it straightforward to explain how either the modern or postmodern concern for justice, fairness, and the righting of wrongs could have sprung, pristine, from the wicked old Church if its moral soil was really as barren as all that. It is also naive to suppose that modern aid programs run by governments and NGOs come with no strings attached. Clearly, this is not true when the aid comes from China, an even less religious regime than any of ours in the West. But neither is it true of secular Western nations. We still see ourselves as the world's great liberators. We are either guiding the benighted natives to the glory of Enlightenment values or offering the critical tools Westerners have contrived to wean them off those same values. Western-educated, often white, middle-class liberals and post-liberals alike are telling Africans and Asians to abandon their convictions, including their religion, and are dismissive when they do not comply. And all the while we protest how different we are from our unenlightened Christian sires.

This new hostility towards Christianity in its former Western strongholds is forcing Christians to recognize the problems Western exceptionalism has caused, and perhaps none too soon. This can end up in a newly reactive exceptionalism of our own, as we look to keep our own company and separate ourselves off from a world that does not understand us anymore. But if we take a wider, more historical, view, we will see that we are not as isolated as we imagine. Many other people also seek a return to tradition of some kind. We are so entrenched in divisive categories and identities, so used to seeing the knots of the old rope cut out and neatly boxed away under the labels of "religions," that we have forgotten the common thread that once united us. Divided and conquered, we have lost sight of the fact that religious people by far make up the majority of the world, that we share many common intellectual and spiritual insights, and that together we have a much greater chance of resisting the ongoing atomization of society, obsession with material gain, and relativization of truth claims than any one of us can do alone.

While we may have paved over the lost way, we can still sometimes see it growing up through the cracks of our straight new roads. We have a truly Western tradition lying dormant which does not isolate us from the world, whether by the modernist strategy of pronouncing Western reason normative or by the postmodern strategy of making the denial of any common norms the one true norm. There is an alternative Western past that could yet be an alternative Western future: one that does not cut us off from the wider philosophical and spiritual traditions of the world, but reconnects us with them. A Platonic approach to our historic Christian faith can unite us with ancient religions and philosophies, living and dead, throughout the world. Platonism offers a once common way of which we have, to the detriment of the whole world, lost sight.

I cannot hope to give an exhaustive account of the interplay of all world religions and philosophies. Even if that were possible in a single book, it is well beyond my competence or wit. There is undoubtedly fruitful work to be done on the comparison between various strands of Platonism and, say, African, native American, or shamanistic metaphysics. Even the multitude of religions and philosophies that stretch from Ireland, via Europe and North Africa, through Central Europe, India, and out to Asia would require far more than a single lifetime to study in depth; and I will be venturing into territory en route which is still fairly new to me. I hope experienced travelers in some of the inner realms will excuse any naivety or oversimplification. One such, my research partner Hasan Spiker, has saved me from several errors in my exploration of the Islamic world, and any that remain are mine alone. My claim to expertise lies at the extreme ends of the trail, and what passes between them makes for a necessary and, I think, illuminating bridge.

In this book you will meet one of the most influential Christian Platonists in the Church, both East and West, who called himself Dionysius the Areopagite. His philosophy is going to guide you down that shared route, following the thread of Platonism as it connects the West with the Church of the East and Islam, and leads us all the way to China. You will see how, even though the thread did not reach Japan, the way it intertwined with Buddhism gives Christian and Japanese Buddhist philosophy enough of a common language to make some mutual sense of the world. Stopping in medieval Kyoto, we will meet Shinran Shonin, founder of the True Pure Land school of Buddhism native to Japan, and see how traditions of the West and East can unite to challenge the relativism and power-obsession of secular modernity, reconnecting us instead to humanity's common and ancient quest for transcendent truth and goodness. We are going to see how a broadly Platonic insight, spread not by the power of empire but by the largely peaceful missionary endeavors of a minority Eastern Church, offers the possibility of mutual intelligibility with Japanese True Pure Land Buddhism and the articulation of a shared, transcendent Good.

The choice of Dionysius and Shinran is not arbitrary. Demonstrating not only a mutual intelligibility but a comparable articulation of a real, metaphysical Good between two religious thinkers from such radically disparate cultures and philosophical backgrounds helps answer objections from both Enlightenment secular modernists and their relativistic postmodern critics. Challenging the Enlightenment's exclusive commitment to scientific empiricism for the validation of truth claims, Dionysius and Shinran together can take the debate on whether sensory data is really enough to guarantee true knowledge outside its usual and rather stale range of self-referential, intra-Western suppositions. There is enough shared metaphysical ground between them to point towards a real, universal goodness, to a reality beyond empirical knowledge but on which such knowledge relies. Western science alone is not enough to ascertain the fullness of truth. However, the inter-cultural and inter-philosophical nature of the comparison also stands against the postmodernist assertion that there is no commonality, that all is particular and culturally relative. Dionysius and Shinran paint pictures of a universe very different from the Hobbesian war zone of bare matter and conflicting power interests in which the West has come, at least implicitly, to believe. Their pictures have far more in common with one another than either has with a materialistic view of the world, and that commonality belies claims of mere cultural relativism.

Japan's place in these metaphysical questions is paramount. Like the West, Japan has certainly been guilty of exceptionalism. In more recent history, this has been a response to Western colonial threats and an emulation of their behavior. From the late-nineteenth to the mid-twentieth centuries, Japan actively absorbed a great deal of technological, scientific, cultural, and philosophical insights from the Enlightenment. What makes Japan unusual in this regard is that it managed this without being colonized and so, more or less, on its own terms. Even the effective colonization of Japan by US forces after the Second World War has not obliterated Japan's deeper cultural and philosophical currents, though it certainly has affected them. The Japanese adoption and mediation of Western thought is unusual, if not unique, in that it is elective rather than coerced. Bringing Japan into our metaphysical deliberations gives us a robust and selective riposte to any Western philosophical exceptionalism. At the same time it subverts postmodern (and at times rather patronizing) expectations of a power imbalance between Enlightenment thought as "white" and colonial, and every other kind of thought from "non-white" nations as necessarily oppressed. Japanese thought does not fit so neatly into that paradigm. The thought of Shinran and his successors shows how traditions of the West and East can unite to call the world back from its decline into relativism and power-obsession, and reconnect us instead to our common quest for transcendent truth and goodness. I hope this will encourage Westerners not to abandon the canon of Western philosophy, religion, art, and literature, but to give it new life, growth, and fruitfulness by re-grafting it onto the great and ancient vine from which it has been untimely sundered.

THE LOST WAY

Nel mezzo del cammin di nostra vita
mi ritrovai per una selva oscura,
che la diritta via era smarrita.

"Midway this way of life we're bound upon,
I woke to find myself in a dark wood,
Where the right road was wholly lost and gone."
— Dante, *Inferno* I.1 [1]

M Y WIFE AND I ARE AMONG THE STRANGE few of our age in the United Kingdom who go to church. Our children are still too young to have been ridiculed out of such reactionary ways by their classmates. I give it a few years. But even our non-religious parent friends fear the impact of today's secular culture on their progeny. That the West has lost its way seems to be the consensus of friends who, like me, have made it to what we hope is the middle of our lives. One worry is the Internet, of course, with its suicide help sites, identitarian "support" groups, and the infinite video library of free hard-core pornography we now bequeath to our children as soon as we cave in and give them a cell phone, often before they even reach puberty. Then there is the consumer ethos it instils in them from infancy as they watch videos on TikTok or YouTube of other children opening consumer goods. Children who might once have aspired to be doctors, soldiers, or some other kind of public servant now aspire to be social media "influencers," serving only themselves, and ideally with the least work possible—an aspiration reaffirmed by the degenerate, blinged-up celebrities whose lifestyles the web throws up for emulation. And woefully, all this seems to be accepted by educationalists, who genuflect to the latest Twitter-inflicted ideological absurdity and stigmatize those who will not conform. Our children are taught in school that the old ways have failed,

---

1 Dante Alighieri, *Hell*, ed. Dorothy L. Sayers (Harmondsworth, Middlesex: Penguin Books, 1949).

I

that the works of men and women of the past are worth only enough of a glance to compare their defects with today's enlightened mores: and if the only way you can be persuaded to ditch the old ways is by being bullied out of them, then frankly, you are getting what you deserve. The only dogma teachers are openly encouraged to proclaim is relativism, especially in the Religious Studies classroom: some people think X, others think Y, but it doesn't really matter, because whatever you think up for yourself is equally "valid." And as we open them up to these supposedly infinite vistas of freedom and self-definition, as we give them the matches to burn the old forests down, as we take away the last stable remnants of their identities and encourage them to start again from scratch, we find ourselves mysteriously unable to explain why the children of some of the most secularized, liberated, technologically abundant nations of the world (the UK and USA among them) are reportedly the unhappiest, most self-hating, self-harming, and body-obsessed. And what do we prescribe as a solution? More of the same.

Many people my age are looking back to old ways. They are longing for a return to tradition, or at least an escape from the consuming glare of the glowing rectangles we so idolize. The problem is that, never having been shown the way, they do not know which fork to choose. Do we go back to Enlightenment values?[2] To the Tridentine Mass? To the Book of Common Prayer? To Steiner and Montessori (wooden toys and organic foods, an infant Walden for the middle classes)? To the front porch,[3] bourbon with the neighbors, a trusty hound and a shotgun by the rocking chair? Or bunker in and cloister up like Culdee monks on some frozen rock, sheltered from the tsunami of liberalism cascading over the Atlantic?

Each of these new traditionalist movements in the West — however laudable — tends towards isolationism. Take Rod Dreher's *Benedict Option*.[4] Dreher sees that Christians are now becoming a minority in the US and exhorts us to form ecumenical communities together to preserve our faith, retreating from state education and the wider world, along Benedictine lines. From where I write in the United Kingdom, the symptoms Dreher diagnoses are all the more evident. We have a national church that claims for itself an historic episcopate in Apostolic Succession, a particular commitment

---

2   Steven Pinker, *Enlightenment Now: A Manifesto for Science, Reason, Humanism, and Progress* (London: Penguin Books, 2018).

3   www.frontporchrepublic.com.

4   Rod Dreher, *The Benedict Option: A Strategy for Christians in a Post-Christian Nation* (New York: Sentinel, 2017).

to Holy Scripture, and boasts both a Reformed inheritance and continuity with its Catholic origins. Yet in practice it is barely differentiable from the liberal Protestant congregations perishing all around it. Its noble claim to sacralize the nation through its role in crowning the monarch is treated with contempt even by its own clergy, who are largely liberal left-leaning. Instead, following in the wake of the Liberationist motifs that rippled out from the *aggiornamento* party of the Second Vatican Council, it prioritizes orthopraxy over orthodoxy, works over belief, form over content, and variety over unity to the extent that it appears less a church than a franchise. There is no consistent sense of identity or mission. Many of the clergy seem to think their primary role is patching up the holes in the welfare state. We are, in the words of Gavin Ashendon (a former Chaplain to the Queen who has recently converted to Roman Catholicism) little more than "a sort of not-too-irritating chaplain to a secular and hedonistic culture."[5]

As a former schoolmaster and a Christian parent, the fear I most share with Dreher is the loss of our children from the Church. Young people are desperately seeking identity and roots. Alas, they will seldom find them in an English church, and so the churches are largely bereft of children. If you need any further evidence for the utter failure of the Church of England to offer anything worthwhile to the young, you might note that despite the Church running a quarter of the nation's primary (what Americans call elementary) schools, only 1% of 18 to 25-year-olds consider themselves Anglican.[6] By this metric, activists in the National Secular Society would be better off campaigning for more Church schools than for their closure.[7] It is tempting for those of us who can afford it to follow Dreher's advice and set up home schools to educate our children ourselves.

Now, I revere St Benedict, founding father of Western monasticism, as much as Dreher does. But as Dreher, himself an Eastern Orthodox Christian knows, Western Christianity is not even half the story of the Christian Church, let alone of the rest of the world that might also want to resist Western secularism. What gives me an unusual angle as a midlife advocate for the restoration of tradition in the West is that about twenty years ago I came to love the tradition of Japan. My Western attitude towards tradition has been formed by my experience of the East. Aikido and Buddhism guided me from atheist materialism to Christianity, and to the study of

---

5   https://www.spectator.co.uk/article/the-benedict-option.

6   2018 British Social Attitudes survey, accessible at https://www.bsa.natcen.ac.uk/media/39284/bsa35_full-report.pdf.

7   https://www.nomorefaithschools.org/.

ancient philosophical texts left by the mysterious theologian who called himself Dionysius.[8]

*   *   *

Dreher is right to say that Western Christians are new to minority status. For centuries, we have enjoyed a privileged relationship with power, both to our boon and doom. Our relationship with actual minorities has at times been atrocious: just ask the Jews. But look to the East and you find Christians who have had to live closely with non-Christians right from the outset: sometimes as a majority, but in proximity to much larger Muslim nations, sometimes as a minority under Muslim rule, and in the case of the "Nestorian" Churches of the East as a missionary church among Buddhists, Taoists, and more. Their methods have ranged from polemical to peaceable, but among the fathers of their tradition we find a reverence for a non-Christian philosophy, one that gave them a language with sufficient conceptual overlap to allow meaningful missionary and intellectual engagement with non-Christians. In the East as in the West, for at least the first millennium after Christ, and despite their differences, pagans, Jews, and Muslims shared a common intellectual and spiritual framework.

Dionysius's philosophy shows us an older, truer path as key to the West as is the path of St Benedict. It once formed a very different Western way of navigating reality, and importantly, it does not isolate us from the rest of the world. In fact it is the secular assumptions of tolerance and neutrality that divide Western philosophy from the traditional philosophies of the rest of the world, and also divide those traditions from one another, conveniently categorizing them as "religion," privatizing their wisdom, relegating it to the realm of unprovable opinion, and so disempowering them. Dionysius's older way gave us an approach which, like an intellectual analogue to the Silk Road, enabled mutually intelligible philosophical dialogue from Ireland to Beijing. It was a path on which St Benedict himself walked. It was the way of Platonism.

My use of the "P-word" will not meet universal approbation. There are those for whom any such Hellenistic intrusions into the pure, Hebraic world of revealed Christianity is an idolatrous anathema, a genuflection

---

8   The most recent translation is the very readable single volume Pseudo-Dionysius the Areopagite, Colm Luibhéid, and Paul Rorem, *Pseudo-Dionysius: The Complete Works* (New Jersey: Paulist Press, 1987). However, this edition can be misleading in the way it paraphrases the text, especially in its elision of theurgic or sacramental themes. For a closer translation I recommend John Parker, *The Works of Dionysius the Areopagite* (London: James Parker and Co., 1897).

to the bloodless god of the philosophers.[9] These are likely to be the more Protestant readers, who tend to see salvation history in terms of irruption and discontinuity. To them I will try to demonstrate that Christian interaction with Greek philosophy itself has biblical precedent and that the line between Jew and Greek cannot be so firmly drawn.

Then there are those who will object on political grounds to the ill uses of Plato in justifying tyranny and despotism. Plato's ideal republic was, after all, the martial state of Sparta. His ideas exercised considerable influence on the political thought of Ayatollah Khomeini in the establishment of revolutionary Iran. Many moderns would side with philosopher Karl Popper in labelling Plato an enemy of the open society. Objectors to Plato on political grounds may, further, attribute his hierarchical ordering of society to the supposed dualism of his thought between the spiritual and the material, in which the former takes precedence by far over the latter. This Platonic dualism, they might opine, is the catalyst for Descartes and for the eventual mechanization of the cosmos in Western philosophy, the abstraction of epistemology from metaphysics, and the ultimate disenchantment of matter, to grave and deleterious effect. Platonism does indeed have its dualizing moments and offers ammunition to those who are skeptical of empirical reason, but as we will see, it is a broader school than just that.

The breadth of Platonism leads to the third category of potential objectors, those assiduous scholars for whom such casual use of the word will provoke the question of which Platonism we are we talking about. By answering their query I think we can sooth some of the political and metaphysical objections. Without doubt, the dualizing strand of Platonism has for many centuries in the West been dominant, but this is not the only Platonism. It will be my task to unravel and display another major strand.

This other, more Eastern, Platonism is exemplified by the fifth-century Proclus of Athens, where he was head of Plato's Academy for fifty years, though his influences were not limited to Greece or Greek thought. They went beyond Europe altogether. Proclus was born in Constantinople and studied for years in Alexandria, Egypt. His philosophical forefather was the Syrian Iamblichus, who claimed a lineage not only from Plato but from Pythagoras and by extension from the wisdom of the Indian and Egyptian sages too. This strain of Platonic thought challenged the dualism between spirit and matter that is today commonly attributed to Platonism as a

---

9   See e.g., Rosemary Arthur, *Pseudo-Dionysius as Polemicist: The Development and Purpose of the Angelic Hierarchy in Sixth Century Syria* (Aldershot: Ashgate, 2008).

whole. In this, it resonates with the non-dualism of Indian and Chinese thought. It was highly influential on the strictly monotheistic thought of Islam. It also influenced the sacramental theology, philosophy, and aesthetic theory of Western Christendom, an influence we can trace to that shadowy Eastern Christian theologian, philosopher, and mystic who wrote under the pseudonym of Dionysius.[10] Via the likes of John Scottus Eriugena (810 – 877), St Thomas Aquinas (1225 – 1274), the twelfth-century Victorines, Meister Eckhardt (1260 – 1327), Nicholas of Cusa (1401 – 1464), St Teresa of Avila (1515 – 1582), and St John of the Cross (1542 – 1591), to name a few, the Areopagite has arguably exercised an influence on Western theology equaled only by St Augustine. In the East, his metaphysics have made the Christian faith intelligible to non-Christians because of the shared ground he offers. For Platonists like Dionysius, the highest orthodoxy is truth, wherever it may be found.

Your heresy radar may be flashing up "relativism" at this point. Christian traditionalists, among whom I number myself, may find it outrageous to suggest that there be any truth beyond the One who is the Way, the Truth, and the Life. Such readers may be instinctively suspicious even of ecumenism, let alone the nebulous aegis of "interfaith" work that covers such a multitude of sins. Without syncretizing or watering down the unique claims of the Christian faith, I mean to show not only that cooperation in the pursuit of truth between Christians and other religious traditions is possible, but that it stands to benefit the world and is rooted in our historic Christian faith. If Christians are to become part of the solution to the problems of secularism, we must begin to work more closely with others, even as we clean our own house. Yet we must go deeper than mere acknowledgement of differences and a gentlemen's agreement to cooperate in social and political projects. Nor is a polite exchange over one another's scriptures enough. Joining the modern Cambridge Platonist Douglas Hedley in both his skepticism towards seeing "all religions as sharing a basic structure" and his commitment "to noticing the surprising currency and universality of theism among different cultures,"[11] I want to take this further and explore the possibilities of metaphysical commonality even in non-theistic traditions. The sacramental metaphysics of Dionysian Platonism offers Christians a language that can help us make allies of others who

---

10   Henri-Dominique Saffrey, "New Objective Links Between the Pseudo-Dionysius and Proclus," in *Neoplatonism and Christian Thought*, ed. Dominic J. O'Meara (New York: SUNY Press, 1982), 64–74.

11   Douglas Hedley, *The Iconic Imagination* (New York: Bloomsbury, 2016), 187.

equally strongly desire and seek the truth, and want to stand against the nihilism of our age. Divided and conquered, we all face the same erosion of our continuity with God, the cosmos, and one another. Dionysius worked with the inheritance of pagan Platonic thought, and most likely even studied together with non-Christian philosophers and spiritual leaders.[12] We can do the same, and we need to. We will rediscover the great tradition of the West only by joining it back to the web of Eastern wisdom. The two, we will see, used to be far more closely intertwined.

Starting from the Areopagus, we are going to walk a way that might help us not only preserve the Christian faith, but discern a common metaphysical language for the re-enchantment of creation: a task as vital for Greeks as for Jews, for Muslims as for Christians, for Japanese as for Americans.

---

12 Saffrey, "New Objective Links."

AT THE AREOPAGUS

S OME TWENTY YEARS AFTER HIS MIRACULOUS experience of divine light and conversion to Christ, in the AD 50s, St Paul stepped for the first time onto mainland European soul to proclaim the Gospel.

It is tempting to set this date as the advent of an Eastern religion in the West: the sect of Jews who for less than a decade had been called by the name "Christian."[1] Yet to pretend that Paul's upbringing had been strictly "oriental," to translate the geographical divide of the Bosphorus into a cultural one between East and West, would be an oversimplification. A native of cosmopolitan Tarsus, a city to the north of Cyprus on the east Mediterranean coast in what is now Turkey, Paul was already a man of overlapping identities: a Jew, yes, but also a Roman citizen who had served in the Army. He spoke Latin and Aramaic, but his native tongue, and so his native way of thought, was Greek.

Thanks to Alexander's conquests over three centuries before, Greek was the lingua franca of the now Roman Middle East, part of the greater empire of which Paul was a citizen. Tarsus was ten miles upriver of the Mediterranean and six miles south of the main trade route to Syria and Asia Minor, so Paul would have known the full diversity of the Empire from childhood. He would have seen the people and heard the languages of traders from all over the Empire and beyond, including those who brought in the riches of North Africa and Asia. Whether they came from Gaul or the Ganges, if they wanted to trade, they would need to speak Greek. The language that gave us the very word and concept of "Europe" was spoken far beyond the bounds of that continent. Today's East-West binary would have seemed less obvious to Paul than it does to us nowadays.

The binary of Jew and Greek was likewise blurred. Jews like Paul spoke Greek, thought in Greek, wrote Greek, studied the Scriptures in Greek, even worshipped in Greek. Many Jews lamented this elision of their culture, but more often it seems they enjoyed living with the freedoms it brought.

---

1   Acts 11:26.

Some feared the Jewish way of life would be diluted to nothing. Maccabees, the Dead Sea Scrolls, and the Christian Scriptures show that some tried to extricate themselves from the Greek way of life, isolating themselves in communities such as that at Qumran, or like Judas and the Zealots, taking up arms against the Roman oppressors.

Paul's approach was different. As far as he was concerned, the Spirit which had opened the mouths of the Apostles and the ears of their hearers at Pentecost, that the Gospel might be known in the languages of all people, was the same Spirit of light which had opened his eyes and breathed to him the voice of the Lord at Damascus.[2] He had been chosen to play a special part in the Spirit's work. He saw the potential of Christ's person and his Gospel to bring to reality the messianic prophecies of the Jewish scriptures, which foretold the day when people of all nations would gather to worship the one God of his fathers, Abraham, Isaac, and Moses. Instead of isolating the Jews from the Greeks, he would make the Greeks into honorary Jews.

So when Paul stepped into Athens in the late 50s he did so not as a stranger, not as a foreigner, but as a fellow citizen of an extraordinarily diverse empire, who spoke the language of the people as his own tongue. An educated and literary man, he spoke not only the utilitarian language of commerce, but was versed in the Greek philosophical and cultural debates of his day. He was well equipped to speak the language of the Greek philosophers in their historic home of Athens. Yes, Paul went first, naturally enough, to his kinsmen, his fellow Jews, to debate with them in their synagogue; but, no stranger to controversy, he then took his conversation into the Agora, as we read in Acts 17:17 onwards.

Generally translated "marketplace," the Agora can have misleading implications for those of us raised with the modern European mindset of a clear division between public and sacred space, or even between mercantile and political realms. We must remember whenever we read texts from the ancient world that secularism is a modern invention. The Agora was where, for centuries, Athenian men had come to spend their mornings in trade, certainly, but also in philosophical conversation, political decision-making and, vitally, in worship of the gods. To them, as to the ancient Jews, it would have seemed perverse to separate such realms. How could anyone trade without political implications, without building or breaking social bonds, relationships, hierarchies of patron and petitioner? And what folly, or worse still hubris, it would be to engage in any such transactions without divine blessing. All these dealings gave birth to and indeed necessitated

---

2   Acts 9:1–22.

philosophical questions, discussion about what life was for and how it should best be lived. The notion that this should be an arbitrary matter for the individual to decide and that commerce could be undertaken in isolation from social, moral, or spiritual considerations would have seemed absurd; and still less that the government should exist only to lubricate the tracks of such transactions. For leisured men in the Agora there was no division between politics, business, and worship, and they could enjoy relaxed discussion of all these things while their slaves toiled on their estates. Paul was not some isolated street preacher of the modern sandwich-board sort. Speaking in the Agora was part of the Athenians' everyday activity.

Even so, Paul's words drew the attention of the authorities. He was summoned to the ancient law court on the Areopagus, a rocky outcrop to the West of the Acropolis. On this hill named after Ares, God of War, Paul would proclaim the God of Peace.

The irony was at home, for this was where in 399 BC the Greek father of irony was famously sentenced to death. Accused of corrupting the young by teaching disrespect for the gods, Socrates could have avoided his fate. His friend Crito offered to bribe the jailers for his release. It would be just, he pleaded: Socrates was innocent of the charge against him. But Socrates replied, according to the dialogue which bears Crito's name, that justice required him to obey the law, even if it demanded his death. [3]

Socrates placed the law of his city above his own personal interest. For Athenians the law was sacrosanct, as was the Torah for Jews. The Attic analogue for Moses was Solon, the legendary lawgiver supposed to have established the city's rules on the very Areopagus where Socrates was tried, and Paul would be tested 450 years later. It is no coincidence that both Solon's law and those of Moses, Socrates, and Paul, were bequeathed in high places, whether the Areopagus or Sinai. All were seen as divine gifts. By Paul's time, Judaism and Greek wisdom had mingled and supported one another in their convictions. Both were seen as fundamentally in harmony with the laws which, by divine governance, were woven into the cosmos: in the movement of the planets, the laws of mathematics, the very growths and surgings of nature itself.

The essential harmony of divine and natural law was professed by Socrates himself, or at least by Plato's version of him, especially in the dialogue *Gorgias*. [4] By St Paul's time the dominant philosophies in Athens were those

---

3 *Crito* 50c ff.

4 *Gorgias* 508a: "Gods and men are held together by communion and friendship, by orderliness, temperance, and justice; and that is the reason, my friend, why they call

of the Stoics and the Epicureans. Plato's Academy, insofar as it was still active, was dominated by Cynics, who seem rather like the relativistic Sophists whom Socrates so famously opposed. Even so, all these philosophies worked in the shadow of Plato's work, in varying degrees of sympathy or opposition to his thought. Neither the memory of Socrates nor the philosophical world of Plato were forgotten.

The philosophers called Paul an "idle babbler" and "proclaimer of foreign divinities." It is tempting to read into their words later European sentiments of cultural superiority or even racism, but this would be anachronistic and miss two references. First, the word translated as "idle babbler" (*spermatologos*) in the Greek of Acts refers to someone who, bird-like, picks up the "seeds of words," scraps of ideas and conversations, in the Agora. Socrates was often accused of such babbling, albeit by a different word.[5] More strikingly, the charge of proclaiming new divinities was directly leveled against Socrates, as he attests in Plato's *Apology*.[6] Luke, by whose name we designate the author of both Luke's Gospel and the Acts of the Apostles, portrays Paul as a new Socrates, challenging the people of Athens as had his predecessor to turn to the natural law of the one God.

There is also a wider cultural point we might easily miss. The word "foreigner" in Greek does not carry the negative connotations we might associate with it in later European contexts. The word *xenos*, which plays a part in the Greco-English compound "xenophobia," means simultaneously *stranger, guest,* and *host*. Each of these senses of the word is apposite to the contemporary Greco-Roman attitude towards gods from other lands. For centuries, during the ages of Greek empire the divinities of the Egyptians had been assimilated into the Greek pantheon. Long before, the Pythagoreans who exercised such influence on Plato had reputedly studied the wisdom of the Indian sages. But in Paul's day not only the Egyptian deities, but also

the whole of this world by the name of order [*kosmos* — a Pythagorean term], not of disorder or dissoluteness."

5   See Socrates' ironic self-reference as a "prattler," *adoleschēs*, in *Republic* 489a and Aristophanes' mocking accusation of the same in *Clouds* 1480 as the "Thinking Shop" is burnt down. *Spermatologos* is a rare word that appears in some fragments of the Pythagorean and in comic poet Epicharmus of Kos, whom Plato is supposed to have admired, but is used rather more literally as a description of the grouse (*Fragments* 56, 59, also quoted in Athenaeus's *Deipnosophists*). The Jewish writer used it in this more metaphorical sense in his *Embassy to Gaius*, written around the early 40s. Presumably it had reached common parlance in this more metaphorical sense by the time Acts was written. Despite the lack of terminological precision, its use fits the general "Socratic" picture Luke is painting of Paul.

6   *Apology* 24b. The same charge is recorded by Xenophon, *Memorabilia* 1.1.1.

those of the Celts, Persians, and others besides, while no doubt foreign in their origin, now served as both guests and hosts in the colonized realms of the Roman Empire. Paul's new foreign divinity might therefore expect to be met with interested curiosity, though hostility or derision may follow.

Nor even was Paul's proclamation of monotheism new. The "divinities" whom the philosophers in the Agora assumed he must be preaching about were not "gods" in the Jewish sense of the word "God" at all, but *daimones*, spiritual beings of the lower, created order. Socrates maintained that these existed, but part of the reason he fell into trouble with the law was that he seemed to suggest a single God above and beyond them.[7]

By Paul's day philosophers who did the same no longer suffered Socrates' fate. The Stoics were among those who acknowledged the capricious divinities of the Greek pantheon but insisted that beyond all these was a single God, whom the pagan Epictetus, only a generation after Paul, would address often as "Father."[8] The Stoics maintained that God's divine *Logos*, the principle of reason and order, sustained the universe. The purpose of life was to discern and to live in harmony with that divinely-imbued law of nature. Signaling his sympathy with the Stoics, Paul quotes at them one of their own poets, the fourth-century BC astronomer Aratus, with a line St Augustine would make much of some centuries later: "in Him we live and move and have our being."[9] The reasoning mind that gives the order to the universe in which we dwell is that of the one God from whom both Jews and Greeks originate: for, as Paul continues to quote the poet, "we too are his offspring."

Some five decades after Paul's mission to Athens, the idea of the Logos was firmly established in Christian vocabulary. The Gospel of St John opened by proclaiming that in the person of Christ, the divine Logos or Word "was made flesh." Here John takes the start of Genesis, the primary source of Jewish metaphysical speculation, and translates the Hebrew *dabar*, the "Word" by which God speaks all being into creation, into terminology understandable by those versed in Greek philosophy. Some scholars used to object that John's Gospel, written towards the end of the first century AD, was a sign of the gradual dilution of an originally pure, Jewish gospel into a Greek philosophical idiom.[10] Nowadays more accept — as St Paul's own life and

---

7 See, e.g., *Apology* 26c, 33c and passim.

8 Epictetus, *Golden Sayings* 1.9; *Discourses* 1.1.3.

9 Augustine, *Sermon* 18; *Confessions* VII.9.

10 See discussion in Martin Hengel, *The Johannine Question* (London: SCM Press, 1989), 113 ff. James D. G. Dunn, *Unity and Diversity in the New Testament: An Inquiry into the Character of Earliest Christianity* (London: Bloomsbury, 1977), chapter XII.

particularly this episode in the Areopagus show — that such a binary is anachronistic. To try to separate the one from the other would be a fool's quest. For almost 400 years the Jews had lived in a Hellenistic culture. Even the earliest Christian literature is couched in Greek ways of thought. Just as a British Jew nowadays is no less British than a British Christian, Paul was native to the Greek culture and spoke the philosophical language of the Stoics and Platonists, not as a second language but as his own.

The Epicureans too would not find the language of Paul's gospel entirely alien. Sometimes atheistic, or at least indifferent to the supposed existence of the gods, the Epicureans are sometimes portrayed as mere hedonists because they made happiness the highest aim in human life, yet the happiness they taught was to be found not in stimulating and sating one's appetites but in taming them. Their word which we translate as "happy" was *makarios*. But there is another place where we translate precisely the same word rather differently. The Beatitudes proclaimed by Christ in his Sermon on the Mount in Matthew 5 each begin with *makarioi*, the plural form. To be "happy" is to be "blessed," and English translations of the Bible use both terms.[11] The Epicureans would recognize something of their own thought in a gospel of self-sacrifice and crucifixion of the flesh in the pursuit of that blessed happiness. Nor had they any more time than Paul for the cavorting of the gods of Greek myth or the worship of their idols.

Paul, then, is standing before the council of the Areopagus, the seat of judgment where Socrates had been condemned, a court in which there was no separation of the political from the theological, and where crimes against the gods might be tried as much as crimes against man. He has been brought by sympathetic company to protest against the worshipping of the idols in the city, not as an outsider but as a Greek-speaker; not in fear of condemnation, but as a Roman citizen protected under imperial law.[12] This protection lets him get away with an ambiguous opening gambit. "Athenians," he says, "I see how *deisidaimonesteroi* you are in every way!" This word, typically translated "religious," properly means "fearful of the *daimones*," the spirits or pagan gods. Taken at face value by a loyal polytheist, it would be a compliment. To the more skeptical Stoics and Epicureans, and to any Platonists loyal to the memory of Socrates, the meaning might, rather, be ambivalent. Hidden behind the praise was the accusation of superstition. But

---

11 "Blessed" prevails in the King James or Authorized Version and its successors, including the Revised and New Revised Standard Versions, whereas the Jerusalem Bible favored in many Catholic parishes prefers "happy."

12 Paul protests to this effect in Acts 16:37.

almost immediately Paul pulls out the barb. Among the plinths of Athens bearing idols to the deities of every aspect of life, of fertility and war, of childbirth and commerce, he has found one that pleases him: the empty plinth dedicated to the "Unknown God."[13]

On Paul's next words rests a tradition of Christian philosophical engagement that flourished in Western Europe until well into the fourteenth century and enjoyed sporadic revivals thereafter to the present day, but which has also exerted an almost unbroken influence on the philosophy and spirituality both of Eastern Christendom and Islam. Rival interpretations of the Apostle's words here are indicative of the great breach between a mainstream philosophical-theological worldview upheld in the West by the Church of the first millennium and the ideas of the late Middle Ages that would in due course lead to the Reformation, the Enlightenment, and modernity, and so to the sundering of faith from reason.

The Pseudo-Dionysius, one of the most influential theologians of the entire Christian Church, but about whom we have no certain biographical data, would find inspiration in just eight of St Paul's words:

> Ho oun agnoountes eusebeite, touto ego katangello humin.
> That which you worship unknowing, I proclaim to you. (Acts 17:23)

A common Protestant reading of this sentence, including that of Karl Barth,[14] is to hear Paul accusing the Greek philosophers of utter ignorance. Without the gospel, he proclaims, you know nothing at all. That is, non-Christian religions are quite simply false, with no truth whatsoever to offer. Worse still, if Barth is to be believed, the closer they seem to Christianity, the more deceptive they really are.[15] Were this really so, we might expect the listeners in the Areopagus to stop listening there and then. But they do not. They keep listening. This is because Paul speaks to them in their own philosophical terms. His use of language is precise: *agnoountes* is a participle, not the adverb "ignorantly," not the noun phrase "in ignorance," but a verbal adjective indicating process: it is, precisely, by the *act of unknowing* that the Athenians give proper honor (which is the meaning of *eusebeite*) to God.

To make the Bible itself the sole vehicle of the knowledge of God seems, on the basis of this passage of Acts, an unbiblical assertion. Rather, there is a proper acknowledgement of the limits of our knowledge of the God

---

13   Acts 17:23.
14   *Church Dogmatics* ii/1. 121 ff.
15   *Church Dogmatics* i/2, 340–42.

whom the Jewish Scripture themselves proclaim unknowable, which leads, paradoxically, to true knowledge of Him; and at least to some extent, this (un)knowledge is accessible in philosophies that lack the full revelation of God in Christ. Socrates is supposed to have said that he who is wisest is the one who knows he knows nothing.[16] It is not at any allegation of ignorance that the wise Greeks scoff. No, they reserve their censure until Paul professes something they really cannot believe: the promise of physical resurrection, and of final judgment by a mere man. For all their wisdom, as St Augustine would later observe, even the Platonists among the pagan philosophers would never accept that the Word could be made flesh.[17]

Still, not all the philosophers scoff at Paul. Some want to hear more. It is hard to see that any would have wanted to do so had Paul not spoken their language, both literally and metaphorically, or had he ridiculed them. He went out not to those whom he knew would be unsympathetic, not into some anachronistically secularized and hostile public square, but strategically, deliberately, to the Agora, a philosophically and spiritually active place where he thought he would meet people who spoke enough of the same language to hear and understand what he had to say. He did so from within the synagogue, from within his own community, but went out to find allies where he could, and if possible to bring them with him.

Even those who could not assent to the ultimate conclusions of Christian revelation became more sympathetic with him. Others went all the way: they crossed over and were baptized into the Church. Among these was Dionysius the Areopagite. Five centuries later he would provide the pen name for a theologian of almost unparalleled influence, who would follow Paul in working in both Christian and Jewish traditions and take the motif of divine unknowing to such an extreme that we do not even know who he was himself. And although his influence waned in the second millennium in the West, his more Eastern strand of Platonism was kept alive among the churches of the East, whose long history of minority, persecution, and proximity to non-Christian believers gave them no choice but to seek the truth with, rather than in isolation from, others who also seek truth. As we will see, the Pythagorean and theurgic principles that informed this

---

16 *Apology* 23a.

17 Augustine, in *Confessions* 7.9.13, as in the *City of God*, Chapter 8, praises the Platonists as those holding the closest philosophy to Christian revelation, but identifies their failure to acknowledge the Incarnation as their fatal shortcoming. Exactly which "Platonists" he has in mind is disputed, but in general terms he seems to have been influenced more by the more intellective school of Plotinus and Porphyry than by the liturgical or "theurgic" teachings of Iamblichus that would inform Pseudo-Dionysius, as we will see.

Pseudo-Dionysius continued on in the living traditions of Islamic Sufi practice and of Middle Eastern minority religions. The path they trace along the silk roads makes for comprehensible conversations with further Eastern philosophies to this day.

The question for modern Western Christians is whether to make allies of these people and learn from them or, in the spirit of Western exceptionalism, remain complicit in the ongoing and almost complete deconsecration of the public square.

St Paul's answer to that question is clear: an answer that some five centuries later would be taken up by the shadowy figure who took the name of his first Greek disciple.

WHOEVER HE WAS...

For centuries it was widely believed that the theologian who wrote as Dionysius the Areopagite really was the Athenian philosopher who had followed Paul. As late as the thirteenth century St Thomas Aquinas seemed to think so.[18] Seeing Dionysius as only one generation removed from Apostles themselves, he treats the writings ascribed to him as second only to the Scriptures, citing them more than Augustine, more even than his beloved Aristotle, whom the medieval Schoolmen admired enough to call simply *the* Philosopher. Yet doubts had been cast on Dionysius's authorship far earlier, even as his writings emerged on the Christian theological scene in the sixth century. By the time of the Reformation his identity was so suspect that Luther could dismiss "that Dionysius, whoever he was" as *plus platonizans quam christianizans*: "more Platonist than Christian."

By the Middle Ages, the Greek language had become almost extinct in the Western Church (Eriugena and some of his fellow monks in Ireland were the exception). What originally Greek philosophical texts were still circulated were now read in Latin translations. It was only with the Christian reconquest of Andalusia in 1053 that the great library of Toledo yielded the treasures of classical antiquity preserved there by Muslim, Jewish, and Christian scholars for the three hundred years of the Umayyad rule in Spain. The monoglot monks of the West had toiled on both classical and biblical texts with great skill, ingenuity, and deeply prayerful engagement, a point missed by those who still entertain the fiction of a European "Dark Age."[19] But even so, the monks' scope could not rival the multilingual tradition of

---

18   Aquinas, *In Quattuor Libros Sententiarum*, 2 d. 10 q. 1 a. 2 co, describes Dionysius explicitly as the "disciple of Paul."
19   For a popular dismissal of the "Dark Age" myth, see Seb Falk, *The Light Ages* (London: Penguin, 2020).

the Islamic world. Islamic universities continued to study and preserve the Greek texts lost to Christendom. This gave the opportunity for scholars of all three Abrahamic faiths to comment on and develop them in Hebrew, Greek and Arabic.

By Luther's day, more European scholars were able to read Greek and Hebrew texts in the original. It gradually became more obvious that Dionysius had relied on some of the pagan Neoplatonic philosophers whose texts were now better known, quoting some of their passages word for word: in particular, Plotinus, Iamblichus, and Proclus. Plotinus had lived in the third century, Iamblichus the third to fourth, and Proclus the fifth. "Dionysius" could not have lived in the first century, unless one rather perversely insisted (as some did) that those three pagan philosophers were actually quoting him. This seemed unlikely, to say the least, given that nobody mentioned him until the first half of the sixth century.[20]

So was Dionysius, as Luther suggested, trying to claim for himself a pseudo-apostolic authority for corrupting the pure gospel with alien, Platonic ideas? Or worse, as some modern scholars have suggested, was he a coward and heretic hiding behind the name to protect himself from orthodox authorities?[21]

Dionysius was undoubtedly a Platonist, and among his pagan peers pseudonymity was an established practice. The Syrian Iamblichus wrote under the Egyptian pseudonym of Abamon, not as some cunning disguise but to place himself in the line of Pythagoras and Plato, who were said to have been influenced by Egyptian, as well as Indian, wisdom.[22] Iamblichus's *De Mysteriis* was an important work to Dionysius, who developed from it his own distinctively Christian sacramental theology, as we will see in the next chapter. So, first, Dionysius's adoption of the pseudonym can be seen as a nod to Iamblichus and an assertion of his role in the universal philosophical quest for truth in which the Platonists claimed their part.

Pseudonymity, though, was also practiced in Christian circles. Take the New Testament: we know that several of the letters bearing St Paul's name were not written by him. The authorship of the Johannine corpus — the Gospel, Letters, and Revelation bearing John's name — is highly disputed, and part of that dispute at least revolves around modern, individualistic assumptions of authorship and testimony that do not readily map onto

---

20 See e.g., Sarah Klitenic, "Theurgy in Proclus and Dionysius," *Yearbook of the Irish Philosophical Society* 90 (2001): 85–95.

21 For an example of this tendency, see Arthur, *Pseudo-Dionysius as Polemicist*, 126.

22 *Iamblichus: De Mysteriis*, ed. Emma Clarke, John Dillon, and Jackson Hershbell (Leiden, Boston: Brill, 2004), xxxiii.

such ancient territory.[23] Scholars do not generally think that the pseudon-ymous writers in the New Testament were frauds trying to claim apostolic authority for themselves. Say the author of the Epistle to the Hebrews did write it in pursuit of his own glory: why, then, would he have let his work, one of beauty and theological sophistication, be ascribed to somebody else? To write in a great saint's name was not to plagiarize, to accrue to oneself their honor or pull the wool over the reader's eyes, but to honor the saint by one's words. It was also an act of humility, since the actual authors of those texts were, and remain, unknown. In this spirit, writes emeritus Pope Benedict, Dionysius "did not want to glorify his own name . . . but rather truly to serve the Gospel, to create an ecclesial theology, neither individual nor based on himself."[24] As Dionysius himself writes, "Paul the Great, in a possession of the divine love and having participated in its ecstatic power, says with inspired lips, 'I live no longer, but Christ lives in me.'"[25] Like Paul and like the Baptist, Dionysius diminished that Christ might grow.

Already we see that there is more to Dionysius's pseudonymity than mere pseudery. His adoption of the ancient saint's name is a practice con-sistent with both Christian and Platonic traditions. But that is not all. It is also a corollary of his specific theological approach to God by mysti-cal unknowing. Dionysius's pseudonymity calls us to a particular way of relating to God.

The Areopagite's writings are most famous for what is called their *apophatic* method of apprehending the divine, later known in the Latin tradition as the *via negativa* or "negative way." Where the *cataphatic* spiritu-ality of the "positive way" focuses on what can be said and known of God, the apophatic way is to "know" God by knowing his unknowability: to recognize that anything we say or understand about the unknowable One is ultimately untrue. The distinction between the apophatic and cataphatic ways can certainly be discerned in Scripture, even if not in such categorical terms. God reveals himself, paradoxically, as unknowable, saying for example to Isaiah, "as the heavens are higher than the earth, so my ways are higher than your ways and my thoughts than your thoughts."[26] He reveals himself to Moses only in the midst of a dark cloud, prompting Moses to avert his eyes and warning him in those words St John will later recall, "there shall

---

23 See the discussion in chapters 14ff. of Richard Bauckham, *Jesus and the Eyewitnesses* (Grand Rapids, Michigan: Eerdmans, 2006).
24 Benedict XVI, *The Fathers*, Vol. II (Huntingdon, IN: Our Sunday Visitor, 2009), 40.
25 *Divine Names* IV.13.
26 Isaiah 55:8.

no man see me, and live."[27] Dionysius's master Paul stresses the same in his
first letter to Timothy.[28] There is a strong tradition of God's invisibility and
unknowability. And yet God does reveal himself, in the images of Scripture,
in the fire as much as the cloud, in the very cosmos that sings his praise, in
the rites of his Temple,[29] and decisively in the person of Jesus Christ. Scripture confronts us with a paradoxical revelation whereby God is revealed as
hidden, and knowable as unknowable. Beyond Scripture, though, ancient
pagan philosophers had intuited the same paradox. Among the Platonists
it was Iamblichus who crystallized the apophatic-cataphatic distinction.[30]
Apophatically speaking, God had to be transcendent, beyond everything;
nonetheless, as origin and cause of everything, He had some relationship
to everything in which He could cataphatically be discerned. Platonic philosophy would help Christian theologians interpret the witness of Scripture.

Dionysius was far from alone in advocating the apophatic way: it was
shared by many earlier Fathers of the Eastern tradition, such as St Gregory
of Nyssa and Origen. In the East, apophatic spirituality would become practically universal, epitomized by the Hesychast tradition of silent meditation.
In the West, similar emphases in the thought of St Augustine are enjoying
reappraisal,[31] and Latin translations of Dionysius would inspire the spiritual teaching of Eriugena, the Victorines, St John of the Cross, St Theresa of
Avila, Meister Eckhardt, the Carthusians and many others. Nonetheless, in
the second millennium, more cataphatic spiritual systems would dominate,
including those of later Franciscans, of St Ignatius of Loyola, and of the
magisterial Reformation often referred to nowadays as "mainline Protestant."
In the Church of England, the more apophatic, Platonic theology persisted
in the theology of the seventeenth-century Anglican Caroline divines and
eighteenth-century Cambridge Platonists. It enjoyed a further revival in

---

27   Exod 33:20; John 1:18, 5:37; 1 John 6:46.

28   1 Tim 6:16.

29   There is a fascinating discussion on the knowledge and vision of God in the Temple
tradition and later rabbinical attempts at eliminating that tradition from the biblical
texts in Margaret Barker, *Temple Mysticism: An Introduction* (London: SPCK, 2011).

30   As related by the Platonist Damascius, *De Principiis* II, 1.4–16.19.

31   Willemien Otten, "In The Shadow Of The Divine: Negative Theology And Negative
Anthropology In Augustine, Pseudo-Dionysius and Eriugena," *The Heythrop Journal* 40,
no. 4 (1999): 438–55. A synthesis with Augustine, generally taken as a representative of
the more Porphyrean intellectualist strand of Platonism, taken together with the more
Proclean, theurgic strand to which I am drawing attention, can be found in John Milbank, "Intensities," *Modern Theology* 15, no. 4 (1999): 445–97. The synthesis is, however,
resisted in Wayne J. Hankey, "One Hundred Years of Platonism," in *Levinas and the Greek
Heritage*, ed. Jean-Marc Narbonne (Leuven/Paris/Dudley, MA: Peeters, 2006), 97–248.

the theology of the nineteenth-century Oxford Movement.[32] Still, among the majority of philosophers, Platonism was tarred by its association with Descartes and treated with contempt.[33] From the late medieval period onward, the apophatic way was sidelined to monks, nuns and poets, and regarded with some skepticism as a reputable philosophical position.

This is not to say that Dionysius excludes a cataphatic approach to God. Certainly, if we think that we can reach God by our own standards and the evidence of our senses, we are led astray; but this is not to say we cannot think or say anything at all about God. We can know God in all things, including in ourselves. All things come from God as their originating cause and are, in a Platonic sense, unfoldings of the One. So absolutely everything "says" something about God that we can name and understand. Dionysius inherits from the Platonic strand of Iamblichus and Proclus an understanding of the creative tension between the apophatic and cataphatic ways of discerning God, divine hiddenness, and revelation — and with it, we will see, an affirmation of the inherent value of the created world.

While our concepts about God are ultimately untrue, some are less untrue than others. Were this not so, Dionysius could not have devoted an entire treatise to the topic of the Divine Names, the highest and least inappropriate of which is the Good. Nonetheless, we must ultimately negate this along with every positive statement we make of God. The positive way must be tempered with the recognition that God is also absolutely transcendent, beyond all things. This is where the apophatic way comes in. As the heavens are higher than the earth, so God's ways are higher than our ways, his thoughts than our thoughts.[34] It is not just that God's goodness is so good as to be beyond any goodness we are capable of imagining, that we are lower beings in a chain of existence and so cannot grasp him in the same way an ape cannot grasp astrophysics. This is not enough. God is so entirely beyond being that he is beyond intelligibility altogether, as a matter of metaphysical truth. It is too much even to say what we cannot know of God, or to describe God by what he is not. Dionysius wants us to negate even such negations of God, stripping away the delusion that our feeble reasoning can aspire to the folly of divine wisdom. Only in dumbness can

32   George Westhaver, "Mysticism and Sacramentalism in the Oxford Movement," in The Oxford Handbook of the Oxford Movement, ed. Stewart J. Brown, Peter Nockles, and James Pereiro (Oxford: Oxford University Press, 2017).

33   Peter Harrison, "Laws of Nature in Seventeenth-Century England from Cambridge Platonism to Newtonianism," in The Divine Order, the Human Order, and the Order of Nature, ed. Eric Watkins (New York: Oxford University Press, 2013), 127–48.

34   Isaiah 55:9.

we be joined with that Word whom words cannot describe, and attain to the knowledge which passes all understanding. True to Iamblichus's tradition, Dionysius brings the cataphatic and apophatic approaches together. God is both all things in all things, and nothing in anything;[35] knowable in all things, and unknowable in any of them. To explain the relationship between these two approaches we can follow Dionysius and Plotinus's precedents and apply the metaphor of a sculptor:[36]

> We pray to enter the darkness beyond light: to see through unseeing that which is beyond sight, to know through unknowing that which is beyond knowledge, even by not seeing, by not knowing. For this is to see and to know truly, and in a way beyond being to hymn that which is beyond being — through the carving away of all beings, just as the makers of natural[37] statues carve out all the obstacles which prevent the clear sight of that which is hidden and, simply by carving away, bring to light the beauty which had been hidden away.

Take a rough block of marble. Looking at its shape and size, you form a plan in your mind for the statue which will emerge from it. At this stage, the idea of the statue is its only reality, unless you want to argue that thoughts are not real. A modern materialist might see the mental plan as less real than the final product. The Platonist would argue conversely: at this stage, the thought of the statue, that plan in your mind's eye, is its only reality. It is far more real in your mind than it is in the block of uncarved marble in front of you. The thought is, moreover, real — whether I make the statue or not.

Now, the statue in your mind is a thing of great beauty. So, it is beautiful even before it is made. You know that it is beautiful even though you have not seen it. This is because you have a sense of what constitutes beauty in your mind already. Yet, however strong your sense of beauty may be, you cannot picture Beauty itself. It is an invisible, abstract idea in which beautiful things share, but it is no less intelligible or real than they are. The materialist would say that we derive the idea of Beauty from the evidence

---

35 Plotinus *Ennead* 5.2.1; Proclus, *Elements of Theology* prop. 142; *Divine Names* 7.3.

36 *Mystical Theology* 2; Plotinus *Ennead* 1.6.9.

37 "Natural": the Greek, *autophues*, is a difficult word to translate. Parker and Luibheid leave it out altogether. Iamblichus uses it to describe a "spontaneous" knowledge of the gods, beyond logic and reason, as they turn us towards the Good in prayer (*De Mysteriis* 47:13–15). The making of statues of the divinities is one such form of prayer, as discussed in Gregory Shaw, "The Chôra of the Timaeus and Iamblichean Theurgy," *Horizons: Seoul Journal of Humanities* 3, no. 2 (2012): 103–29.

of our senses, because only the physical world is real: there is no reality that is not material. The Platonist, conversely, would argue that Beauty itself is prior to and so more real than any actual beautiful thing. Nor is its reality confined to the mind of the observer. It is more real even than any beautiful idea in our minds, such as the plan we have for our sculpture.

The notion that Beauty is more real than beautiful things may seem an odd proposition to moderns, with minds entrenched in materialist presuppositions. Yet it follows the same logic as the relationship between your imaginary sculpture and the solid block of marble. The imaginary sculpture is more real than the marble sculpture at this stage. The marble will share the pattern you have in your mind, and indeed several more blocks of marble might share the same pattern, if you happen to have many of marble blocks and plenty of time. They will eventually participate, as Platonists would put it, in your idea of the sculpture. Furthermore, that idea itself participates in higher ideas still: just as those several blocks will participate in your idea of the sculpture, so your idea of the sculpture participates in a higher, unifying idea: the idea of Beauty. Your mental sculpture is not the only beautiful idea in existence. What it has in common with all the other beautiful ideas and beautiful things is its participation in the idea of Beauty. That idea is therefore real, and like the mental statue it is real whether or not any actual beautiful ideas or things come into existence.

Platonists do not stop with the assertion that ideas are as real as physical things: they say that in fact the ideas are *more* real. Physical and even mental representations are only reflections of the universal realities beyond, flickering like the shadows on the wall of Plato's famous cave. Perhaps you are a great sculptor. But even if you are a new Michelangelo, your statue will never reach the perfection of your mental image of it. What artist is ever completely satisfied with his or her work? Even if you were Leonardo da Vinci reborn, you could not draw an absolutely perfect square or circle: the perfect square, the perfect circle, or the perfect statue can exist only in abstraction. Even a Malevich, Mondrian, or Rothko square will only participate more or less in the idea of the square. It will not be a perfect square. Likewise in the plastic arts, a statue you make will bear more or less of a relation to the beautiful idea you had, depending on your skill as a sculptor. That is, it will participate more or less in the idea of the statue. Yet however perfectly our concept might accord to the idea of the statue, even Michelangelo's *David* is base and ugly in comparison with the idea of Beauty itself. Beauty is more beautiful, and hence truer, than any of its instantiations.

What is more, the ideas are more lasting. A statue carved in stone, even in marble, will not last forever. It will deteriorate. Still more so and more quickly, will the beauty of a beautiful person. These things change and die. Yet beauty itself is imperishable. Its reality is not only purer than any physical instantiation, but eternal. The implication of resisting the reality of such invisible and perfect forms is that it reduces existence to nothing but sheer multiplicity, which is to say in the end nothing but a mentally imposed construct unites, say, one tree with another, or more problematic still, one human with another. There is no real human nature, only an agreed code which we, as language-using animals, choose to designate things that seem similar but are ultimately absolutely different. Language, on this view, becomes the rules of a mental game, and the physical realm its board and pieces.

Dionysius does not spell all this out in his analogy. He shifted its focus from the image we want to carve to the marble we are carving away. In carving, we do not build up an image from nothing. We create by stripping away, which Dionysius calls *aphaeresis*. The block, with all its veins and granulations, its texture and shape, suggests a statue to us. Perhaps we see in a certain block the shape of an arm or head, or note in its hue some redolence of human character. An image begins to develop in our minds. This corresponds to the cataphatic affirmations about God. What we perceive tells us something of him. It also resonates with the Buddhist teaching of Buddha-nature and its outworking in traditional schools of woodcarving, where images of reality's true, internal nature as nondual with Buddha are brought out of the wood by working with its natural grains, twists, and shapes rather than imposing an image onto it.[38]

Once we have discerned the image, we must chisel away everything that occludes it. From the outset, the act of carving is not meant to impose our will on the marble, or to create something we have uniquely conceived. The matter has suggested the form. So, we cut away all that is not beautiful, carve away the imperfections, smooth it down, until all that remains is the closest approximation to the beautiful idea we had in mind. Yet the beauty was always there, latent, before it entered our conscious mind. We might say that the capacity to recognize beauty is part of the original architecture of our mind, and that the beauty it recognizes is an essential part of the original architecture of the universe. Like reflects like. Order and harmony are constitutive elements of human memory rather than arbitrary impositions upon it, as much a part of the formatting of the mind as of everything else

---

38   See some examples of the tradition at work today and find out more about the philosophy behind it at https://www.carvingthedivine.com.

in existence. The alternative position, which would render the mind a blank slate, ignores the question which, as the German-American theologian Paul Tillich points out, "empiricism never can answer, namely, the question of the structural presuppositions of experience."[39] In Dionysius's analogy of carving, we do not impose anything on the marble; rather, we bring its latent beauty to light. It is a recognition that, in the words of Professor Douglas Hedley, Director of the Cambridge Centre for the Study of Platonism, "we are forged of the same stuff as all other creatures and, as such, share the similitude of the created order with the author of all things."[40]

Yet as we carve, we come to realize that the idea we had was imperfect. We try to bring out the shape and contours of this beautiful image we have glimpsed through the stone, but it is never quite right. We cannot capture it. It is difficult enough even if we are trying to carve only a mortal subject, say a beautiful person, but if we are trying to carve Beauty itself, and thereby to carve God, we will keep carving and carving and carving — until there is nothing left at all. The marble is every concept of God that we have; the chisel, our recognition that each of these concepts is related in metaphors to material, created things, and is therefore ultimately untrue of God, who is beyond them. And in the end the statue is no idol, but the Unknown God who reveals himself in the divine darkness Moses found on Sinai and St Paul on the empty plinth in Athens.

The emptiness of the plinth is essential to Dionysius's understanding of God. Only by unknowing can we attain to the knowledge of God: but to unknow, we must first know. We must look and see and name and then systematically carve away all the images, negate all the words and names we use of God. We must negate even the negations. The physical world gives us, cataphatically, the very images of God which, apophatically, we must cut away. Affirmation and denial are equally necessary. A purely cataphatic model over-identifies God with creation and leads to pantheism, the domestication of the transcendent to the material sphere; a purely apophatic model denies any continuity whatsoever between God and creation, and removes any basis for knowledge beyond the merely experiential and empirical. Dionysius's move to preserve both the immanence and transcendence of God, and both his knowability and unknowability, is just as Christian as it is Platonic. In the Divine Names, Dionysius describes the great paradox of the Divine Fullness of God self-emptying into Christ, and yet remaining unaffected in its eternal plenitude:

39　Paul Tillich, Philosophical Writings (Berlin, New York: De Gruyter, 1989), 384.
40　The Iconic Imagination, 35.

So, since for the sake of the love of humanity (*philanthrōpia*) the Beyond Divine has come all the way to the natural realm, and truly come into existence, and taken the name of man (may the Divine be gracious towards such matters beyond mind and word which we are hymning!), the one who is beyond nature and beyond being therefore shares in these things: not just because he has entered communion with us without alteration or confusion, and without suffering any effect on his superplenitude by this unutterable act of self-emptying (*kenōsis*), but also because this newest of all new things was supernatural *in* our natural characteristics, beyond being *in* things of being — transcending all things which belong to us, all things which derive from us, all things which are beyond us. [41]

Here, Dionysius offers a commentary on that profound meditation on the nature of Christ in St Paul's letter to the Philippians 2:5–11, where Jesus is described as "emptying himself of divine glory." Biblical scholars broadly agree that in this letter, one of the first and therefore one of the earliest parts of the New Testament, written before any of Gospels, Paul is citing a hymn already well-known to his Christian correspondents. So, the divine act of "self-emptying," or *kenosis* in Paul's and Dionysius's Greek, comprises one of the earliest Christian understandings of who Christ is and how God works in him.

But why does God empty himself in this way? At this question, Dionysius the Christian departs from much pagan Platonic precedent. For while Plotinus would heartily agree that created beings are drawn to God by their desire or love for him, he could not have accepted Dionysius's conclusion that God is drawn out of himself because of his love for us. It is, for Dionysius, only because God is love that he empties himself at all: first, in the ongoing act of creation, but then in the Incarnation of Christ, and conclusively in the Crucifixion.

From our time-bound perspective, these may appear to be three separate "events" in chronological sequence, but for Dionysius, they are aspects of the sole outpouring of grace that constitutes not only an action of God, but God's very nature. It is not just that self-emptying for the sake of love is something God does: it is what God is. As the prologue of St John's Gospel expounds, the divine Logos or Word by which God gives shape and order to creation is not something separate from and subordinate to God, but is with God and is God. We can conceptually distinguish the Logos as the "mind" of God from God the Father, but to posit the separation of God

---

41 *Divine Names* II.10.

from his mind, his Logos, is nonsensical. As God, the Divine Logos entirely transcends creation, both in its spatial and temporal dimensions. That is to say, the Logos, there "in the beginning," is beyond time. And yet it is this selfsame Logos which is Incarnate in time as Christ, and manifests the same, self-emptying "philanthropic" love. It is out of God's *philanthrōpia*, his love for humanity, that Christ, the Divine Logos, comes down and takes on himself our nature.[42] Plato had attributed such "philanthropy" to Socrates, and Iamblichus later thought it a great virtue in political leaders,[43] but it was Paul who applied this quality to God himself in his Epistle to Titus, "when the kindness and *philanthrōpia* of God our Savior shone forth" for our salvation.[44] Building on these biblical and Platonic foundations, Dionysius speaks of the entire divine hierarchy by which reality is ordered as "philanthropic." Christ's Incarnation is the realization in time of God's eternal, unchanging, transcendent yearning to draw the created order into the uncreated heart of his divine love.

As he does so, pulling the world into his own self-emptying, he does not however compromise the integrity of creation. The self-emptying of God into which all being is called is not a destructive act, not an emptying out to a nihilistic nothingness. Rather, it is the realization that any given being, including humans, have no existence at all except in relationship to one another and to God. In their own right, all things are already empty. It is only in relationship that they can be said to have any existence at all, and in this, they are reflections of the Trinitarian God who by nature is mutually self-emptying relationship. God empties himself through creation, not despite it, and in doing so brings it to its fullest being and value. "It does not belong to providence to destroy nature,"[45] writes the Areopagite, a sentiment on which six hundred years later St Thomas Aquinas would beautifully build his memorable maxim, *gratia non tollit naturam, sed perficit*: "grace does not destroy nature, but perfects it."[46]

It is in the Divine Word emptying himself of glory for the sake of love that all things are bequeathed their truest nature and the possibility of

---

42   Despite later scholars' attempts to paint Dionysius as basically a Platonist with a slight Christian veneer, the philanthropic love of God is not an isolated theme in the Dionysius Corpus, in which it appears 31 times. See especially Epistle 4, where Dionysius designates *philanthrōpia* Jesus's predominant characteristic.

43   The reference can be found in a letter of Iamblichus preserved by Johannes Stobaeus (III, 3, 26).

44   Titus 3:4.

45   *Divine Names* 4.33.

46   *Summa Theologiae* I. I.8 ad 2.

perfection. For humans, this means becoming saints. So, while the empty plinth is a metaphor for Dionysius's pseudonymity, his self-negation by the taking of another name also reveals a deeper aspect of the spiritual path to which he calls us down today.

Abbot Christopher Jamison's popular book, *Finding Happiness*, proclaims self-reflection the very first of his *Monastic Steps for a Fulfilling Life*.[47] He tells an ancient story of the desert fathers, in which three friends set out in the service of Christ. The first seeks to serve as a doctor, the second as a broker of peace between warring tribes, the third as a hermit. After some years the first two, burnt out by their work and seeing there will be no end of the sick to cure or wars to end, seek out their third friend for advice. He listens to them in silence, then takes down the water skin from its hook in his tent. He pours water into a bowl and asks them what they can see. Swirling and full of sand, at first the water reveals nothing, but when it settles they can see their own reflections clearly. The message is that in our busyness, the relentless swirling activity of our lives, we are blind to our true reflection. Unless we make time to rest and to examine ourselves with honesty and clarity, we are unable to see how ravaged we are by sin.

Like the Benedictine Abbot, the Areopagite calls us on a journey of personal holiness too, but the self-reflection he advocates goes much further than recognizing our moral flaws. As we contemplate our image in the clear water, we must recognize not only our deficiencies but our absolute inability to resolve them. For Dionysius, as a student of Paul, "the foolishness of God is wiser than men."[48] Human wisdom falls so far short of the perfect wisdom of God that we cannot reach true knowledge by our own efforts. This not only limits our capacity to know God, but even to follow the Delphic maxim to "know ourselves." As Augustine saw, if our souls are made in the image of God, then they too are incomprehensible to us. Here Platonism and Christianity cohere, for unlike the Aristotelian empiricists, both Plato and St Paul were wary of the evidence of our senses. Our self-reflection is unreliable. We must go beyond reflection, beyond cognition, to embrace a foolish unknowing if we are to enter into the wisdom of God.

Both the Catholic and Reformed churches of the West have adopted St Augustine's doctrine of Original Sin and the recognition that we humans are unable to save ourselves. We must depend entirely on divine grace. Despite

---

47   Christopher Jamison, *Finding Happiness: Monastic Steps for a Fulfilling Life* (London: Orion, 2008).

48   1 Cor 1:25.

this, Western Christianity has often lapsed into systems of moralism that reify evil and imply that we are able to save ourselves from it. Conversion from sin still ends up being understood as a personal choice, a test of our individual moral sternness. To this day, advertisers exploit this in their marketing of temptation and "harmless" indulgence. Sin is seen as a kind of naughtiness that we can exorcise with the right regime. We can have the cake as long as we go to the gym afterwards; take the long-haul flight as long as we plant a tree. Mechanistic interpretations of the Sacrament of Reconciliation have not helped to dispel this popular image of religion as a kind of spiritual calorie-counting. Hence the popular image of Catholics sinning all week, going to Confession and Mass for a weekly top-up of forgiveness, and then getting back to bad habits.

Yet for Platonists, including St Augustine himself, evil is not so much a reality as a deficiency of reality — that is, of the true reality, which is God. Evil is an absence, a lack of divine goodness. This is more than just a Platonic trope. In the Greek of the New Testament, sin is called *hamartia*, a term used in archery to mean "missing the mark." For Dionysius, the Christian response to sin is not just self-chastisement and trying to do better next time. It is, rather, bound up in the realization of the reality of Divine Goodness and the awakening of our need, our desire, and our love for God. Repentance is not just "saying sorry," but a turning of our entire deficient being towards the full reality, and hence absolute goodness, of the One who is Being beyond Being.

Here we might turn the sculpting metaphor around and make ourselves the blocks. Oriented towards God, we let him sculpt away all the attachments to non-being that weigh us down, carve and smooth us into a nearer representation of his divine image as self-giving One, the Christ whose image lies buried within the stone of human hearts.

The Areopagite calls us not only to see our sin, but to develop the sense of our absolute need for and dependence upon God: a corrective to the modern technocracy that ravages the world with its inventions and does not see the irony in trying to cure the world by the same means. This puts our individual sin into its wider context. I do not mean the all-too-human sense of "structural sin" popularized by Liberation theology, with the semi-Pelagian implication that we humans can "solve" the problem of evil once and for all by the manipulation of social conditions. We are fundamentally incapable of perfection, not because we differ from God in scale, but because perfection resides in God alone. This is a metaphysical point before it becomes a social one.

Dionysius chose the name of the Athenian convert to show his commitment to the philosophy of the Platonists, but his pseudonym is just as much a marker of his Christian faith. Pseudonymity is the first challenge to those who would walk the Areopagite's path. It constitutes a call to absolute humility, to walking the Way of the Cross with no concern for one's own glory, to putting all earthly pride and approval aside for the sole aim of aspiring to mystical oneness with God in love; to emptying ourselves that we may live, and so to become one with the eternal, creative life of self-emptying, which is God revealed in Christ Incarnate, Crucified, Risen, and Ascended.

The call of the Areopagite does not end in some quest for personal holiness via Platonic meditations upon the nature of God. It is not a call for a secret Christian spiritual elite to engage in mind-bending acts of intellectual acrobatics. Far from it. The Areopagite's negative way frames the self-emptying God revealed in Christ in terms of Platonic metaphysics, but then builds on that foundation to reveal the Church as the vehicle of salvation, the communal, sacramental, and liturgical means of opening this negative way to all believers. Exploring this will help us understand who . he is, who he wants us to be, and how his way can reconnect the West to the wider world.

SALVATION IS COMMUNAL

All is righteousness and there is no equality. Not as when stones lie
side by side, but as when stones support and are supported in an
arch, such is his order; rule and obedience, begetting and bearing,
heat glancing down, life growing up. Blessed be He!
— *Perelandra*, C. S. Lewis

IN THE 12TH CENTURY, CHARGED WITH THE REBUILD-
ing of the ancient Basilica of Saint-Denis in Paris, the French Abbot
Suger took the teachings of the saint to whom the church was dedicated and developed a new architectural style: the Gothic. Its pointed arches,
clusters of columns, and vaulted ceilings would sculpt light into an allegory
of the divine ascent proclaimed by the Areopagite.

The Dionysian spiritual quest has not met with universal approbation
over the years. The theological college where I studied for the priesthood
bears the name of the nineteenth-century Anglican bishop, Brooke Foss
Westcott. He was not fond of Dionysius, accusing him of teaching a selfish
spiritual path at odds with Christianity, something "essentially individual
and personal and subjective."[1] It is as though Dionysius was just window
dressing the shopfront of his pagan forefather Plotinus, often considered,
by the final words of his *Enneads*, to have a taught a solitary mystical path,
"a flight of the alone to the alone."[2] St Augustine tried this path, with
some fleeting and ultimately unsatisfactory success.[3] Passages of Dionysius's *Divine Names* read in isolation may seem to commend such a lone
spiritual quest.

So, is Dionysius essentially professing pagan Platonism with some Christian flourishes? Does he mean for us to meditate our way to salvation
through private efforts of affirmation and negation of the Divine Names?

---

1 Quoted in Andrew Louth, *Denys the Areopagite* (*Outstanding Christian Thinkers*), 2nd
ed. (London: Continuum International Publishing Group Ltd., 2001), 130.
2 *Ennead* 6.9.11.
3 *Confessions* 7.10.16, 7.17.23.

Is he really just a pagan in Christian dress, his pseudonym an apostolic guise to con credulous Christians into a foreign spirituality?[4] Various motives lie behind these accusations. One is a skepticism towards sacramental theology. Though Colm Luibheid was Catholic, his popular translation in the *Classics of Western Spirituality* series[5] was undertaken with the Protestant scholar Paul Rorem, and tends to downplay the theurgic and liturgical aspects in favor of a more scripturally oriented approach. Related to this Protestant skepticism is the suspicion of "magic." This aversion to theurgy risks sundering nature from grace, so that the physical realm ends up disenchanted, a no-man's-land waiting to be seized, exploited, and given its meaning by the strongest competitor, or a board for our linguistic power games of contested definition and control.

Dionysius challenges any theory of radical discontinuity between the divine and the created, but without merely conflating the two, as though God and the universe are one and the same. This connects him — and through him, much traditional theology of the West — with that majority of world philosophies which, albeit in a great variety of ways, recognizes the cosmos as in some sense mediating the sacred rather than isolated from it. If we read beyond the *Divine Names* we can find plenty of counterexamples to the objections against Dionysius, and at least two reasons to contest them. First, those suspicious of Dionysius's reliance on Platonism rely in turn on an overly narrow account of that broad and variegated philosophy, focusing on Plotinus at the expense of the later theurgic, liturgical, Eastern strand of Iamblichus and Proclus, which exercised such great influence on Dionysius. Second, Dionysius's philosophy is grounded in Christian theology. Like the convert whose name he adopts — the Athenian brought to Christ by the words of an itinerant Jewish preacher — Dionysius discerns the fulfilment of the apophatic theology of the Platonists in specifically Jewish lore. He uses this to stress the necessity of apostolic continuity through the bishops of the Church, and makes the Church the communal locus of salvation. People sometimes see Platonism and Buddhism as denying the salvation of individuals, as though all sense of self is merged into the higher reality without any individual distinction. We will question whether that insight is universally true of Buddhism in detail later on, but it is certainly not so with Dionysius.

That said, becoming one with God is a Platonic theme, and Dionysius does develop it. The pagan Platonists tended to call this *henosis*, meaning

---

4   As argued, for instance, in Arthur, *Pseudo-Dionysius as Polemicist.*

5   Luibhéid and Rorem, *Pseudo-Dionysius: The Complete Works.*

oneness or unification. Later Christian Platonists moved towards the term *theosis*, or divinization.[6] Dionysius himself uses the term *theosis* but also the word *koinonia* or "communion." Now, this is by no means an alien term to the pagan Platonists, even to Plato himself. But for Dionysius, as for any Christian, it rings with the specific cultic resonances of the Eucharist. Communion is more than just union. Communion implies commonality, and that means relationship between others. To call *theosis* communion is to make clear that it does not obliterate the individual. Neither, however, does it end in a straightforward dualism of the individual human versus God.

In the *Mystical Theology*, that terse summary of his work, Dionysius follows an established patristic tradition. As St Gregory of Nyssa had before him in his *Life of Moses*, Dionysius takes the ascent of Moses up Mount Sinai as a metaphor for the spiritual life. At the highest peak of unity with God, Moses' identity shifts so that he becomes neither himself nor someone else,[7] echoing St Paul's words in Galatians 2:20 about that state of spiritual Crucifixion where it is "no longer I who live, but Christ who lives in me." The true self is found in becoming neither self nor other.

Yet this allegory of Moses is not merely the ascent of an individual, to be imitated by the faithful. Dionysius himself makes a clear parallel between the ascent of Moses and the eucharistic rites of the Church. The mystical ascent is communal and participatory. No private mental exercise, oneness with God works through the material elements of bread and wine.

Dionysius frames the *Mystical Theology* as a letter to Timothy, who is a bishop, though Dionysius favors the Eastern term "hierarch." The bishop is Eucharistic president par excellence. In chapter 3 of the *Ecclesiastical Hierarchy*, Dionysius's treatise on the Church, he identifies Moses as the "type" of the ideal bishop. Like Moses, the bishop does not represent just himself before God as some kind of exalted spiritual soloist, but the body of the new Israel, the Church. The basic ecclesial unit of the Catholic Church is a bishop, his presbyterate and his people. You cannot have the Eucharist without either a bishop or a priest in communion with him. Nor can you have a bishop without people. The framing of the *Mystical Theology* as a letter to a bishop,

---

6 St Clement of Alexander (150–211) first used the verb *theopoieō, make divine*, from which St Athanasius (293–373) derived the noun *theopoiēsis, divinization*. The Cappadocian fathers Sts. Gregory of Nazianzus (329–390) and Gregory of Nyssa (235–295) moved to the more direct verb *theioō* and noun *theōsis*.

7 Gorazd Kocijancic, "The Identity of Dionysius Areopagite. A Philosophical Approach," *Sobornost Incorporating the Eastern Churches Review* 29, no. 2 (2007): 75–84.

and particularly its set-piece on Moses as a "type" or model of the bishop in his liturgical role, straightaway indicates Dionysius's sacramental, communal intent for the work.

Moses' ascent into the divine darkness is a metaphor for the apophatic way as practiced through the liturgy of the Church. Dionysius links the ascent to the liturgy with specialist vocabulary which could easily be missed if we read the *Mystical Theology* in isolation from the rest of the corpus:

> Even the divine Moses is himself ordered to be first purified, and then to be separated from those who are not so. After total purification, he hears the many-voiced trumpets, and sees many lights, flashing forth pure, diffusive rays. Then he is separated from the many, and with chosen priests leads on to the highest of the divine ascents. Yet even by these, he does not intercourse with God himself. Nor does he even see him, because he is invisible: just the place where he is. This, I think, signifies that the holiest and highest things we can see or conceive of are, as it were, hypothetical accounts of the things subject to the one who transcends all things. Through these is shown a presence of him, a presence beyond all power of thought, which mounts the intelligible heights of the holiest places. Then and only then Moses is freed from all that is seen and sees. He enters the cloud of unknowing . . . by the act of knowing nothing, knowing above intellect. [8]

The ascent, though it may not be immediately obvious, begins with baptism. Moses has to be purified before ascending the mountain. Dionysius describes baptism as "purification" in the *Ecclesiastical Hierarchy*.[9] He is not unusual in this. St Gregory of Nyssa uses exactly the same terminology in his *Life of Moses*. Moses is then separated from the unpurified, as we know happened in many early church communities during every Eucharist, when the unbaptized were dismissed before the consecration. An appendix of this practice remains in the liturgies of the Eastern Church, after what Western Christians would nowadays call the Liturgy of the Word, when the Deacon proclaims, "Catechumens, depart." Catechumens are those preparing for baptism, and while the exhortation is nowadays ignored, historically only the baptized were allowed to remain for the Liturgy of the Sacrament. Hence the "trumpets" Moses hears as he ascends. Exodus 19:19 reports the sounding of the shofar as Moses climbed, but in Gregory's *Life of Moses* these are given an

---

8   *Mystical Theology* 1.3.
9   *Ecclesiastical Hierarchy* 2.3.1, 397B.

allegorical significance with the angelic music of the heavens proclaimed at the beginning of Psalm 19. Dionysius adds yet another resonance. Elsewhere he describes the sacraments as "trumpet-calls" of the sacraments to which the uninitiated — such as the catechumens — are deaf. [10] So, the trumpets contribute to the sacramental frame of the passage.

Next, Moses sees "many lights." In early churches the baptistries were often separate from the main body of the church, sometimes even in caves. Baptism was traditionally held at what we now call the Easter Vigil, so that the baptized would literally emerge from darkness into a church newly illuminated by the Paschal light as they joined the congregation for the first time. Likewise, Moses, the model of apophatic ascent into the divine unknowing of union with God, does not go alone. We have seen already that he leads a band of select priests, but he goes also as a prototypical celebrant of the Eucharist, a proto-bishop, standing for all the baptized via the Blessed Sacrament which he and they share. Oneness with God is given via the Church, not outside, despite, or in isolation, from her.

Only after his initial liturgical purification can Moses ascend to what Dionysius calls the "highest of the divine ascents." Following Gregory of Nyssa and Origen before him, Dionysius portrays baptism as the first of three spiritual stages: purification, illumination, and perfection. The purification of Baptism serves as a preliminary for illumination by the Holy Spirit through anointing with holy oil in what the Western Church would call Confirmation, and leads ultimately to perfection in the Eucharist.

The Dionysian sensibility of liturgical ascent defined the aesthetics of Gothic architecture. Medieval altars, elevated up several steps, represented the holy mountain Dionysius describes, designating them as the proper place of the bishop or his priests. The architectural device and eastward orientation of the altar guided the eye to where Moses beholds the "holiest and highest of the things we can see or conceive of," namely the "holy of holies," the elevated Sacrament of the Eucharist. This, Dionysius recognized, is the "head" or "crowning point" of all the sacraments, again indicating its elevated nature. [11] God's "presence beyond all power of thought" is mediated not through the power of lone meditation, but through the Church communally venerating these holiest of things. It is on reaching the Sacrament, this holiest and highest of material things, in the company of the Church, that one finds the gateway to oneness with God. "Then and only then," writes Dionysius, can Moses break free from the visible and

---

10   Ecclesiastical Hierarchy 3.6.
11   Ibid., 3.1, 424D.

conceivable and plunge into the "cloud of unknowing," so that, like St Paul, he becomes "neither himself nor someone else."[12]

Dionysius is saying that we can reach spiritual oneness with God, *theosis*, not despite the created world, but through it; not despite one another, in isolation, but through one another in the Church; not despite the matter of the cosmos, but through the matter of bread and wine, itself as much the work of seasons and ecosystems as of human hands. The liturgy of the Church is a stripping down of the greater liturgy of the cosmos to its bare, suggestive forms. Just so, the arches of the cathedral are figures of the order and stability, ascent and descent, we find inscribed in the natural world: in the canopy of trees reaching for the sky or in the cascading plummet of a waterfall. In stone, humans carve these natural forms down into their elemental icons, at once concealing and revealing the harmonious interdependence of being that can exist only in difference, inequality, and hierarchy, without which the stones would lie next to one another in a formless heap of rubble.

As in stone, so in flesh. The liturgy we celebrate with our minds, voices, and bodies is a deeper stripping still, a carving down to the very invisible ideas at the heart of being. Not despite but *through* the music and movement of the sacraments, the lights of the Church, one ascends to the unspeakable action of the altar, offering, breaking, receiving, and consuming the forms of which the silent matter sings. The call God makes through the ancient rites is not a matter of "worship style," as though the form of the liturgy has no necessary connection to the matter of our faith. Rather, liturgy is the mediation of the likeness of God, as far as possible, in the created order. Through inanimate matter, the most unlike of all things to God, the likeness of God is consummated in us. In matter, Christ dwells among us. Bread is his tabernacle, the "place where God is." This is no superficial gloss on some pagan mystical scheme. Only by the place where God sets camp in being can Moses be lifted to that realm beyond being where sacraments shall cease.

Whatever else may still be shrouded in gloom, it should at least be clear now that Dionysian spirituality is not individualistic in the negative and exclusive sense. His truly Christian method of negative ascent is inextricable from the communal action of liturgy and the role played within it of material things. Baptism and the Eucharist happen through inanimate matter and other people. Oneness with God is realized, not in isolation, but through communion. Not only with each other, with fellow human beings, but with bread and wine, made of grain and grapes, nourished by

---

12   Galatians 2:20.

the sun and rain, as dependent on nature and its rhythms and as much part of them as we are. Salvation is more than just communal: it is cosmic. It is that by which nature is consummated in grace, losing itself, that it may become truly itself.

Nor is Dionysian ascent an "escape" of the soul from the body. There are such dualistic strands of Platonism, to be sure, and Plotinus's thought at least bears such dualistic traces, though scholarly opinion on this point is divided.[13] Even so, for him, Iamblichus, Proclus, and Dionysius, oneness with God is brought about, not despite, but *through* the physical realm, which mediates and in a sense is God's presence. Dionysius's spiritual teachings have both social and environmental consequences. They are not about abandoning the physical world to reach the spiritual, but about discerning the spiritual in and through the physical. The created world mediates and radiates God's saving grace. Whatever the reservations of Bishop Westcott, Dionysius tells us that salvation is far from a lonely business. Salvation is communal, cosmic, and iconic.

---

13   Eric D. Perl, *Theophany: The Neoplatonic Philosophy of Dionysius the Areopagite* (New York: SUNY, 2007), for example, sees Plotinus, Proclus, and Iamblichus as fundamentally in harmony with one another; Armstrong's notes to his Loeb translations give a more ambivalent picture, while trying always to emphasize that Plotinus overall has a positive view of the material world.

THE CONSUMMATION
OF THEOLOGY

IONYSIUS ARTICULATES A COMMUNAL PATH
of spiritual ascent through the Christian liturgy. He was not
alone in this, or even original. His Christian Platonist predecessors, especially the Cappadocian Fathers, said much the same. Even the
motif of "divine darkness" for which Dionysius is perhaps best known is
much indebted to St Gregory of Nyssa's *Life of Moses*, where it becomes an
expanded inversion of Plato's famous Allegory of the Cave: while Plato's
prisoners are to escape into daylight and so see truly what they have only
ever known by shadows cast on the wall, Gregory and Dionysius would
have us flee further still, into the divine vision where darkness and light are
both alike. So far, then, we have not seen much innovation on Dionysius's
part. But where he is original, and where he goes further than his Christian
forebears, is in his use of a newer strand of Platonic wisdom to articulate
his Christian sacramental vision of reality: the ritual practice called *theurgy*.
Meaning *divine work* or *activity*, theurgy provided the intellectual framework
for Dionysius to expound (as far as due reverence allows) how God works
through the liturgical action of the Church.

The father of the theurgic strand of Platonism was Iamblichus, the Syrian
pagan priest. In common with many of his contemporaries, Iamblichus
understood what we now call Platonism as one strand in a universal tradition of wisdom that was not restricted to the Greeks alone, but by way
of Pythagoras was shared with the Egyptians, Indians, Zoroastrians, and
even Moses.[1] Platonic philosophy gave Iamblichus insight into the cult of
his fathers, which he maintained.

Even in Iamblichus's day, theurgy was not universally welcomed by his
fellow pagan philosophers. Much of Plato's own thought denigrated the
material realm as inferior to the spiritual, a dualism even further exploded

---

1 Iamblichus, *The Life of Pythagoras*, 3–4, describes Pythagoras's sojourns among the
Jews, Syrians, Phoenicians, Egyptians, and Babylonians before returning to Samos.

by the influential Aristotle, for whom the divine and the material had completely different purposes and trajectories. How, one might ask, could the merely material mediate the divine?

Iamblichus abhorred such dualism. He emphasized the Platonic doctrine of participation, as discussed in the previous chapter: all causes contain their effects, and so the physical mediates the spiritual rather than being isolated from it. This helped him answer another objection. Porphyry, an acolyte of Plotinus, wrote a letter criticizing theurgy for, among other things, suggesting that mortals might be able to manipulate the wills of the gods through their rituals.[2] Until recently scholars have read this letter as proof of a clear bifurcation of Platonic tradition into two rival schools: whereas the pristine Greek Platonists had moved towards a rationalist approach to philosophy divorced from traditional religious practice and homage to the gods, the likes of Iamblichus and Proclus were adopting pagan ritual elements, perhaps as part of a popular pagan resistance to the now official Christian religion and its far more accessible rites. This tells us rather more about modern proclivities than those of the ancients themselves. The great twentieth-century Platonist E. R. Dodds firmly demarcated the "rationalist" Plotinus from the likes of his pupil Porphyry, who, "deeply religious by temperament . . . had an incurable weakness for oracles."[3] Thanks to these unfortunate religious tendencies, Dodds writes, Porphyry's letter "made a dangerous concession to the opposing school." Whether two such resolutely divergent schools can really be so clearly identified is debatable. The Neoplatonist Damascius does delineate the more theurgic from the more philosophical strand of Platonism, but understands both as present in Plato's thought as a whole. The ancients were far less ready to oppose reason to religion or philosophy to magic than we are. Dodds knew, for instance, that Plotinus is said to have taken part in a theurgic divination and to have taken some pride in its result, which proclaimed him the reincarnation of a god. But because this was reported by Porphyry,[4] Dodds says it is to be disregarded as schoolyard chatter. His equation of theurgy with the séances of Blavatskyite spiritualists perhaps reveals why he protests so much.

There is, it must be admitted, a certain rather Hegelian orientalism at play here: credulous Eastern "superstition" and spiritualism was supposed

---

2   Porphyry, *Letter to Anebo*.

3   Eric Robertson Dodds, *The Greeks and the Irrational* (Berkeley and Los Angeles: University of California Press, 1951), 287.

4   *Life of Plotinus* 10.

to give way to the mature rationalism of the West. We will see that scholars of Japanese Buddhism of Dodds's vintage have likewise downplayed or denigrated the supposedly "irrational" elements of its founding fathers in order to emphasize their own rationalistic credentials and thereby avert Western condescension. But rationalism is an obsession of modernity, not antiquity. More recently a compelling case has been made that Porphyry's and Iamblichus's correspondence is part of a more formal, intra-traditional debate purposely designed to teach the value and importance of theurgic ritual.[5] Leaving aside the debate whether such rivalries existed among Platonists in the days of Plotinus, Porphyry, and Iamblicus, we may rest content in this book to speak broadly of Western and Eastern "streams" of Platonism, with the caveat that however they may diverge, they spring from a single source.

Whether Porphyry's accusation against theurgy manipulating divinities was heartfelt or a didactic tool, Iamblichus's retort stands either way: theurgy, he writes, is absolutely not a matter of mortals manipulating divine energy using matter, but rather, divine energy working through matter to bring the material realm closer to its spiritual perfection. Theurgy was not us working on the gods. It was opening the channels for the gods to work in us:

> It is not the case that such activity draws down the passionless and pure into proneness to passion and impurity; on the contrary, it renders us, who have come to be subject to passions by reason of birth, pure and immutable.[6]

In other words, we do not call down the gods: the gods lift us up. Nor is theurgy in any sense an act of domination, whether by humans of the gods, or by gods of humans. Rather, Iamblichus calls it a "communion of friendship based on like-mindedness"—using the exact word, *koinonia*, we met above in Dionysius—bringing its practitioners into such harmony that the invoker and the invoked are unified while nonetheless retaining their distinction. One can see a basic connection between this theurgic ritual and the Eucharist as Dionysius describes it. The celebrants of Christian liturgy and pagan theurgy alike claim not to affect the immutable and transcendent, nor to manipulate it, but to establish communion with the divine such that the divine might divinize the practitioner, in this

---

5   Crystal Addey, *Divination and Theurgy in Neoplatonism: Oracles of the Gods* (Aldershot: Ashgate, 2014).

6   Iamblichus, *De Mysteriis* I.12.

way effecting that *henosis* or oneness[7] that Dionysius will call *theosis* or divinization.

Despite these caveats, it would be an understatement to say that theurgy's reputation has been mixed in Christian circles, too. St Augustine was most decidedly not fond of it,[8] which may suggest that there is at least some truth in the divergence between theurgic Platonism and the more exclusively intellective kind he encountered and praised. More recently, especially since the Reformation, theurgy has been written off as "magic," and while this sobriquet increased interest in esoteric circles, their attention did not necessarily help its cause. Modern scholars may have seen theurgy as a foreign blight upon the pure Hellenic gene pool of Platonic and Aristotelian philosophy, engendering a sort of folk-religious hick cousin of unsavory ritual magic, an unfortunate degeneration of the older and purer intellectual Platonism of Plotinus. Yet neither Iamblichus nor Dionysius himself show any sign of regarding themselves as importing a foreign system into their religious practice. For Iamblichus and Proclus it is simply a question of the proper interpretation of Plato.

Philosophy in Plato's day was never a solely intellectual enterprise to be pursued in isolation from life and spiritual experience. The love of wisdom was a way of life and the best possible expression of realities experienced, however dimly: the "most probable" ways of seeing the world, as Socrates puts it, when he renders his insights in the language of myth and parable. We have lost that capacity for myth and reduced our interaction with reality to empiricism or metaphor, with no room for anything in between. This leads to a dualism between myth and fact, imagination and reason, metaphysics and physics, grace and nature, which Iamblichus himself warned against: a disenchantment that "spells the ruin of all holy ritual and theurgic communion between gods and men," leaving the cosmos "a desert, without gods."[9] Order is seen as something to be imposed or opposed, rather than discerned. There is no fundamental architecture to the universe, nothing that can yield meaning. Where arches were, there is only rubble stretching beyond the horizon in endless and utter equality.

Such is the apartheid in Western thought between the spiritual and the physical. As we will see, Reformation priorities of scripture over reason, faith over works, and grace over nature contributed to a binary worldview

---

7 *De Mysteriis* 41.4–11.

8 *City of God* 10.9–10.

9 *De Mysteriis* 28.4-8, translated in Gregory Shaw, *Theurgy and the Soul* (Kettering, OH: Angelico Press, 2014), xxii.

where the supernatural and natural realms are mutually exclusive, and speculation about the former was relegated to realms of irrational "mysticism." The Reformers rejected relics and the Real Presence of Christ in the Eucharist; modern materialists reject the miraculous altogether. For the Reformers, inheriting the late medieval doctrine of voluntarism, God can be known by his will alone; for moderns, the historical-critical approach to Scripture has removed any confidence in the Bible as a consistent revelation of that will. The difference is only one of degree, and that degree has expanded via deism to a *de facto* atheism: if God exists at all, he is safely inscrutable in his heaven, not troubling this world, so that this world need not trouble much with him. The notion that humans might invite his action into this realm seems like little more than make-believe, with a suspect whiff of sorcery.

Like Iamblichus, Dionysius does not only believe in miracles, but practices them — with the caveat that whatever magic is done in theurgy, it is done by God. We and the material elements involved are the vehicles of that work, and at best only indirectly its agents. Thus, with its parallels to the Christian priority of grace, theurgy offered Dionysius a way of articulating sacramental theology in the philosophical language of his day. His use of it, however, was not just pragmatic. Theurgical principles resonated with the Christian doctrine of the Incarnation. Whether or not we can so neatly identify two opposing Platonic "schools," there were some Platonists committed to an impassible divide between the superior realm of the spirit and the inferior material realm. As we read earlier, Augustine tells us that these could never countenance the Word, the Divine Logos, becoming flesh in a human person.[10] Nor, perhaps, could they countenance the working of the Divine Spirit through materials such as water, bread, or wine. For Dionysius, the latter followed naturally from the former. Iamblichus's and Proclus's theurgy offered the perfect philosophical interface between the universal wisdom Iamblichus shared with the Egyptians and the Greeks, and the specific revelation of God in Christ.

Theurgy unites Dionysius's Platonic apophatic theology with his Christian commitment to the Incarnation of Christ. It gives clarity to the revelation of the Divine Word made flesh once as a man, and until the end of the world in the matter of bread and wine. It exhorts the spiritual progress of the individual believer, but only through the communal sacramental life of the Church. And more, it discovers the cosmos charged with divine presence. In short, theurgy makes matter matter.

---

10 *Confessions* 7.9.13.

Theurgy evidently does not belong to Christianity alone. Its origins connect Christianity to a wider metaphysics which one might tentatively describe as sacramental or iconic, and in which other spiritual and philosophical traditions continue to share. That Christianity has largely eschewed, marginalized, or demonized theurgic Platonism is the result of later tendencies in Western theology: tendencies that have given rise to negative consequences of modernity, including the technocratic subjugation of nature and of one another. A recovery of a participatory metaphysics and its practical outworking in theurgy offers Christians a means to oppose the dualistic worldview of materialism — the division of spirit and hence meaning from matter. This will help us answer some of the challenges other religions rightly make of Christianity, and stand in greater unity with them to help redirect modernity to its proper course.

The Negative Way is an antidote to the culture of celebrity that has infected even the Church: a prophylactic against celebrity preachers and megachurch personality cults, and also to the veneration of the clergy that has led to such infamous abuse of station and of vulnerable people. It means a move away from the Church being used as a platform for wannabe gurus or poor-man's therapists. It means a reorientation away from what a learned friend calls "Breakfast Television" church, where the charismatic priest talks over the altar like the host of a cookery program addressing a live audience over a kitchen table. It means an end to petty power struggles among lay volunteers who see their domain, whether the cutlery drawer or the flower rota or the home group, as a way to exercise the authority they either had at work before they retired or never had at all. It means finding oneself by dying to self, and the paradox of living in and through the material world and yet in Christ alone.

Theurgy takes Dionysius's apophatic path, his call to self-offering, deeper still. It makes his pseudonymity a sacramental act. Not merely an homage to St Paul, Dionysius's self-effacement takes him into the heart of Christ himself, and so into the self-emptying inner life of the Trinity. One with the Communion of Saints in Christ, "Dionysius" shares their identity, and so might well take any of their names, as Catholic Christians take a saint's name at Confirmation.[11] But his particular choice of name is instructive: he loses himself to find a shared identity with that Greek philosopher who was converted by Paul's approbation of "worship by unknowing." Worship, that

---

11   An insight for which I am indebted to Gorazd Kocijancic, "The Identity of Dionysius Areopagite. A Philosophical Approach," *Sobornost Incorporating the Eastern Churches Review* 29, no. 2 (2007): 75–84.

is, the liturgical worship inherited from Our Lord and transmitted through the apostles to the bishops of our day, is at the heart of Dionysian theology, not an optional addendum over some otherwise self-sufficient meditative scheme. He is not trying to turn the Church into a mindfulness class. The Divine action of and in the liturgy is paramount, eclipsing all words and images, even those of Scripture itself, for "theurgy," he writes, "is the consummation of theology."[12] Taking the name Dionysius is a baptismal act, an act of worship offered to God, a reorientation of the self to the cult of the saints, a Christening of Platonic apophatic theology. So it is thanks to his theurgic theology, even more than his better known apophatic philosophy, that Dionysius fulfills the word of Pope Benedict and is able "to put Greek wisdom at the service of the Gospel, to foster the encounter of Greek culture and intelligence with the proclamation of Christ."[13]

The influence of Dionysian Platonism has indeed extended far beyond the Greeks. It has informed the spirituality of the many Eastern churches and helped their ideas flourish along the Silk Road. It has helped them survive and, in some cases, thrive as minorities under Muslim rule. It has also had a profound and lasting influence on Islam itself. These are the themes to which we next turn.

---

12   *Ecclesiastical Hierarchy* 3.5, 432B.
13   Benedict 2009:79.

A MINORITY CHURCH

It is difficult to find a name to express the excellence of the true and unchangeable doctrine; but as its meritorious operations are manifestly displayed, by accommodation it is named the Illustrious Religion. Now, without holy men principles cannot become expanded; without principles, holy men cannot become magnified; but with holy men and right principles, united as the two parts of a signet, the world becomes civilized and enlightened.

— from the Stele of Xian

WHAT IS THIS RELIGION, DECLARED "ILLUStrious" by decree of the Chinese Emperor? This civilizing faith of true and universal teachings, expounded by holy men, which brings enlightenment to the world? The words on the 8th-century stone stele unearthed in Xian could refer to Taoism, Confucianism, or Buddhism—but they do not. This was the imperial verdict on a new arrival: Christianity.

It is hard to imagine the Chinese authorities giving religion such a good name these days, especially in the lands of the Uighur people, now being systematically "re-educated" out of their own monotheistic faith of Islam, while Christian churches are meanwhile bulldozed for failing to secure state approval. The court of 7th-century China viewed religion in general and Christianity in particular rather more favorably than its Marxist successor today; and, for that matter, more favorably than much of 21st-century European and American officialdom.

Rod Dreher's *Benedict Option* calls Christians to form ecumenical communities with a common life focused firmly on God in prayer. In the face of marginalization by the secular powers, we can no longer afford division and disunity, if ever we could. Catholics, Orthodox, and Evangelicals need not set aside their important differences, but do need to see that we have plenty enough in common to support one another in maintaining our families' and communities' life of faith.

If the example of the Areopagite is anything to go by — an example set in turn by St Paul himself — then we are called to go further than ecumenism. Orthodox Christians of all stripes are finding, through initiatives like the *Benedict Option* and journals like *First Things*, that we have more in common than divides us. We also have more in common with traditional adherents of other faiths than we have with the sea of liberal secularism that surrounds us.

The history of the Christian faith extends much further than Europe or America. By the time the gospel had reached Britain, it had already reached the frontiers of China, spread along the Silk Road by Nestorian missionaries who encountered Persian and Indian religions along the way. The diverse origins of Platonism gave them the needed concepts to engage with the advocates of these sophisticated intellectual and spiritual systems in an intelligible language. Plato's thought itself did not develop in an ethnic or national bubble, but by way of Pythagoras Platonists could claim Indian, Persian, and even Semitic influences. Nor were the stories and ideas of the Old Testament conceived in a vacuum. They bear traces of the Canaanite, Babylonian, and Assyrian cultures around them. By virtue of both its Greek and Jewish inheritance Christianity was from the outset bound up with the wider quest for truth that until very recently occupied the best minds not only of Western Christendom, but of the world.

When school textbooks tell us that Christianity is a "Western" religion, they are over-simplifying. Christianity is no less Eastern than Western. Even the name "Christian" is not of European provenance, even though it is in the European language of Greek. It was in Syria, not in Europe, that the followers of Jesus were first called Christians. They had fled to Antioch from Jerusalem in around AD 35 after the stoning of Stephen, in which Paul himself had taken part. Sometime before AD 44 the apostle himself went to Antioch. His letter to the Galatians[1] describes his falling out and reconciliation with St Peter there over the extent to which gentile converts should adopt Jewish practice. This was all going on in Antioch *before* Paul set foot in Europe. Christianity neither began in the West, nor need it end there.

Antioch had marked the beginning of the Silk Road. The trade this brought made it the third largest city in the Roman Empire. Wealth lay in the East, not the West, as any Roman soldier would have told you. A dreary outpost like Britain was certainly not seen as a plum posting. Only much later, when Christian monks smuggled silkworms back down the Road to Byzantium in AD 552, would the West break its dependency on

---

1 Galatians 2.

the sericulture of the East. Yet the mission of these monks, their several generations of forebears, and the hundreds of thousands of converts they won from Antioch to China is practically forgotten by western Christians as much as by advocates of secularism: whatever the facts, they are determined to believe that Christianity is a "western" religion.

The West has a poor memory of the past outside its bounds. Recent popular histories including Peter Frankopan's *Silk Roads* books and Gerard Russell's *Heirs to Forgotten Kingdoms* have helped cure the West of some of its exceptionalism, showing how it is really only in the last few hundred years that Europe ceased to be a fairly insignificant sideshow in world history, before it (and later its colonies) took center stage.

The Western belief that our way of thinking is the neutral, default position of the world is too deeply engrained to be revised overnight. This Eurocentricity begins not with Christian exceptionalism per se, but specifically with *Western* Christian exceptionalism, and the fourth-century *Ecclesiastical History* of Eusebius. Focusing on the Christianity of the then burgeoning Roman Empire, Eusebius overlooks the swathe of contemporary Christianity that existed and flourished outside the Empire, in the East. Indeed, the very definition of the East was soon circumscribed by the division of the Empire: to the western province of old Rome, the "East" meant the new Rome, Constantinople, and extended no further than its bounds. The existence of anything further eastward was relegated to the periphery of this intra-imperial West-East binary.

This amnesia resulted partly from the dominance of Greek, the language of the Eastern Empire, in Eastern Church affairs. When the Church fell into controversy in the fifth century over the nature of Christ, Greek was the language in which the arguments were aired. Given that Syrian Christians spoke dialects of Jesus's own language, it is ironic that those arguments lost so much detail in translation. This led to some of the Church's earliest schisms. Despite the fact that their tradition was grounded in the Semitic languages and culture of Jesus and his apostles themselves, from then on they were marginalized and forgotten in the annals of both Latin and Greek Christianity, reduced to the status of heretics. [2]

Pope Gregory sent St Augustine to Canterbury in the sixth century, marking the furthest westward frontier of the early Church. By that time the Syriac Church had spread as far east as China. Our forgetfulness is partly

---

2   For further details, see the discussion in chapter 3 of Christoph Baumer, *The Church of the East: An Illustrated History of Assyrian Christianity* (London, New York: I. B. Tauris, 2016), 44.

accidental, in that formal communications between the Catholic Church and Syrians were cut off, but it is also down to the dogmatic decision to designate them as heretics, followers of the disgraced Nestorius. These "Nestorians" were not real Christians, so their missionary endeavors did not count.

This is a shame, because the success of the missions of the churches of the East is remarkable. You would think they had a harder time of it than the Western Church. Western missionaries went out to poor pagan peoples with no written records of any systematic philosophy behind their practices and devotions. Meanwhile, the Church of the East was spreading through lands of great wealth and highly sophisticated philosophies that had been refined for centuries, and in writing. Moreover, Western Christians went with the might of the Roman Empire and, for better or worse, its armies. There is plenty of scope for criticism that Christianity was spread by the sword in Europe and later by Europeans abroad, though there are often one-sided and polemical tendencies at play in such arguments nowadays. It is harder by far to make this criticism of the Church of the East. Their missionaries lived and preached from the start among Zoroastrians, Manicheans, and Buddhists. At various points they suffered considerably under Persian Zoroastrian rule. Later, they and their sundered Orthodox brethren would become minorities under Muslim rule, with mixed fortunes.

Christianity was eventually suppressed altogether in China. Nonetheless, by the time St Augustine reached Canterbury, Christianity was flourishing at the opposite end of the known world as part of a vast, international Christian community in the East. The success of that community lay not in the power of the sword or even commerce, but in its ability to have meaningful philosophical interactions with its neighbors and their native traditions.

At the far end of the Silk Road from Antioch, on the northern border of the Taklamakan Desert in Xinjiang, lie the ruins of the oasis and trading outpost of Gaochang, known to its ancient Uighur inhabitants as Chotscho. Here, East Syriac Christians, Buddhists, and Manichaeans lived together. Murals on a ruined church there dating back to the seventh century depict what seems to be a Palm Sunday procession, including a deacon wielding a thurible, dressed and drawn in Persian style, attended by palm-bearing worshippers in Turkish and Chinese dress. Texts from the area, written in the ancient Sogdian tongue of Iran and old Turkish, reveal intellectual interplay. Jesus is portrayed as Buddha, the Resurrection interpreted as entering Nirvana. The Flower Festival marking the Buddha's birth was reinterpreted as marking Mary's gift of a rose to Elizabeth.[3] It may be tempting to reject all this as outright syncretism and dilution of the Christian faith. But first, we might recall how Christians in the West adopted the Greek philosophical language of their day to express their doctrine, or how they adapted pagan festivals to those of Christian saints or even feasts of the Lord. As a well-known example, evidence for the dating of Christmas to December 25th goes back only to AD 354 and coincides with the birthday of the Roman god Sol Invictus, the Unconquered Sun, whom Emperor Constantine venerated before his conversion to Christianity. The use of Christmas trees and even the name of Easter itself are similar baptisms of pagan practice. The use of contemporary language and religious practice by the Church was a practical missionary imperative, whose effectiveness is borne out in the East as much as the West. From Chotscho the faith spread to Kitan in North China and the tribal Naiman, Kerait, and Ongut peoples, some of whose amulets show motifs bearing a mixture of Christian, Buddhist, and native shamanistic symbols.[4]

The theology and spiritual life of these eastern Christians was formed by Greek thought, and transmitted the apophatic, Platonic principles of Dionysius. One of the most revered fathers of the Antiochene tradition, Theodore of Mopsuestia (350 – 428), was an exponent of Aristotle. Since 489, when the poet-theologian Narsai took over Nisibis theological college (which still exists in what is now Turkey), Theodore's writings were taught as the standard for the Church of the East, supplemented by the study of Aristotle's own work. But before long Platonic texts would also enter this academic world. In 529, the Roman Emperor Justinian closed down the Platonic Academy of Athens, forcing an exodus of pagan Neo-platonist scholars. Many of these fled east. Christians paraphrased, compiled, and translated their works into Syriac.[5] They continued to establish more schools further east, disseminating Platonic texts and also translating and integrating Persian and Indian thought. Among the Greek texts translated were the complete works of Dionysius. Sergius of Reshaina's Syriac version, translated in the second half of the 6th century, may in fact be older and closer to the original than the Greek text we have now.[6] Without doubt it

---

3   Wilhelm Baum and Dietmar W. Winkler, *The Church of the East: A Concise History* (Abingdon: Routledge, 2003), 76.

4   Ibid., 78.

5   Yury Arzhanov, "Plato in Syriac Literature," *Museon* 132, nos. 1–2 (2019): 1–36.

6   István Perczel, "The Earliest Syriac Reception of Dionysius," in *Rethinking Dionysius the Areopagite*, ed. Sarah Coakley and Charles M. Stang (Oxford: Wiley-Blackwell, 2009), 27–42.

influenced the theology of the Church of the East. The 7th-century bishop
St Isaac the Syrian quotes Dionysius's *Mystical Theology*,[7] and Dionysian
references to the divine darkness can be found in letters of the 8th-century
monk John of Dalyatha.[8] We also find traces of Eastern Platonism in its
broadest sense at the end of the Silk Road, among literary evidence of the
Christian missions in China.

The missionary Bishop Alopen arrived in the imperial court of China
in 635. If he met hostility, there is no record of it. We know from Chinese
texts that he was granted freedom to preach and to establish a monastery
in the capital, Xian.[9] These texts refer to his faith as the "Persian religion"
or the "religion of Enlightenment." There was a brief period of persecution under Empress Wu, who reigned from 690 to 705, and wanted to
eliminate any competition with Buddhism, but Christianity was legalized
again in 745 by Emperor Hsüan-tsung. Christians had been actively living
and worshipping in China for almost 150 years when their most impressive literary remain was carved: the so-called Nestorian stele. Made in 781
and rediscovered in 1625, this stele is our most extensive extant record of
the history of the East Syriac mission in China.[10] Written by the Syrian
priest known in Chinese as Qing Qing, it makes use of Buddhist language
to explain Christian doctrine.

The stele begins with a concise doctrine of the Triune God as true,
invisible, eternal, without origin, a perfect intelligence beyond all sacred
intelligences, and source of all that is honorable or good. The influence
of Platonic thought on Christianity cannot be deduced from these terms
directly, but the concepts of God as mind, source of the Good, and beyond
being are resonant of Dionysius's Platonic tradition, especially when combined with a reticence toward referring to the Divine as "God." The use
of the Chinese equivalent might have caused confusion or even derision,
since the "gods" of Buddhist and Taoist belief were thought of as created
and finite spiritual beings, lesser intelligences rather than that which is
beyond being or the source of being. Instead, the Syriac word "Allaha" is
transliterated into Chinese characters and left untranslated, as though it

---

7 Jason Scully, *Isaac of Nineveh's Ascetical Eschatology* (Oxford: Oxford University
Press, 2017).

8 Serafim Seppälä, "Angelic Mysticism in John of Dalyatha," *Parole de l'Orient* 41
(2015): 425–33; Alexander Treiger, "From Dionysius to Al-Ġazālī," *Intellectual History
of the Islamicate World*, 2019, 1–48, 2; István Perczel, ibid., 27–42.

9 For a list of these Chinese works, see Baumer, *The Church of the East: An Illustrated
History of Assyrian Christianity*, 188.

10 Baum and Winkler, *The Church of the East: A Concise History*, 48.

were a proper name. Like the cognate Arabic word Allah, it means not just "God" but "the God." The definite article places God beyond any multiplicity of gods.

Dionysius and the non-Christian Platonists were also wary of describing the One as God, for fear that he might be mistaken for one of the many gods of popular pagan belief. This is not a Platonizing aberrance from the Christian faith. The Old Testament itself rarely describes God as "God," preferring Elohim or the sacred and unspeakable name Yahweh revealed to Moses in the burning bush. Jews do not read this name out loud, reading "Adonai" instead, a tradition that older English bibles continue by printing "LORD" in capital letters wherever Yahweh is written in the Hebrew text. Modern Christians might heed this precaution: so limited is contemporary secularists' understanding of religion that many assume the God of whom Jews, Christians, and Muslims speak is a god, and much modern atheism makes the point of dismissing belief in any gods, as though the Divine One could fall into the same category as Hecate or Thor, or one of those statues on the plinths Paul saw in the Agora. Emulating the missionaries of the Eastern Church of old, one of the first things Christians need to impress on those around us is that God is not a god.

The stele goes on to describe God as the cause of all things that are good, a notably Platonic designation. As the Good, God cannot be the cause of evil, and all that is truly said to exist does so only insofar as it participates to some extent in goodness. For the Platonist, to be is itself good. Evil is a privation or lack of goodness, and so of true being. Dionysius writes extensively on this in chapter 4 of the Divine Names. At one point, developing a theme of St Gregory of Nyssa, he insists that even demons, insofar as they exist, are good: their evil is a falling away from true reality. To take another example, an utterly evil person who desires to live at all costs, even if he thinks that means killing off all the competition, still ultimately desires something good, namely to continue to exist; however perverse and wrong his chosen means of achieving his end, the end is still good. It is a corruption of a fundamentally good desire. The Goodness of the One is the Platonic reason for anything to exist at all, and so existence and goodness are intractable. Apologists for the Church of the East emphasize their lack of a doctrine of original sin, often seeing this as the root of Western Church doctrinal flaws, and blaming St Augustine. In common with the Eastern stream of Platonism we find in Proclus and Iamblichus, the Church of the East stresses instead the essential goodness of creation. This Platonic inheritance makes sense of the stele's sequence, starting with the unknowable source of all things, identifying this source in terms of goodness, and next, moving onto creation.

Here, the stele's account takes a decisively Christian turn, as it begins the story of creation with the Sign of the Cross. To a westerner used to a linear, chronological rendition of salvation history beginning with Adam, this may seem odd. The stele represents salvation history primarily in its spiritual and transcendent dimension. Its use of the Cross marks the centrality of God's salvific intent as the whole purpose of creation, but it is also using local tradition as an evangelistic motif. The Cross is a four-armed shape, and the number four is as important to Buddhist numerology as three is to the Pythagoreans, Neoplatonists, and Trinitarian Christians. Curiously, East Asian countries that used the Chinese script would develop a lasting tetraphobia akin to the Western superstition against the number thirteen. Until recently in Japan, you would never buy gifts for someone in a pack of four, but it seems that the convenience of mass-produced packaging has overcome such ill omens. The reason for the old aversion is that in Chinese characters the number four is a homophone for the word for "death," *shi*. These local superstitions notwithstanding, in Buddhist cosmology the number four signified universality, both physical and spiritual. As well as the four directions of the compass, classical Buddhist cosmology speaks of Four Dhyānas and the Four Formless Abodes as metaphysical realms of consciousness. Time is said to pass in cycles of four periods.[11] The Four Noble Truths of the Buddha share this metaphysical significance. The author of the stele adapts this Buddhist cosmic numerology to the Cross on which Jesus died. Its particularity as the vehicle of salvation is derived from its universality as a symbol of the goodness and salvific intent that underlies and motivates the cosmos. By beginning their account of creation in terms of its salvific metaphysical significance rather than with its merely physical origins, these Christian missionaries were showing that their teaching crowned the wisdom of the native philosophies they encountered, fulfilled those teachings rather than replaced them.

The tendency to work from higher, universal, abstract forms to their specific instantiations is also typically Platonic, as opposed to the more Aristotelian approach that relies on sensory evidence to draw universal conclusions from specific phenomena. One of the intellectual problems Christianity faces in the West is the dominance that the more empirical mold has had on the way we see the world since the late Middle Ages. Christian apologists struggle to "prove" the existence of God and the historicity of

---

11   Akira Sadakata, *Buddhist Cosmology* (Tokyo: Kōsei, 1997).

the Resurrection from the ground up, as it were, using the evidence of the senses. Despite being a minority in the regions they traversed, the Eastern Church succeeded because they, like the Taoists and Buddhists they met, began instead from the abstract and universal. Modern Christians in the West, now a minority in our traditional homelands, need to show the universal rationality of Christian belief, which has far more in common with the spiritual and philosophical traditions of the rest of the world than it does with the narrow empiricism of our compatriots. We need to remember that Christians are not, overall, the odd ones out: the empiricists and materialists are a minority in face of the collective weight of the world's philosophical traditions.

After the cruciform creation narrative, sin is the next subject of the stele. It takes us back to the story of Adam and the Fall, but without mentioning Adam by name. Westerners attuned to demythologization may be tempted to see this as sweetening the pill, removing the incredible element of an original couple whose names have been handed down to posterity. To do so would be both anachronistic and a failure in translation. In the Hebrew of Genesis, Adam is the word for "human," and Eve for "life." They are not proper nouns. As native speakers of Syriac, a fellow Semitic language with Hebrew, the Christians of the Church of the East would not have needed this pointing out, as we do. They are not pulling the wool over anyone's eyes when they paraphrase the story of the Fall as follows:

> To the first man [God] granted perfect harmony with himself. The nature [of man] was left in its original state and did not well up [with ambition], his pure heart knew no desires.[12]

Again, in common with Platonism and the theology of the Church of the East, the stele insists on the essential goodness of the human soul. It frames sin in Buddhist and Taoist terms of harmony and freedom from attachment: sin is delusion, in Buddhist terms *avidyā*, literally "unseeing." This corresponds with Platonic readings of Christianity in which evil is only ever a privation, a lack of the goodness proper to Being, a view to which both Sts Augustine[13] and Thomas Aquinas[14] subscribed. "Insofar as they exist," writes Dionysius, "all things are good and are from the Good."[15] All desires are for some good, even if those specific desires are misdirected. Ultimately,

---

12 Baumer, *The Church of the East: An Illustrated History of Assyrian Christianity*, 190.
13 E.g., *City of God* 11.9.
14 *Summa Theologiae* I, Qu. 49.
15 *Divine Names* 4.20.

all desires tend towards the desire for life and being. Thus, through our desires, God as the fullness of being and of well-being draws us to himself and to our end in him.

After the Fall, the remedy. Next on the stele, Christ emerges from the Trinity, truly divine, "radiant" yet "concealing his true eminence."[16] This takes us back to that very early Christological hymn of Philippians 2:5–11, so important to Dionysius and his fellow Christian Platonists because of its teaching of kenosis, the self-emptying of Christ, who, though equal to God, "takes the form of a slave." The stele proclaims how, hidden in lowly human form, Christ overcomes death, removing "the impurities" of human nature and re-establishing "its sacred purity." So, connected with the divine hiddenness and manifestation, we find the classic Platonic motif of procession and return. The hidden God reveals himself in Christ to bring fallen humanity back to its Edenic origins.

This "radiance" attributed to Christ on the stele has Buddhist connotations, referring to the Buddha's benevolence which enlightens all realms, and so returns sentient beings to the true seeing of reality. Buddhism presents itself often as a teaching of enlightenment or illumination. In Dionysian terms, *theosis* or oneness with God is also a kind of enlightenment, a knowledge beyond knowledge reached through the sacraments: "Enlightened with the knowledge of visions, being both consecrated and consecrators of hidden understanding, we shall become luminous and theurgic, perfected and able to bestow perfection."[17] Despite the lack of any direct textual links between Qing Qing's stele and Dionysius's works, we can see a family resemblance in the way they use the language of metaphysical goodness and illumination. Loyal to St Paul's affirmation of the Unknown God in the Agora, Dionysius wants to show that Christianity is no novelty, but crowns the wisdom of the ages. Likewise, Qing Qing does not present Christianity to the Chinese as a mere innovation. He does not, as an advocate of a minority religion, enter someone else's land and denounce their philosophy or religion. Rather, he continues the stele by describing the teaching of Jesus contained in the "twenty-seven books" of the Bible as the "Great Reform" of what has come before.

The stele alone may give us a somewhat too eirenic picture of Christian life at the eastern end of the Silk Road. There were points of disagreement and conflict. We can find out more about these from six Chinese Christian scrolls in which Bishop Alopen and his successors make use of Chinese

---

16 Baumer, op. cit., 191.
17 *Ecclesiastical Hierarchy* 1.1, 372B.

philosophical concepts to portray the salvific importance of Christ's self-sacrifice.[18] This was difficult. Confucius had taught that because humans are essentially good, we are capable of right action of our own accord, without reliance on divine grace. Buddhism and Taoism taught that one might save oneself largely by one's own power, albeit in the Mahāyāna Buddhist teaching prevalent in China and Japan this progress might be assisted by bodhisattvas or deities. Suffering could be overcome by proper application. Despite their insistence on humanity's fundamental orientation towards goodness, the Church of the East still had a greater sense of the human propensity towards sin than the native traditions. After all, if we could escape sin entirely by ourselves, there would be little if any need for the Crucifixion. There was the further issue of reincarnation in an endless cycle of death and rebirth versus to the linear eschatology of Christianity, in which the universe has a beginning and end and humans have only one life, death, and resurrection. Finally, the Church would not want to abandon Christ's claim to be the only means of salvation.

Nonetheless, modern Christians might learn from Bishop Alopen's evangelistic approach in face of these contradictory claims. The oldest of his Chinese writings, The Book of Jesus, the Messiah, begins (like the stele) with concepts sympathetic to the local traditions: God as omnipresent, rather than a discrete "being," and as the source of all life. From here, Alopen reveals God's commandments, reordering them to emphasize first the common moral teachings of Confucius, namely honoring God, Emperor, and parents, and the Buddhist commandment to be merciful to all living creatures.[19] Having established this base, he builds on it the life of Christ, including an uncompromising account of the Crucifixion; but note that he establishes commonality and trust before moving onto disputed doctrines.

Later, Alopen's On the One God continues with the same methodology. He draws on Buddhist teachings about the need to live righteously and virtuously, but unlike Buddhism, which teaches multiple reincarnations, he restricts the scope of these actions to a single life on earth. This life is our only opportunity for salvation. Karmic seeds cannot be put off until a later life but must be sown here and now. Sin he explains as confusion and a lack of understanding, drawing on Indian philosophical understandings of moral failure as ignorance. In these, he shares common ground with some of the Platonic tradition, if not with the Augustinian notion of original sin: Proclus, for instance, maintains in his On the Substance of Evil that sin is a

---

18 Baumer, The Church of the East: An Illustrated History of Assyrian Christianity, 188.
19 Ibid., 188–89.

weakness of the soul, a failure in its act of contemplation to focus properly on the Good. A weakness in knowing is precisely a weakness in being. So, the Church of the East recognizes the innate tendency of humans to sin, but does not join Augustine in seeing this as directly transmitted in the act of generation. The image of God within us is stained, but not completely broken. True knowledge of God can restore the image in us. This salvation is open to all sentient beings, whom Alopen calls to lives of holiness in his *On the One Heaven*. Here, he echoes both the universalist soteriology of Origen and St Gregory of Nyssa, who said that even demons had the potential to repent and reach salvation.[20] This doctrine would resound with Mahāyāna Buddhists, who strove to see the inherent Buddha nature awaiting realization in all things.

Leaving aside the question whether the Christian East or West has the right doctrine on original sin or universality of salvation, we can appreciate the methodology of Alopen's evangelism. Always, he moves from the universal to the particular, establishing continuity before declaring rupture. Instead of smashing idols he pointed to empty plinths.

It worked. The effect of Bishop Alopen's mission was such that in AD 638 the Emperor proclaimed:

> The Greatly-virtuous Alopen, of the kingdom of Syria, has brought his sacred books and images from that distant part, and has presented them at our chief capital. Having examined the principles of this religion, we find them to be purely excellent and natural; investigating its originating source, we find it has taken its rise from the establishment of important truths; its ritual is free from perplexing expressions, its principles will survive when the framework is forgotten; it is beneficial to all creatures; it is advantageous to mankind.

Thanks to Bishop Alopen's dialogical missionary methods, unaided by sword or empire, Christians remained active in China for several centuries after him. The Uighur, who seem to have a taste for monotheism, were Christian before they were Muslim, and we have eighth-century evidence of Uighur Christian texts translated into Chinese by an Indian scholar. In AD 872 a merchant in Basra reported the Emperor I-Tsung showing him a picture of Jesus.[21] Ninth-century inscriptions, churches, crosses, and Christian manuscripts in Persian, Syriac, and Turkish have been found in Tibet. In

---

20   Origen, *Peri Archon* 3.6.5; Gregory of Nyssa, *Catechetical Orations* 26.
21   Baum and Winkler, *The Church of the East: A Concise History*, 48.

the same century, writings of the Arab cosmographer al-Masudi reveal that in Kashgar, Christians, Jews, Muslims, and Zoroastrians lived together with Buddhists and Taoists. By the end of the millennium, over 500 Christian texts had been translated from Syriac into Chinese.

Six hundred years later, new Christians arrived. They found little trace of their forebears who had one flourished there. Not that they had expected to find any, because they had no idea about the historic extent of the Church of the East and little interest in their "heretical" missions. Yet these new missionaries, the Jesuits, applied quite similar methods in their evangelism to those of Bishop Alopen and his clergy. This caused some consternation with their western brethren, suspicious that they may be syncretizing the Christian faith with the idols of barbaric, foreign cults. For all the hostility they faced from their peers, however, the Jesuits succeeded much as the Church of the East had done, in China and in Japan, until later persecution drove them out. The sad irony is that if Latin and Greek Christendom had paid greater — or any — attention to the Church of the East, the Jesuits may not have needed to go there at all. Christians might still have thrived and flourished alongside Buddhists and Muslims in cities like Kashgar. Perhaps it would have been a happier place than it is now, in the euphemistically monikered Uighur Autonomous Region. The Muslims of Kashgar are being imprisoned and persecuted for their belief in the same Allaha whose belief was once proclaimed by Bishop Alopen and welcomed by the Emperor.

Neither the Syrian Christians nor the Jesuits were explicitly invoking Dionysius, but his Platonic heritage ran through their methodology and spirituality, as well as the philosophy undergirding both. As Aquinas paraphrases Dionysius, "grace does not destroy nature, but perfects it." Western Christians might pay more attention to this dictum. Trends of postmodern thought have trained us to prioritize particularity and regard with extreme cynicism any claims of commonality or universality. This has led to an all-too-convenient categorization and partition of historically overlapping metaphysical traditions into rival and mutually exclusive "religions," a hermeneutic of suspicion that pushes us into competition with each other like rival products vying for space on the same supermarket shelf. We must not leave aside our genuine, mutually exclusive truth-claims; but unless we recover some common ground, we will neither be able to resist the debilitating fissiparity that has been imposed on us, nor to contest those truth-claims except by making arbitrary assertions of "belief." Adding our grace, our Christian salt, to the shared goodness we find in non-Christian religions, we can form an arch of many stones to help uphold our societies' fundamental structures against the jackhammers of Western exceptionalism and relativism. But we have first to acknowledge that Western secularists learned their exceptionalism from the Western Church. Dionysius calls us instead to recover an appeal to the common reason postmodernists deny, but that in the time of Alopen was so persuasive to the Chinese authorities. This offers far more than any atheistic political system of West or East. In the end, it is not by communism, or any other utilitarian, technocratic model of society but, as the Emperor proclaimed, "with holy men and right principles" that "the world becomes civilized and enlightened." Much of what passes for the European Enlightenment is simply staring into our own shadow.

A Tale of Two Islams

THE UIGHUR GET BETTER PRESS IN THE WEST THAN some of their co-religionists. Islam is mentioned only twice in Dreher's *Benedict Option*, and both times in relation to acts of terrorism. An American book, it reflects American concerns. Conservative American Christians particularly tend towards a negative view of Islam, fueled by the attack of September 11, 2001 and by the US's part in the conflicts in the Middle East. In Europe the attitude is more ambivalent. Michel Houellebecq's novels are not much loved by the left-wing world of letters, but sell so well that a publisher would be foolish to turn them down. Readers presumably have some sympathy with his thought, which in earlier books was highly critical of Islam, but now approaches a grudging admiration.

Submission[1] is the most obvious example. A Muslim premier is elected thanks to France's large immigrant minority from its former North African colonies. The protagonist is an academic, who cannot keep his job in the now privatized Islamic university of the Sorbonne without converting to the new creed of the day. He retreats to the Catholic monastery of Martel, a name notable for its association with the Frankish ruler Charles Martel who in 732 repelled the Umayyad invasion of Gaul in the Battle of Tours. The monastery evokes some nostalgia, but ultimately he finds the Church a spent force with no future. In the end, finding certain benefits — polygamy chief among them — he converts.

Many Muslims come to the West, but judging by how they persevere in their religious practice, it is not the ideologically purged public squares of godless secularism that attracts them. For now, they seek something more like the divinely-blessed Agora than the secular public square, where they might openly practice and promote their minority faith among a sympathetic majority. My experience in both state-funded and private church schools, poor and rich, has shown me that Muslim parents often send their children deliberately to Christian schools because they hope that, at least there, God will not be a dirty word and Christian moral ideals will be taught

---

1   Michel Houellebecq, *Submission*, tr. Lorin Stein (Portsmouth, NH: Heinemann, 2015).

and upheld. They are often disappointed, and I can sympathize. Though Anglicans, my wife and I have sent our daughter to a Catholic primary school to ensure a firm grounding in the faith. As even church schools genuflect to the latest ideological absurdities of critical theory, I wonder how long it will be before Muslim schools will be a better option for Christian parents.

My sentiments are shared in *The Possibility of an Island*,[2] where another of Houellebecq's middle-aged male protagonists channels his perennial sense of emasculation by secular modernity, saying:

> It's sad, the shipwreck of a civilization, it's sad to see its most beautiful minds sink without trace — one begins to feel slightly ill at ease in life, and one ends up wanting to establish an Islamic republic.

This encapsulates the more European style of angst about Islam: a double fear that Islam threatens Western liberties, along with the dawning suspicion that many of its reasons for doing so may in the end be right. No doubt, we must protest with all our strength against the murder and forced conversion of Christians in fundamentalist Islamic regimes, the violence against homosexuals and apostates, and the repressive controls over women in some Muslim countries. The sense of threat is not unjustified. But even if such Wahhabist interpretations are in vogue today, we would be fools to believe that this represents the historic spiritual and intellectual heritage of Islam. When Westerners see Muslims settling together in tight communities with well-disciplined, devout families, when we hear the power and beauty of the muazzin's call to prayer, when we discover the austere beauty of Islam's artistic and musical heritage, many find something to admire, even to envy.

Reading the European press, you might wonder whether Islam is really two different religions: one the Wahhabi religion of the fanatic, behind 9/11 in the US, Drummer Rigby in the UK, Charlie Hebdo in France; the other, the school textbook "religion of peace," historically a model of proto-Enlightenment tolerance and brotherly love. The latter is popularly associated with the name of the twelfth-century Andalusian jurist Ibn Rushd, known better in the West as Averroes. According to this "two Islams" story, Averroes' forward-thinking Aristotelian, logical, scientific worldview was crushed by the fanatics in his Islamic homeland, signaling the death of philosophy in the Muslim world; happily, he passed on the baton to European Christians and so paved the way for the Enlightenment utopia we now enjoy. A British Muslim commentator, Ed Husain, writes in a recent article

---

2   Michel Houellebecq, *The Possibility of an Island* (New York: Vintage, 2007).

that "many Muslims have been dragged into a new Dark Age of fanaticism, unable to accept modernity."[3] Averroes, Aristotle, and the Enlightenment, he says, offer the way out.

The story of a "medieval" (read: "backward and regressive") Islam in need of a Reformation is one often aired in the pub or at the dinner party, but it has been discredited in academia for decades. Rightly so. It is dangerous, ahistorical, and more fundamentally, untrue. To tell Muslims that their only worthwhile thinkers are those who most resemble 18th-century European rationalists is condescending; but worse, it blinds the West to its own flaws, and to the possibilities of redemption from them. Averroes is not the answer.

True, there was a time when Christians lived far more happily under Muslim rule than vice-versa, but this was not because Islam presciently fostered Enlightenment values. Christians of both the Orthodox and Eastern Syriac Churches lived as minorities under Islamic rule long before Averroes' ideas came into vogue. We have seen already how the Church of the East flourished along the Silk Road. This continued even after the sixth-century advent of Islam, and Christian patriarchs continued to send their missions from within Muslim-controlled lands. In the late eighth century, Patriarch Mar Timotheos I saw the Islamic rule under which he lived not as a threat or imposition, but as a "purifying strength for Christianity."[4] Maintaining good relationships with the five caliphs under whom he worked, he was able to procure their blessing for missionary activity to the extent that he built six new ecclesiastical provinces and sent bishops to Tibet and China. Under him, the Church of the East numbered tens of millions of worshippers in 230 dioceses. In Syriac letters between him and Caliph al-Mahdi, now translated into Arabic, he cites Aristotle, whose philosophy offered common ground, but often what passed for "Aristotle" was in fact the work of Neoplatonists. Certainly there is no indication of some fully-fledged empirical method that might foreshadow the European age of Enlightenment.

East Syriac Christians were not only tolerated but highly valued in the caliph's courts of eighth-eleventh century Iraq and Assyria, especially in the field of medicine. The leading medical school was a Christian foundation in Gundeshapur, Persia. A monastery since the fourth century and theological school from the sixth, the medical school boasted a vast library and a scholarly tradition. There, Christians translated not only medical but

---

3   Ed Husain, "Macron is preparing for intellectual battle against Islamism," The Spectator: https://www.spectator.co.uk/article/macron-is-preparing-for-intellectual-battle-against-Islamism.

4   Baum and Winkler, The Church of the East: A Concise History, 61.

mathematical and philosophical works from Greek into Syriac and Arabic, including works of Aristotle, Galen, Euclid, Archimedes, and Ptolemy.

One seventh-century Deacon, Hunain bin Ishaq, became personal physician to Caliph al-Mutawakkil. He had mastered Arabic, Persian, Syriac, and Greek, and as well as translating over 260 works, wrote over one hundred of his own. These included *The Way to Recognize Truth in Religion*, in which he asked, "from where does a person know that what he believes is the truth, and that what someone else believes is falsehood?" He wants to go beyond relativism or mere appeals to ancestral tradition:

> Indeed, if someone says that that belief has come to him by way of his ancestors, or if he says that that belief has come to him by way of a book, or from a prophet who has performed miracles, or from his own opinion, since he holds to a certain viewpoint, and to him his own religion is confirmed to be true through it, all the adherents of the religions who disagree with him would be able to say something similar. If that response is common among all the adherents of the (different) religions, it must be necessary then for whoever accepts his religion on the basis of this argument to embrace any other religion on account of this same argument.[5]

Life would have been far easier for Hunain if he had converted to Islam. However, part of his argument for the truth of his own minority religion was that any religion imposed by kings and threats of violence would lose one vital criterion for the suspension of disbelief. The perseverance of Christians who abandoned the possibility of high status and even went to their death for the sake of their faith was what demonstrated the true power of their religion:

> The true religion has not invited people from lowliness to high standing, or from humiliation to great might. But rather, it has called them from great might to humiliation. And yet, it has been accepted, even to the extent that whoever has accepted it would rather die than live at its cost.

Deacon Hunain saw Christians' minority status not as a mark of divine disfavor: he saw it as a vital witness to the strength of their faith. Without that strength, today's Christians living in the Middle East would not have survived the horrendous persecution they have endured in the last few decades: persecution that has accelerated thanks to Western-sponsored

---

5   http://www.tertullian.org/fathers/sbath_20.1_Hunain_ibn_Ishaq.htm.

"regime changes" which left Islamist warlords in charge. An Iraqi Christian priest I met on pilgrimage told me how his city of Mosul, home of thousands of Christians since the sixth century, was purged of Christians by the Islamic State, their churches destroyed, and their women seized as slaves, to return pregnant if at all.[6] I have spoken online to Iranian Christians imprisoned for converting from Islam and now living in diasporas in Turkey and Italy. Make no mistake, the fideism of Wahhabi ideologues is responsible for great evils. That said, even their persecution of Christian minorities hardly compares to the scale of the atrocities committed by Communist regimes, and the Bolshevik influence on the Wahhabi Jihadis themselves is arguably stronger than Islamic tradition, which, we might note, had preserved innumerable Christian churches, monasteries, and cultures intact for fourteen centuries before. It is likely that more churches were destroyed by these revolutionaries in the three years between 2014 and 2017 than all the previous centuries of Islamic rule combined.

In essence, Islamic rule was and is nothing like the recent revolutionary distortions of the Islamic State and its ilk. It has been more tolerant, and if that tolerance was at times fickle and limited, it was less so than its contemporary Christian regimes. At the opposite end of the Islamic world, the five centuries of Muslim rule in Spain which began in 711 are especially instructive. Under Muslim rule in Córdoba in 951, a Christian monk, a Spanish Jew, and Arab doctors would gather to revise one of Hunain's medical translations. In later years, Andalusia would yield such thinkers as the Jew Moses Maimonides, the broadly Platonist Ibn 'Arabi, and the great Aristotelian commentator, Averroes. Nor was it just Jews and Muslims who lived by and large peaceably in Andalusia. Until the ascendancy of the Almohad dynasty in the mid-twelfth century, Christians in Andalusia, known as Mozarabs, also flourished as part of the celebrated *convivencia*, a fruitful "cohabitation" of the three Abrahamic faiths.

While some Jews and Muslims were just about tolerated in Latin Christendom at times if they had some especially useful skill to contribute, this degree of scholarly interplay was not replicable in a polity where even internal diversity within the Catholic faith was suppressed. Indeed, the unique Mozarabic rite of the Andalusian church was replaced after the Catholic reconquest of Spain with the uniform Roman liturgy — though it has enjoyed some revival and can be heard in Toledo today. Back in the East, the Christians' tactic of making themselves indispensable worked well.

---

6   You can find out more about the Church in Iraq and donate to reconstruction efforts at https://acnuk.org/iraq/.

By 1015, for example, the Syriac metropolitan of Cairo had jurisdiction over three suffragan bishops, forty-seven priests, and 7,300 families; the Alexandrian metropolitan, two bishops, twenty-three priests, and 4,025 families. At both the Eastern and Western extremes of the Islamic world, Christians were by and large able to enjoy a respected and important role in medieval Islamic society: more than can be said for Muslims and Jews who came under Christian rule at the time.

This respect Muslims accorded to Christians had nothing to do with Enlightenment values *avant la lettre*. Nor had it anything to do with Averroes, who was not born until 1126, and in any case made almost no philosophical impact at the Eastern end of the Islamic world, and rather little even in his native Andalusia. While his legal work remained highly influential, his philosophical work may not have even survived until today were it not for Hebrew and Latin translations used by Jews and Christians in Christian Europe. For them, his extensive commentaries were an exciting new window into what had been for them long-lost works of Aristotle. But for scholars in the Muslim world, with a long tradition of Aristotelian exegesis behind them, Averroes' scrupulous return to the sources was decidedly old-fashioned: "the equivalent of silent films made after the invention of sound," as Peter Adamson, author of the History of Philosophy without any Gaps podcast, puts it in his very readable introduction to philosophy in the Islamic world.[7]

Christians survived and often even thrived because they made themselves invaluable. In times of persecution, they used their medical expertise to their advantage. This is something Western Christians may think on as we face further curbs on the exercise of our religious convictions. On the basis of Western monasteries in the so-called Dark Ages of Europe, the Benedict Option exhorts Christians to group together and preserve the literary and philosophical heritage of the West. This is well and good, but the Eastern Christians, who have lived always as a minority, raise the challenge: if Christians are going to be a minority, it is not enough simply to preserve knowledge. We need to be in the position to offer something unique, something valuable enough to the wider world that we become a respected minority. Christ has told his followers that we can expect to be hated: look at Matthew 10:22, for example. So be it. Muslims are hated, too; and for any Christian in time of trial, the question should never be "Why me?" but "Why not me?" Perhaps we need to be more willing to accept the contempt of the world if we also wish to be its envy.

---

7 Peter Adamson, Philosophy of the Islamic World: A History of Philosophy without Any Gaps (Oxford: Oxford University Press, 2016).

Christians living in the West should expect missionary activities to be curtailed. Already in the UK, Catholic adoption agencies have been forced to close on the grounds that they would not in good conscience offer children to same-sex parents.[8] Campaigning peacefully outside abortion clinics has been tightly restricted.[9] Scotland, at the time of writing, is in the process of effecting legislation that would effectively ban public reading of Scripture as a hate crime.[10] It will not be long before Christian schools have to choose between wholesale adoption of critical gender ideology or withdrawal from the public sector and possibly even the private. Individual Christians will no doubt be allowed to continue in public life as long as they are silent about their principles, but church-run charitable and social organizations will face pressure to conform and, depending on who is in charge of our countries, the possibility of complete closure. The social services which have justified our existence to a secular society, such as homeless shelters, women's refuges, Alcoholics Anonymous meetings, or chaplaincy work in prisons, hospitals, and the Armed Forces, will continue to come under criticism and may prove unviable or be taken over by the state.

So what to do? There would be nothing uniquely valuable in Christians following Deacon Hunain's example and training as medics, especially in countries with state-funded hospitals. Nor can or should the Church try to justify its existence by plugging the gaps of the welfare state. Mission to the poor and vulnerable is a core vocation of the Church, to be sure, but if that is its only purpose, it can and will be superseded. Our unique and exclusive calling is to offer worship to the Triune God; but what we can also offer in support of this is to follow Hunain's example of scholarship. We guard unique knowledge more precious than any of the missionary services we might offer: the deposit of the Christian faith. As theological faculties in universities close down and faculties of the liberal arts are overtaken by ideologues hostile to the faith, we may find that we have an even more extensive inheritance to safeguard. We can no longer expect secular schools and universities to be fit places for the education of Christian children. They are in the hands of people who would brainwash our people into nihilistic relativism. Religious institutes may be the only places willing to

---

8   See, for example, the 2012 BBC news article *Catholic Care loses gay adoption fight*, https://www.bbc.co.uk/news/uk-england-leeds-20184133.

9   "Anti-abortion protesters lose appeal over clinic buffer zone," https://www.bbc.co.uk/news/uk-england-london-49421766.

10   "Bishops fear owning a Bible could be hate crime offence under new Scots law," https://www.scotsman.com/news/politics/bishops-fear-owning-bible-could-be-hate-crime-offence-under-new-scots-law-2927927.

preserve the growing literary and philosophical corpus of the West, which is otherwise being consigned to oblivion by left-wing intellectuals in the name of "decolonization" of the curriculum: perhaps even literally to save books from the pyres. As the *Benedict Option* warns, there may be a great work of preservation to be done.

Hunain shows us that Christians have a greater task than just preservation of knowledge. The deposit of the Christian faith and the wider intellectual inheritance of the West is not to be guarded jealously, but shared. Hunain's ideas flourished in company with those of the ancient pagan philosophers and his contemporary Muslims and Jews. As Christians become a minority in the West, we will join Muslims, Jews, Buddhists, and Hindus, among others, in that minority status. But together we are considerably less a minority than we might be divided. We may need to set up institutions where people of prayer and a high level of shared theological, intellectual, and ethical commitment can continue to pursue truth, beauty, and goodness in a world from which these dearest values have been ruthlessly exorcised.

*   *   *

The first problem with the tale of two Islams is that the mythical proto-Enlightenment, Averroist paradise version of Islam, where faith and reason were neatly separated and priority given always to the latter, never existed. The *convivencia* of Christians and Jews in the Islamic world had nothing to do with those presuppositions, which in fact prove unconducive to genuine diversity of thought. We will see why in the next chapter, when we look at Averroes' influence on Europe's Aristotelian turn. His strict Aristotelianism led to the skeptical sundering of the material world from any sense of transcendent value, and this has proven both a boon and curse to the post-Enlightenment West: a boon in its openness to empirical experimentation and the great scientific benefits we have enjoyed therefrom, but a curse in its technologization of the world and one another, the false belief that science offers the solutions to the very problems which it causes. Such reasoning has been used not only for medical and technological advances, themselves a two-edged sword, but also to justify racialism, slavery, sexual inequality, social Darwinism, and eugenics. A disenchanted cosmos cut loose from the divine nature leads to greater social autonomy, as we see ourselves not so much as part of a whole, oriented towards a common good, but as the independent definers of our own goodness, our own personal truths. Yet this autonomy quickly unravels into solipsism and a war of absolute wills. "Religious freedom" presented as part of this package of personal autonomy serves only to divide religious people from one another, as our faith recedes ever further into the private sphere.

The second problem with the tale of two Islams is its claim that philosophy died in the Islamic world with Averroes, and this is because the triumph of a kind of "Averroism" in the West has blinded us to the surge in the Islamic world of a different kind of philosophy clearly influenced by Platonism.

Platonic philosophy was the intellectual and spiritual engine of what we might call a "third Islam," which stubbornly refuses to conform to the Western binary of Enlightenment values versus fideism. That binary owes its existence to the wedge Averroes' successors drove between philosophy and theology. While Latin Christendom perpetuated that divide, the spiritual and theological world of Islam integrated scripture, Sufism, and the rational intellect in a far more Platonic manner, even if it was seldom explicitly branded as such. In this, Muslim sages were following the example of Plato himself, for whom philosophy was no matter of proofs and stale syllogisms, but the love of wisdom as a living, spiritual practice. Where Western mysticism was treated with increasing suspicion and relegated to the monasteries and convents, Muslim sages found that what was ultimately a Platonic approach to philosophy helped them express their inexpressible experiences of the divine. Even in its broadest sense, Platonism had never completely vanished from Islamic thought, since the most influential of all Muslim philosophers, the great Aristotelian Avicenna, had read the philosophy of the Stagirite through a lens colored by pseudo-Aristotelian Neoplatonic glosses. Although Avicenna rejected Plato's doctrine of forms and saw himself very much as an Aristotelian, it was his ultimately (and unconsciously) Platonic elements to which Averroes most objected.

The distinction between Platonism and Aristotle in Islamic literature is not at all straightforward, given that much of what the Islamic world considered Aristotle was in fact Neoplatonic material misattributed to the Stagirite, and also that they had texts of Aristotle now lost to posterity. The textbook distinction between Platonism and Aristotelianism should therefore be treated with extreme caution: first, because medieval notions of Aristotle were filtered through later Arabic philosophy; and second, because we have so little of Aristotle's total output that we cannot with any certainty establish what he thought. The ancients may well have been right in thinking that Aristotle was far more of a Platonist than his extant works suggest. The few of his works that survive amount to little more than lecture notes, which may even have been written down by his students rather than by the Stagirite himself. Still, without falling into the trap of an anachronistic division between "Platonism" and "Aristotelianism," we can say that in the twelfth century a more conscious revival of explicitly Platonic thought surfaced in the spiritual teachings of the Persian Suhrawardi, who found in the thought and character of Plato an antidote to Averroes' supposedly "Aristotelian" separation of faith from reason. Under similar influences, the Andalusian Ibn 'Arabi and Persian Mulla Sadra, in the thirteenth and seventeenth centuries respectively, found Neoplatonic philosophy conducive to their contemplative insights into the nature of reality. The existence of Arabic translations suggests that the works of the Pseudo-Dionysius are likely to have been among their many influences, [11] along with many Platonically-inclined thinkers in between, such as Mulla Fenari, Mulla Jami, and Ibn Turka. Highly sophisticated metaphysical speculation both informed and was refined by their spiritual disciplines and exercises. As little as they may be known in the West today, Ibn Arabi's doctrines and practices live on among Sufis to this day, and Mulla Sadra remains the preeminent philosopher-theologian of Shi'a Iran. Plato is still studied in earnest in the madrasahs of Qom and more widely in Iranian universities, while he is neglected in the West.

Nor was this Platonic tradition a minority belief or niche pursuit in the Islamic world. Platonic theology was very much the mainstream throughout the Islamic world until the end of the nineteenth century, insofar as Ibn ʿArabi's metaphysics, widely recognized as the ultimate synthesis of spirit, scripture, and intellect, came to dominate the intellectual milieux of both the Ottoman and Mughal worlds. Aristotle was not forgotten, as advocates of Averroes might have us believe, but his thought continued to exercise influence through the tempering lens of Avicenna. The reason Islamic philosophy since Averroes has so largely escaped Western attention can be gauged by certain Orientalizing assumptions of scholars in the last century, who wrote it off simply because it was more Platonic than Aristotelian, and so (to their thinking) bound up with an ill-defined "mysticism" or "theosophy" no more deserving of attention than the works of Madame Blavatsky: not so different, then, from the sorts of accusations leveled against Proclus and Iamblichus, and as we will see, against apparently fideistic elements of Japanese Buddhism which twentieth century rationalists found distasteful. Each of these sophisticated systems has been measured against the West's Procrustean bed of broadly Aristotelian and empiricist presuppositions about what constitutes proper philosophy, while having their perceived excesses either ignored or suppressed.

---

11   Treiger, Alexander, "From Dionysius to Al-Ġazālī," *Intellectual History of the Islamicate World*, 2019, 1–48.

Averroes' influence on the Western Enlightenment bifurcation of faith and reason has something to do with this marked closure of mind. But worse, it has played a part in whittling down the once dominant Platonic stream of Islamic theology to the threatened minority status it has today. The kind of fideism that spawns today's Islamic fundamentalists was not, we should emphasize, the result of Muslims abandoning Averroes eight hundred years ago. It was provoked far more recently, in the nineteenth century, by Western empires invading Muslim lands. Given modern Middle Eastern affairs, it may be hard to believe that until the twentieth century, Jews were generally seen as allies of Muslims, and that both they and Christians lived largely peacefully in Muslim lands. The birth of the Muslim Brotherhood and the hardline reforms of Islamic countries did not happen in the aftermath of Averroes, eight centuries ago. They started much later, with Muhammad 'Abduh, whose influential 1897 *Epistle on Unity* urged measures to combat westernizing influences. This, in turn, was a response to the Islamic renaissance in Egypt earlier that century, when the introduction of Western technological and social innovations divided Islamic thought. Some welcomed every aspect of European modernity. Others wanted to adopt helpful technologies but were wary of their potential application and social consequences. Elsewhere in the Islamic world, the last Ottoman Shaykh al-Islām, Mustafa Sabri, expelled from Turkey after the rise to power of Ataturk, wrote an influential four-volume defense of traditional Islam and critique of modernism, calling for a repristination of Islamic ideals. Such caution was not unreasonable. It is surely uncontroversial to point out that Western technological innovations have had, and continue to have, an ambivalent effect on societies that embrace them, sometimes destabilizing entire nations and playing them into the hands of European empires. The myth of progress is so ingrained in the Western mindset that it can be hard to sympathize with alternatives, and easier simply to dismiss them as regressive mentalities yet to catch up with our civilized ways. The truth, as Aristotle himself may well have averred, most likely lies between the two extremes: but if we are stuck so deeply in one extreme that we cannot see the other, we will never find the middle way.

We will later encounter a similar story of responses to Western influences in Japan. In the Islamic world, as there, philosophers have continued in their work to this day, varying in their degrees of interaction with Western thought. Some, like the contemporary Iranian Seyyed Hossein Nasr, are skeptical of Western science and the attitudes behind it, criticizing the ecological consequences of a worldview indifferent to God. That the West cannot distinguish between such criticism and fideism is a sign of our loss of perspective, born from the assumption that philosophy should have nothing to do with religion.

The reader might have noticed that "religion" is a word I do not very often use. It is a post-Enlightenment notion of dubious provenance. By using it, we risk falling into the Aristotelian habit of categorizing everything as though it were an encyclopedia entry, subdividing reality into genus and species, conquering the world by annotation like the Judge in Cormac McCarthy's *Blood Meridian*. With this encyclopedic mentality we find things that seem cosmetically similar and so name them "religions," determining that each is just one different example in one definitive set. But this distinction is artificial, and was once quite alien to the mindset of Islam, as it was to the Christians, Taoists, and Buddhists along the Silk Road. While a Muslim was one who had submitted to the One God as proclaimed by the Prophet Muhammad, a "muslim," uncapitalized, was anyone who submitted in peace to God. For a Muslim with a capital M, those who did not acknowledge Muhammad as the final prophet are certainly in error, but their error was not absolute. There was a sense that Jews and Christians too were sharing in the pursuit of truth and in the worship of God. Likewise, the ancient Emperor of China saw the new Christians in his realm, despite their differences in important details, as exponents of a shared truth. St Thomas Aquinas saw that Muslims, Jews, and pagans could arrive at some knowledge of God, even though they lacked the full knowledge Christian revelation alone could give. We do not need to lapse into perennialism to see that the idea of "religions" as badges of identity or products to be picked from a supermarket shelf is a modern one, born of Enlightenment proclivities, and has proven divisive. It is used by secularists to keep we "religious" in our place, our own separate sphere from an otherwise secular neutrality, but also from one another: to divide and conquer, relegating our pursuit of truth to private and irreconcilable opinion. There may be an ironic justice in the deposition of Christians to the kind of ghettos we once imposed on others, but this should give us all the more reason to join those whom our forefathers may have persecuted in resistance against their new secular successors.

The great error of the West, whether in its Christian or its new secular history, has been its exceptionalism: the idea that whether because of its religion or its science, "we" are superior to the cultures of the rest of the world. Medievalists like to stress that the so-called Dark Ages were rather more illumined than we have hitherto thought.[12] Yet now, we sink into

---

12 For a popular presentation, see Falk, *The Light Ages*.

the barbarism of a real Dark Age, where the autonomy of the individual is the sole measure of all things. The academy and the Church, appointed guardians of Western civilization, are apparently in the business of breaking it up for spare parts. It is time we wake up, not to anguish about our early modern exercise of empire, but to the philosophical suppositions which held then and continue still to let us think we can dictate terms to everybody else. For all the well-meaning toppling of statues, the idol of Western superiority remains firmly in place. It is by this idol that Westerners have hitherto deigned to measure the philosophy of the Islamic world, and sentenced it to death with Averroes. The very westerners who decry the imperialism of early modern Christendom and the imposition of so-called Western religion in foreign lands are the same who blithely proclaim the universality of Western liberalism and Western science, who insist on class or racial conflict as the only means of interpreting history, or who promote a nominalist discontinuity between sex and gender as the sole permissible understanding of human identity. Such claims rest on the supposed neutrality of a disenchanted public square. In this, the West remains out of kilter with the majority of the world's people, who maintain their stubborn habit of traditional religious adherence.

The *Benedict Option* of forming communities with fellow orthodox Christians is a vital antidote to secular modernity, but it can only be the beginning. The first word of the Rule of St Benedict is the command, "Listen." Dionysius urges us to listen deeply and more widely. If we really want to resist the secularist agenda, we will need to make allies further abroad: to find those wider common spaces, like the sacred Agora of old, where the search for the unknowable, transcendent Absolute is still taken seriously; to guard the knowledge of our faith, but to seek out the common ground with others doing the same; to find our role as a respected minority, not in dismissing other minorities but in using our special status in Western society to show the world the lost but better, reasonable, common way. The Agora for us today may be the space around the mosque, the gurdwara, or the temple. The Stoics, Epicureans, and Platonists might be Muslims, Jews, Hindus, Buddhists, or even pagans. If we listen, we will find friends, and the language of the Areopagite will help us speak with them the truths we share.

But before we do that, and put Dionysius into conversation with a philosopher and sage from beyond even the furthest Eastern reach of the Silk Road, let us further examine the root of the rot in the West.

The "Aristotelian" Turn

T HE WEST INHERITED THREE THOUSAND YEARS of collective tradition, spanning from Moses, through Plato, to the Western Middle Ages. The edifice of Western society had its foundations in ancient Middle Eastern and Greek philosophy. Now we stand like victorious barbarians in its rubble. Platonic theology is written into the architecture of cathedrals we can no longer afford to maintain, let alone to build. Tales of wisdom are inscribed in windows, icons, signs, and sculpture, yet the number of those who can read them has dwindled. Stones from ancient arches once calibrated to bear each other's weight are reduced to equality, resting in their crumbled heaps on level ground. Like them, we isolated individuals gaze forlornly at broken bosses and finials we are no longer equipped to understand. How have we come to this?

A Renaissance fresco offers a clue. To those who have succumbed overmuch to popular portrayals of the Catholic Church as an anachronistic bastion of intolerant and narrow-minded fideism, one of the finest paintings in the Apostolic Palace in the Vatican may come as something of a surprise. Raphael's *School of Athens* fresco, painted between 1509 and 1511, is a visual ode to philosophy. At its center is the famous depiction of Plato and Aristotle, as might be expected. The master and his student seem to be locked in scholarly dispute. Plato points upwards, as though arguing for the priority of higher things, of universals over particulars. Aristotle, in reply, stretches his hand palm-down over the ground. For the forefather of empiricism, our knowledge of higher things can come only from our study of the lower. We can know the more universal only by reference to the particular.

Surrounding Plato and Aristotle, as we might also expect, is a venerable cast of many of the great names in ancient philosophy. We find the likes of Archimedes, Heraclitus, Parmenides, Socrates, Diogenes, and Epicurus, all modeled by friends of the painter. But who is that behind the balding Pythagoras: the turbaned, green-clad fellow peering over his shoulder to look at the notes the old mathematical mystic is so intently penning? He is an unexpected figure: a Muslim, no less. For one of the most highly venerated philosophers of Raphael's Renaissance milieu was Averroes, that Cordovan acolyte of Aristotle we met in the last chapter. As we have seen, his influence in the Islamic world did not last long. But in Europe, Averroes' work threatened the Platonic consensus of the first millennium and heralded the great sundering of faith and reason which would characterize the Enlightenment. Despite the attempt of both Muslim and Christian scholars to reconcile Plato and Aristotle, it would be Averroes' firm commitment to the downturned palm of the Stagirite which came to rule European sensibilities.

Averroes was born Abu al-Walid Muhammad ibn Ahmad ibn-Rushd, in Cordova, then capital of Islamic Andalusia, in 1126. The Caliphate at this point extended all the way from India to Spain. Since at latest 830, when Caliph al-Ma'mun al-Rashid founded the *Bayt al-Hikma*, "House of Wisdom," in Baghdad, Islamic, Jewish, and Christian scholars had preserved and continued the work of the ancient Greek philosophers, translating, annotating, and commentating in Arabic. Though thousands of miles away, this was the same intellectual tradition into which Averroes was born.

Averroes would become influential in Latin Christendom, but he was as controversial there as he had been in his homeland. We see this ambivalence in another great work of Renaissance art, this time in the literary form of Dante's *Divine Comedy*. There we meet Averroes, neither exalted to heaven nor yet relegated to hell, but in the limbo reserved for the virtuous heathen. Dante puts him there with his Persian philosophical forefather, Abu Ali al-Hussein ibn-Sina (980 – 1037), known to the West as Avicenna.

Avicenna was born at the opposite end of the Islamic empire from the later Averroes, in the small town of Balkh in what is now Uzbekistan. In his day, philosophy and Aristotle were nearly synonymous. A prodigious and not entirely humble innovator in medical science and philosophy, Avicenna reworked the Aristotelian inheritance with insights from Islamic theology and Neoplatonic sources into what he called a new "Eastern Philosophy." Ever after, Avicenna effectively displaced Aristotle as the representative philosopher of the Islamic world. His work continued to influence Islamic philosophy and theology long after the death of Averroes, even among the more explicitly Platonic likes of Suhrawardi and Ibn 'Arabi, and occupied the attention of such great medieval European philosophers as St Thomas Aquinas and Duns Scotus, who borrowed his "ontological proof" of God's existence with little alteration. In the Islamic world, Aristotle would no longer be read and understood so much in his own right, but rather through the lens of Avicenna. If anyone wanted to make a target of philosophy, it was Avicenna rather than the Stagirite himself whom they would have in their sights.

To be sure, there were plenty who took aim, among them Averroes, for whom Avicenna was not Aristotelian enough. Long before Averroes though there were those who had disputed Avicenna's findings for quite the opposite reason, for under Aristotle's influence he appeared to reject traditional and essential Islamic doctrines. These included the creation in time of the world by God and the bodily resurrection of believers. Aristotle had argued that the universe was eternal, without beginning or end, and that any afterlife could at best be purely spiritual. Also, Avicenna was simultaneously committed both to Aristotle's priority of sensory data for knowledge of particulars and to the pseudo-Aristotelian (but actually Neoplatonic) theory of knowledge as emanation. This left him in the awkward position of reconciling God's lack of physical senses with his knowledge of particular things: He knows them universally and by intellect alone.[1] It seemed to some of his critics that the rather bloodless Prime Mover of Aristotle had come to replace the God whom the Qur'an proclaims as "closer to [man] than the jugular vein."[2] Avicenna saw scripture as a divine revelation of philosophical truths. Averroes, though, took Avicenna's Aristotelianism further still, and arguably further than Aristotle himself. He found parallel truths in philosophy and religion, but saw the latter as essentially a crude version of philosophy for those who could not aspire to its subtleties. Ironically, though, like the return of a pendulum, his criticism of Avicenna was itself a response to other critics of Avicenna who had swung out in the opposite direction.

Averroes toiled in the shadow of one of Avicenna's greatest critics, Al-Ghazali (1056 – 1111). If the casual Western reader has come across him at all, he will most likely have featured as the "baddie" in the polemical *Tale of Two Islams* I outlined in the last chapter. He, it is commonly supposed, was the fundamentalist who ultimately killed Islamic philosophy, despite the valiant attempts of Averroes to effect a revival. He did indeed describe "philosophy" as a kind of sickness debilitating our ability to perceive truth from falsehood. But to understand this claim we need to ask what exactly he meant by "philosophy." That he did not mean to reject Aristotelian logic outright is readily demonstrated by his use of it to make his argument. Nor indeed did he oppose Avicenna *tout court*. Rather, Al-Ghazali's sharp polemics were directed specifically against those Aristotelian precepts of Avicenna that violated the divine revelations of the Qur'an.

---

1   Adamson points out that this is a disputed question, for Avicenna simultaneously posited a theory of knowledge closer to Neoplatonic theories of knowledge as emanation from the divine Intellect. Adamson, *Philosophy of the Islamic World: A History of Philosophy without Any Gaps*, 138.

2   Qur'an 50.16.

Teaching in Baghdad, Al-Ghazali found aspects of the dominant philosophy — namely, that of Avicenna — incompatible with divine revelation. Finding himself at an intellectual impasse, he left to join a Sufi order. There, a mystical experience of God gave him insight into the fundamental incapacity of reason to comprehend the divine nature. Only the free gift of divine light could ultimately unveil truth. St Thomas Aquinas had a spiritual experience the year before he died, after his lifetime of prodigious theological output, so profound that it determined him to stop writing. He said that it showed up his life's work as so much "straw" fit only for burning. I wonder, was Al-Ghazali's awakening of a similar order? If so, it did not have the same effect. Moving on from his earlier polemics, he devoted the rest of his life to writing Iḥyā' ʿUlūm al-Dīn, The Revival of the Religious Sciences, an encyclopedic work on Sufi praxis, rooted in the Qur'an and hadith but explained in terms of Avicennan psychology. This became one of the most influential books in all the subsequent history of Islam. But before his "conversion," his main effort had been the more apologetic defense of those key Islamic doctrines that Avicenna had challenged or denied on Aristotelian grounds, notably the bodily resurrection and the creation of the universe. Al-Ghazali agreed with Avicenna that there was indeed an order to the universe, but solely on the grounds that Allah willed it to be so. The Qur'an, after all, directly attributes will to God, yet Avicenna seemed to suggest God lacked any agency because he created by necessity, as of his nature. On the contrary, Al-Ghazali argued, absolutely everything that happens, including human acts we suppose are freely willed, are in fact directly willed by Allah in their minutest detail. Things may appear to follow a rational order as causes and effects in their own right, but in fact this is so only as the result of direct divine causation, because God wills such an order into existence at all times. He might equally will otherwise, which is why miracles, for instance, are possible. He generally does not, for of his goodness he gives us the sense of causality we need in order to live meaningful and sane lives. The ordering of existence is providential.

Because it is ordered by the divine will, the world can be subject to rational and therefore philosophical enquiry. Yet after his turn to Sufism, Al-Ghazali insisted that to understand the relationship between the divine and human will was properly a matter for mystical vision rather than philosophical reasoning. In making his case he was himself engaging in what we might call "philosophy": in fact, he applied insights from Galen, and even Aristotle himself, against Avicenna as well as the venerable school of Asharite theology. It has recently been suggested, albeit not without controversy, that Al-Ghazali was directly influenced by Dionysius.[3] So, it is easy to be misled by the title of his pre-conversion polemical treatise *The Incoherence of the Philosophers*, little read in the West but often used as evidence to support hanging its author. It is arguably better translated as something like *The Stumbling into Error of the Philosophers*. It is a criticism only of certain aspects of philosophy, and by philosophy Al-Ghazali mostly means Avicenna. A manifesto of skepticism, the *Incoherence* has rather more in common with modernity than some of Al-Ghazali's detractors might admit. The absolute emphasis in his pre-Sufi work on the sovereignty of God's will is problematic, and arguably this idea has contributed more to the mindset of secular modernity than Averroes, as we will see when we come later to the influence of Duns Scotus and William of Ockham. Still, I am told this strict advocacy of divine command theory can no longer be found in the works of his later Sufi period. In any event, both the philosophical tenor of the *Incoherence* itself and the metaphysical turn of his later, more Platonic works rather undermine the all too convenient accusation that Al-Ghazali "killed off" Islamic philosophy.

One extreme often invites another in the history of ideas, not least in those of the religious category. If, at risk of oversimplification, Al-Ghazali can be seen as swinging the theological pendulum away from reason and towards mysticism, then with Averroes it swung back with equal and opposite force. Averroes reacted to what he saw as Al-Ghazali's obscurantism by doing the opposite. Where the old Sufi had sought to chip away at Avicenna's Aristotelian excess, the young jurist wanted to augment it.

One of Avicenna's best known philosophical positions was the distinction he made between essence and existence. Essence means the necessary properties of any given thing which distinguish it from other things. However, this essence could apply readily to things that do not exist: I can, for instance, define the set of characteristics, or "essence," of a unicorn or balrog without either actually existing. Essence does not cause existence. Rather, Avicenna taught, the existence of otherwise merely potential essences must be actualized, or caused, by a necessary existent. Since everything must have an existent cause for it to exist, there must be a necessary existence as first cause: namely, God. All other causes necessarily trickle down from this original one. The first cause takes no further part in proceedings. Progress might thereafter be construed as more or less mechanical, and so, Al-Ghazali

---

3 Treiger, "From Dionysius to Al-Ġazālī." For rebuttal, see Michael Chase, "Porphyry and the Theology of Aristotle," in *Reading Proclus and the Book of Causes: Translations and Acculturations*, ed. Dragos Calma, vol. 2 (Leiden & Boston: Brill, 2021), 163 fn. 30.

thought, compromise the freedom of God's will. Hence his rival proposition: the doctrine of the direct divine causation of all things. Averroes was so set against Al-Ghazali's teaching that he wrote an entire work specifically to refute it, called *The Incoherence of the Incoherence*. Al-Ghazali had found Avicenna too Aristotelian; for Averroes, Avicenna was not Aristotelian enough. Where Avicenna had prioritized philosophy over divine revelation in the pursuit of truth but sought a rapprochement between the two, in his *Decisive Treatise* (*Faṣl al-Maqāl*), Averroes widened the gap. Philosophy and theology may come to different conclusions. It seemed, though, that where scripture conflicted with philosophy, it must be read only as an allegory. Later Latin readers, perhaps unjustly, accused him of subordinating divine revelation to philosophy. He could give the impression that the Qur'an was a wonderful divine gift generously bequeathed by Allah to give a general outline of truth to the dull masses who could not grapple with philosophy. Certainly, he felt justified joining Avicenna in rejecting the scriptural tenet of physical resurrection after death. This came with an even more disturbing corollary. We creatures are distinguished from one another not by universal and immutable participation in the incorruptible and unchanging truth of the divine Intellect, but by our physical and corruptible nature. That is to say our individuality is maintained only by our physical embodiment. Averroes' wrestling with Aristotle led him to conclude that all minds shared in a single intellect into which they would be absorbed on death, with no individual afterlife at all. When the body dies, he thought, we are absorbed into the single Intellect, which is the only ultimate locus of truth.

These controversial theses explain why, having enjoyed the protection of the caliph for decades, Averroes was deemed to have gone too far. If anything, it was he rather than Al-Ghazali who brought Aristotelian philosophy into disrepute in the Islamic world. In 1195 the caliph ordered that Averroes' books be burned and the study of philosophy forbidden throughout the realm. Fortunately for Averroes, the caliph later relented, so that by the time he died in 1198, he did so in freedom as a respected jurist; but there is no doubting the tumultuous wind that whipped around him, and would do likewise in Latin Christendom for centuries to come. His work does not reflect a widening of Islamic thought into great new vistas of tolerance and imagination, as some would suppose. Where Avicenna had applied Qur'anic and Platonic insights to Aristotelian metaphysics, and Al-Ghazali had weighed up a range of philosophical positions in the light of apophatic spiritual experience, Averroes wanted to narrow philosophy down to Aristotle alone — and a hardline empiricist reading of the Stagirite at that.

It is only because the thought of Averroes — or at least, a version of it — flourished in Europe that Westerners now make him the measure of Islamic philosophy. Those who call on Averroes as the potential savior of Islam from medieval benightedness are not in the end calling for tolerance, unless by tolerance they mean the denial of divine revelation, whether Muslim, Jewish, or Christian, and with it the effective abolition of Islam. There is nothing tolerant about making philosophy synonymous with Aristotelianism and relegating Plato to the bin of mystical mumbo-jumbo. Platonic philosophy enjoyed a great revival in the Islamic world even as Averroes' hyper-Aristotelianism faded there.

Averroes achieved fame, or notoriety, in Europe primarily as an exponent of Aristotle. As Aristotle was known as "the Philosopher," Averroes was known simply as "the Commentator," a testimony to his renown. For centuries, while Aristotle's works on logic remained in circulation in Europe, his philosophical and what we would now call scientific works had been lost. The Islamic universities, however, had retained and translated his works, along with the geometrical treatises of Euclid and the medical texts of Galen. By the twelfth century a great treasure-trove of these ancient texts preserved by the Islamic world was being translated into Latin in the great library of Toledo, Spain. Established as a provincial capital under Islamic rule, Toledo had been part of the Caliphate since 712. Taking advantage of internecine warfare between Muslim rivals, the Christian armies of the Reconquista finally took the city back in 1092. For all the failings and intolerance of Christian government in Spain, this opened a new wealth of ancient knowledge to the West, including the philosophical works of Aristotle. Or, at least, what the Arabic writers thought was Aristotle. As mentioned earlier, some of the works that went under Aristotle's name were falsely attributed. The *Theology of Aristotle*, for instance, was in fact some of Plotinus's writings, and "Aristotle's" *Book of Causes* was a redaction of Proclus. Thanks to this Arabic inheritance, Aristotle received a medieval makeover in Latin translation as a Neoplatonist before his time. This would lead to attributions of "Aristotelian" tendencies to what we might now consider rather un-Aristotelian Christian Platonists, Dionysius included — though again, with the caveat that today's common distinction of Platonism and Aristotelianism is based on limited textual evidence.

The introduction of Aristotelian philosophy into the mind of the Western Church was explosive. We can only imagine the wide eyes of medieval monks, raised on a diet of Platonic meditations on scripture, as they read some of those contentions we saw in Avicenna and Averroes. According to what we know of Aristotle, the world had no beginning or end but had always co-existed with God. The Platonic forms have no existence of themselves, but only insofar as they are instantiated in matter. God and creation have completely separate purposes and ends, which should not be confused, and so nature can be studied without reference to God. God, if Aristotle's "Prime Mover" can reasonably be described as "God" at all, is the necessary uncaused cause of the universe, but plays no active role sustaining it.

That these contentions were supported by a clearly sophisticated Islamic tradition only aroused further interest — and suspicion. Some scholars, such as St Thomas's younger contemporary Siger of Brabant (1240 – 1284), were so enthusiastic in their adoption of Averroes that they argued for a complete separation of philosophy from theology. St Bonaventure (1217 – 1274) was one of the many Latin theologians who saw this "new" Aristotelian thought as a threat to the free agency of God implied in the Christian doctrine of creation.

This set the stage for the greatest medieval theologian of Latin Christendom, St Thomas Aquinas. By the time of the foundation of the University of Paris in 1215, the teaching of Aristotle's metaphysics and natural philosophy had been forbidden by papal authority for five years, although study of his logic was required at all universities. In practice, Paris ignored the prohibition, even after it was renewed in 1263 specifically for fear of "Averroism" by Urban IV. Were it not for this Parisian hauteur, Aquinas may never have completed his introductory theological and philosophical textbook, the Summa Theologiae. Eventually the Summa would become the core text for the formation of all Catholic clergy, and arguably remained secondary in importance only to the Bible in the Latin Church right up until the twentieth century. Yet at the time it was deemed to contain enough dangerous traces of Averroism that parts of it would be condemned in 1277 by the Bishop of Paris. Fortunately for its author, this was three years after his death. Not, I suspect, that he would have been too worried by that stage of his life. He had, after all, declared his life's work mere straw.

Long before he lay down his quill, Aquinas was sympathetic to the older, more obviously Platonic position of such figures as St Bonaventure. This had, after all, formed and nourished him as a Benedictine novice, where the liturgy of the Hours and the practice of Lectio Divina immersed him in the contemplation of Scripture. The study of the sacred page was no less paramount when he broke with his parents' wishes and left the comparatively comfortable monastic life to join St Dominic's new mendicant Order of Preachers. To flee the cloister and go out among the poor armed only with the Word of God, to challenge attractive heresies that were leading the flock astray, the Dominican needed a courage that only utter identification with Christ in his poverty could afford. For Thomas as much as for Franciscans like Bonaventure, the fullest revelation of divine truth would be found in Christ, incarnate and crucified, yielding himself for the sake of world in self-giving sacrificial love; God revealed as absolute self-gift, as life lived entirely for others:

> The passion of Christ completely suffices to fashion our lives. Whoever wishes to live perfectly should do nothing but disdain what Christ disdained on the cross and desire what he desired, for the cross exemplifies every virtue. If you seek the example of love: "Greater love than this no man has, than to lay down his life for his friends." Such a man was Christ on the cross.[4]

No less than St Francis's more famous Cross in the chapel of San Damiano, the image of the Cross which St Thomas paints draws the gaze into divine reality not as some isolated and other "being" but as fundamentally and essentially consisting in a relationship of self-gift to others. His God is unmistakably the God of Trinity, into whose inner self-relationship the Cross invites us. This reality emerges all the more fully in St Thomas's sacramental theology of Christ's self-gift in the Eucharist, and finds expression in his well-known prayers and hymns used in eucharistic adoration to this day, not least the *Tantum ergo*.[5]

In this, St Bonaventure could well agree. His *Journey of the Soul into God* plants the Cross more firmly into older, Dionysian soil. To him, though, the rediscovered "Aristotelian" philosophy in the form mediated by Averroes jeopardized this whole iconic vision. St Thomas did not find it so. Instead, he would attempt a synthesis of Platonic thought, including that of Dionysius, with the exciting new rediscovery of Aristotle and his Muslim commentators. While truth would be found primarily through the more Platonic, contemplative mode of prayerfully studying the sacred scriptures, as practiced for centuries in the monasteries of the Western Church, what

---

4 *Collatio 6 super Credo in Deum.*
5 As translated in the *New English Hymnal*:
> Therefore we, before him bending,
> this great Sacrament revere;
> types and shadows have their ending,
> for the newer rite is here;
> faith, our outward sense befriending,
> makes our inward vision clear.

we now think of as more Aristotelian philosophical reasoning was to be invaluable in the interpretation of those scriptures and the exposition of that truth. Philosophy was not an alternative to divine revelation, and certainly not superior to it, as Averroes and arguably even Avicenna supposed, but was a handmaid to theology, which held its place as Queen of the Sciences.

Responding to Bonaventure's concerns, Aquinas explicitly refuted two of Averroes' most contentious doctrines while still insisting on the value of philosophy for the pursuit of truth. First, St Thomas's early *De unitate intellectus*, "On the Unity of the Intellect," was a direct riposte to Averroes' teaching that humans did not have particular intellects but shared in one collective intellect. Al-Ghazali and Bonaventure alike had discerned the scandal of this teaching. If it were true, souls would have no enduring individual identity after the death of the physical body, being "merged" instead into a unitive consciousness. Worse even than denying any bodily resurrection, Averroes was teaching the dissolution of the person's soul after death. Yet his teaching did not come from nowhere. Averroes had built the doctrine on Aristotle's *De Anima*, "On the Soul." Where Bonaventure saw this as an instance of the pernicious influence of Averroes, Aquinas wanted to show that philosophical thought was of value in the pursuit of Christian truth. As Averroes had done to Avicenna, Aquinas turned Averroes' own weapon against him, arguing for the futility of his position on the basis of Aristotle's *De Anima* itself. So keen was St Thomas in these early days to defend Aristotle from being read solely through the lens of later Islamic thought, that in his *De unitate intellectus*, he accuses Averroes of being a *depravator* or "corrupter" of Peripatetic philosophy. Focusing its argument solely on a philosophical text, the *De unitate intellectus* was meant to show that intra-Aristotelian philosophy afforded enough diversity of thought to pacify sceptics like Bonaventure. In writing it, Aquinas was inhabiting the critical tradition of Avicenna, Al-Ghazali, and Averroes themselves.

However, philosophy alone was not enough to refute Averroes' second most contentious point: that the cosmos was co-eternal with God. This was an indisputably Aristotelian doctrine from which the Peripatetic system itself offered no obvious route of escape. Aquinas's *De aeternitate mundi*, "On the eternity of the world," therefore offers a more ambivalent appraisal of Aristotle. Bonaventure argued that the doctrine of an eternal world is incompatible with the Christian doctrine of creation from nothing, and thus with the divine revelation of Scripture as it was then understood. Aquinas hedges his bets. He answers that the teaching of creation from nothing does not necessarily exclude the possibility of creation being co-existent with God: it expresses the causal dependence of creation on God rather than necessarily relating to a moment in time. Aristotle's position is defensible within the realms of Christian orthodoxy. Yet conversely, Thomas argues, the doctrine of creation in a moment of time that Bonaventure defends is also philosophically possible. So how can one arbitrate between these two incompatible hypotheses? In the end, he admits, philosophy alone cannot judge on the matter. Either possibility could be true. We must appeal to a higher authority to answer such disputed questions: and this is divine revelation, in particular the contents of sacred scripture. When in doubt, consult the Bible. Hence, he will ultimately side with Bonaventure and defend the traditional doctrine of *creatio ex nihilo*, creation from nothing, while maintaining that Aristotle's position is at least theoretically defensible. The implication that orthodoxy need not be compromised by what we would now call scientific discovery is an important one, but Aquinas's attitude to Scripture is different from that of Averroes, for whom even the Holy Qur'an, the direct revelation of Allah, could at best offer allegorical explanations for truths that were properly the province of philosophical reason.

St Thomas Aquinas is clearly not a Latin Averroes. Nonetheless, he had drunk from Averroes' well. His now famous cosmological and teleological proofs for the existence of God are almost entirely borrowed from Avicenna, via Averroes. Averroes' theory of intellect might also be detected in St Thomas's adoption of the Aristotelian principle that "there is nothing in the intellect that is not first in the senses."[6] Read in isolation, this marked a radical departure from the Platonic priority of forms in the mind of God over their physical instantiations in the cosmos. Echoing Averroes, Aquinas seemed to suggest that knowledge was primarily, even exclusively, to be based on the evidence of the senses. The door was open to the empirical methods of modern science, for all their good and ill.

Further, Averroes' formulation of the "single intellect," combined with his refutation of a physical resurrection, had implied the dissolution of individual souls after their bodily death. Aquinas's position, without going this far, did still raise the question of how disembodied souls awaiting resurrection can have any knowledge at all. This raised concerns and eyebrows. For if the souls of the dead were essentially sleeping or vegetative until a later bodily resurrection at the end of time, what would that mean

---

6 *De veritate*, q. 2 a. 3 arg. 19.

for prayers for the dead or invocation of the communion of saints? Once asked, such questions would not easily go away, and finally erupted with epidemic persistence at the Reformation.

And yet for all Aquinas's reputation as the great Aristotelian of the West, he is at least as much dependent on Platonism.[7] Some of what he considered Aristotelian was in fact the work of Neoplatonists. The mistaken attribution of Proclus's thought to Aristotle led St Thomas to think that even Dionysius was an Aristotelian, given how often Dionysius quoted this Proclus in disguise. Aquinas cites Dionysius second only to Sacred Scripture — more than he cites "the Philosopher" himself. It is ironic, then, that it should be Aquinas who opened the door to the decline of the participatory and sacramental Platonic theology he had inherited and worked so doggedly (or bullishly?) to sustain.

The late medieval paradigm shift from the Dionysian Platonism to the Aristotelianism of a more Averroistic mold turns on the question of "being." Dionysius, given his inheritance from Plotinus, had rigorously avoided equating God with being. For him, as for his pagan predecessor, the highest name of God was the Good, and God is beyond being. Yet however carefully Aquinas dealt with this Dionysian caveat, he followed Avicenna and reprioritized God's highest name as Being over the Good. Aquinas was careful to clarify that God is not in any sense *a* being, nor "Being" in any static way, as though God were somehow identical with existence or its underlying substance: rather than use the noun "being," he referred to God by the infinitive verb "to be," *esse*, indicating that God was the *act* of being rather than an object. To speak of God as Being and us as beings was not to use the word "being" in exactly the same way; rather, we could refer to concrete beings only by *analogy* to that incomprehensible act and source of being which is God. Aquinas develops this point with an unexpected comparison to bull's urine (surely an "unlike likeness" in which the Areopagite would rejoice).[8] We may determine that a bull is healthy because its urine is healthy, but the word "healthy" does not mean exactly the same thing in both instances. The use of the word is neither univocal nor equivocal — that is, we are not using it either strictly in the same sense, nor in a totally different sense, when we apply it to both the bull and its urine. Rather, we are using it analogically. There is conceptual overlap. The health of the one indicates the health of the other,

---

7   Wayne J. Hankey, "Aquinas, Plato, and Neoplatonism," in *The Oxford Handbook of Aquinas*, 2012, https://doi.org/05.
8   *Summa Theologiae*, I.13.5.

even though the word "health" does not mean the same thing in each case. As with the health of bull and the urine, so with our being and God's.

There are scholars who harmonize Dionysius's phrase "beyond being" with Thomas's "supereminentist" reading of it as an incomprehensible *excess* of being, rather than in the more literal Neoplatonic understanding of God transcending even the distinction of being and non-being. They would argue that Aquinas's definition of God primarily as Being is, in the end, not all that different from Dionysius's definition of God as essentially Good.[9] The great Christian Platonist Augustine had, after all, equated God's goodness with his Being long before Aquinas. Nonetheless, Aquinas arguably gave higher prominence than ever before in Christian theology to "being" as a metaphysical concept in its own right. So, Aquinas's thought, influenced by his Islamic precursors, inadvertently set off a radically new chain of thought. Quite against his intentions, Being itself would become an idol, a concept used to contain, tame, and push God to the periphery, rather than an icon of the participation of creation in the creative Good. After his death, St Thomas's Averroistic moments would be picked up on, at times condemned, but ultimately amplified by successive generations. Where Aquinas had participated in a wider shared intellectual culture with Jews and Muslims, his successors would take the Aristotelian scholarship of one Muslim thinker who was ultimately marginal in his own milieu, and sow the seeds of a revolution in Latin Christian thought. The irony of this is that it took the Latin West further away from the developments of Platonic philosophy that were going on contemporaneously in the Islamic world and continued to provide fruitful grounds for interaction with philosophies further afield.

So it was that St Bonaventure's fears would come true. We were led off the old, shared Way to the Good to beat our own haphazard path. The single finger of Plato, pointing up to our shared, higher reality, would be swept away by a brush of Aristotle's down-turned palm, its five fingers spread over the great multiplicity of beings, as though sowing the seeds of an intellectual revolution: seeds blown by the turbulent winds of empire from Baghdad, via Al-Andalus, to Naples, where Aquinas would water them, but his successors would train them into something quite unlike the older shoots. The plants that grew might flower beautifully, blooming into the wonders of modern medicine, technology, respect for civil liberties, and freedom of religion. But like many medicinal herbs, with ignorance or

---

9 Among them, William Riordan, *Divine Light: The Theology of Denys the Areopagite* (San Francisco: Ignatius Press, 2008).

misuse they could prove poisonous, leaving the acid tang of technocracy, the black fruits of racialism, the charnel fumes of nuclear war. These are only some of the symptoms of an intellectual virus that still courses through the world in three cross-contaminating strains: voluntarism, nominalism, and individualism.

We will address these in turn before we continue our journey to medieval Kyoto and see how even such apparently remote philosophies as Christian Platonism and Mahāyāna Buddhism can work together towards a cure, and graft the severed limb of the West back onto the old green tree. But first, an interlude. We must come back to the present, as we look at some of the symptoms of the West's enduring philosophical alienation.

CONFESSIONS OF
A MODERN MISSIONARY

"T HERE'S A FOREIGNER HERE," GRUNTED THE
Deputy Head from behind his desk, ignoring my Japanese greet-
ing. "Get an English teacher."

I first went to Japan in 2002 as a missionary. Not a Christian missionary,
I should point out. At the time, I was firmly atheist. In fact I didn't know
that I was a missionary and would certainly never have called myself such,
but that's what I was: an unwitting ambassador for Western modernity.
Only later did I discover that this had in fact been part of the founding
intention of the government scheme I was on. I had taken its name, the
Japanese English Teaching or "JET" Program, at face value. The limited
value to this end of a young Englishman with no Japanese and no teaching
qualifications had not really crossed my mind. Many would call it "white
privilege" now, I suppose, though plenty of us were not white. Even if I
had thought that way, the generous salary and promise of adventure would
have dispelled any doubts. But it turns out that the scheme had originally
been put in place not for the sake of English teaching, at which it frankly
was not all that effective, but rather to get young foreigners to live in Japan
so that the Japanese could get a bit more used to us. We were to be living
exhibits of Western life, specimens for an anthropological zoo right on the
doorstep of even the most rural Japanese. English language teaching was an
afterthought, an excuse to justify using taxpayers' money to pay foreigners
to be guests in Japan. By the time I joined the scheme, what had been an
appendix was treated as the primary organ. Teaching was what we were
there for, however ill-prepared or unsuited.

It was a great scheme for me, and I look back on those years fondly,
but I do now wonder whether the benefits to the Japanese taxpayer were
commensurate. Perhaps that explains the reaction of the aforementioned
Deputy Head when I walked into his staff room ready to deliver a one-off
English "lesson" to the Japanese teenagers at his fishery college, who were

after all most likely to spend the rest of their lives working in the local docks. Their need to meet someone who was in effect paid just to be a foreigner may not have been so obvious to them. I did not see it that way at the time.

Nobody had explicitly told us this, but to me and my mostly American, Australian, and New Zealander peers, it was clear that behind the language teaching, our real job — no, our moral duty — was to reform the minds of the benighted natives into greater conformity with our Western, enlightened, liberal mores. We would scoff or sigh over our beers in the evenings about the backward ways of the Japanese, most of whom were still at work generating the tax money that we were putting behind the bar. As young and "free-thinking" university graduates, we all held identical leftist political views, and sneered at the traditions and values of our own countries. Faced with the ubiquitous national pride of the Japanese people, we would insist on how different our homelands were from our host nation. In presentations we were asked to give about our countries' history, cuisine, and character, we would take pride in how multi-cultural we were in comparison with Japan. Asked to demonstrate an English recipe in a school cookery class, I instinctively opted for Chicken Tikka Masala, just to break down the expectations of roast beef or fish and chips and show off the glorious diversity of the United Kingdom. Bowler hats and pinstripes out, David Beckham and Blairite Cool Britannia in. When asked what "British people" think about any topic, I would pontificate that all British people think differently, and no two of us would presume to think the same way — as every other young British graduate on the scheme would have agreed. In my lessons I would find ways of showing up Japanese gender disparities and challenge their collectivism and cultural conformism with reference to the shining example of the West. At no point did I realize that in so doing I was merely an agent of another, no less constrictive conformism. We young missionaries took it as gospel that we were there to open closed minds. I hope, in hindsight and slimly, that we achieved something more than confirmation of Japanese stereotypes about the arrogance and superiority of Westerners.

Since I went to Japan, Western educationalists have kept at their work of cultivating cultural amnesia in the young. We have no tradition, they say, or no tradition that is any good. Tradition is an obstacle to progress, best buried and forgotten. But amnesia is the death of identity. Who we are is what we remember, and this is not limited to the memories of the head but of the whole body, our muscle-memory, and especially the memories of the heart: how it felt when our mothers stroked our hair; the smell of a childhood pet; early experiences of revulsion and attraction; a dislike for the texture of mushrooms or baked beans; the music of our teenage years; abuses and humiliations that sloped our shoulders then and even now twist our stomachs at their recollection; the triumphs and celebrations that stood us tall; the lover's "Yes"; the birth of our first child; our first encounter with God.

Yet behind all these fleeting memories, in their momentary particularity, we discern — in hiding — things more universal and enduring. Not only behind, but in and through our many loves, we glimpse something of love itself. Through and in beautiful people and places and songs, we espy an underlying beauty that belongs exclusively to none of them but joins them, paradoxically both beyond and within them all, and as real in its universality as any of its particular instantiations: for is it not true to say that even after our lovers are dead and all their beauties faded, love and beauty will still exist? It would be impossible to recollect all the particularities without remembering the universals behind them. If my mind were incapable of categorizing, say, the Great Buddha of Kamakura, the poetry of Rumi, the stones of Venice, and my daughter's face as instantiating a universal "beauty," I would have no memory at all, just a jumbled bundle of random and unconnected sense-data.

My younger self, the one who went on mission to Japan, would object that these supposed universals are dictated by upbringing, by our culture, and in particular by the language in which one speaks and thinks. If I had read Locke, I might have modernized his conjecture and opined that the infant mind is like a blank hard drive, just waiting to be formatted by society; that what is considered beautiful, or good, or virtuous, or just varies according to place, culture, and context. In other words, I would have subscribed uncritically (but no less dogmatically) to the creed of relativism. This, the young are taught, is the way of tolerance: the way that says there is no one way, no universality, only the freely chosen multiplicity of individual wills, and that the ideal society is whichever maximizes their exercise. With its insistence that only the particular exists, relativism amounts to a forgetfulness of the commonality that binds us to one another, to the world and all existence, and to our origin. It results in the breakdown of the traditional ties of family, locality, and nation. Enlightenment modernists tend not to want this breakdown, but unwittingly drive us to it by their insistence that only the empirically verifiable is worthy of serious public discussion. Many postmodern activists on the other hand are quite open in their desire for the overthrow of all such "oppressive" constraints.

Relativism ultimately falls into its own trap, for by its own logic it is itself only one culturally conditioned way of thinking, incapable of claiming hegemony over any other. But if relativism itself cannot claim to be true, on what basis can it establish itself other than by the victory of the most powerful will? This is why Pope John Paul II and Pope Benedict have condemned it as the greatest danger of modernity. Had I thought a little more about it at the time, I might have seen that this exercise of power was precisely what was happening politically in the Blairite years, as Western liberal relativism was imposed on other nations by trade sanctions or by military might. Friendly nations like Japan welcomed our exports of cultural capital: for instance, paying graduates from prestigious universities to come and proselytize. I was one small pawn in the sheer assertion of a set of values which, by its own demonstration, are arbitrary.

The West has abandoned the sense that there is any absolute truth, goodness, or beauty. It's all a matter of opinion. Worse, the belief in such absolutes is increasingly seen as a sign of bigotry. There is no real continuity between culture and nature or humanity and the cosmos, let alone between us and God. Even our minds and bodies are so divided that we can talk about rights over our bodies, as though they were somehow separate from our purely mental selves, just another piece of property. This dualism between spirit and matter, between sentient and non-sentient being, has led to a worldwide relegation of the created order to the status of value-free stuff for the use and abuse of the human will. The political sphere becomes a war zone in which the majority or the most powerful will takes charge. History is rendered the story of conflict and domination, always to be viewed with the question *cui bono?* at the front of the mind. We live with the belief that we can tame the world by technology, control everything by human intervention, redefine everything according to our will, perhaps even medicate and augment ourselves into eternal life. It is this technocratic mindset, seeing the physical world as just so much dead and meaningless, manipulatable matter, which leads to eugenics and abortion, the use of medication or even irreversible surgery for ailments of the mind, calls for the abolition of *any* connection between sex and gender. There are of course harmful conventions and expectations around gender, age, race, disability, and wealth, but when people say that anything is *just* a social construct, the word "just" is made to do a lot of work. It excludes the middle ground of analogy and of participation of the social in the natural and supernatural realms. But without this, by denying that there is any reality *at all* to the relationship between nature and culture (and claiming that truth is entirely defined by

88

the exercise of power), it is hard to see on what grounds any challenges to the damaging status quo can be made. It seems the solution to power imbalances is to point out (or contrive) corrective balances and then either appeal to the better nature of those who wield power and persuade them to relinquish it, or seize it by force. The first option is not really an option if one denies there is any true goodness, because to appeal to a "better" nature would rely on the existence, or at least consensus, on what comprises a good nature. That leaves only the second, which is equally self-defeating: because if the supposedly powerful really do have so much power, there is really nothing that the oppressed can do about it; and if the oppressed in fact have enough power to overthrow the oppressor, the original assertion of a power imbalance begins to look rather suspect.

Such relativism is not the historic home of Western thought. Nor did it come from nowhere. It did not spring fully armored like Athena from the skull of its father. It is not a neutral and perennial presupposition on top of which alien ideologies have later been imposed. It has its own very specific and traceable intellectual genesis. We will see how it was born, along with its siblings of materialism and utilitarianism, as the incestuous spawn of three closely related late medieval theological errors.

In England, the likes of the Cambridge Platonists, the Romantics, the Arts and Crafts Movement, and the Inklings resisted these erroneous influences. They had recourse to the Christian Platonic intellectual inheritance of the West. J. R. R. Tolkien's *Lord of the Rings* and C. S. Lewis's *Narnia Chronicles* portray magical worlds where nothing is without significance and all is sung into being. Yet we can find analogues as far afield as Japan in the cartoons of Studio Ghibli, replete with their Shinto allusions. Young Westerners admire these and yearn for the world they depict, but their minds have been strictly trained to demythologize all supernatural content, to what little extent they are equipped by modern education to understand the references in the first place. There is a deep inner thirst for a re-enchanted world, but the means to sate it have been lobotomized by an excessive emphasis on empirical knowledge. Blinkered to the supernatural within our own religious and folk culture, we grope naively for half-understood titbits from "exotic" cultures, but are careful as we do so to distance ourselves from their philosophical content by relegating them to the realms of alternative health regimens (yoga, mindfulness, martial arts), or of entertainment ("the Force be with you!"). The supernatural must be held at bay, controlled and categorized in terms that do not threaten the hegemony of our vitiated Western reason over the world. And yet, all the while, unsettling but persistent noises just beyond earshot remind us that there are forces beyond our control. We cannot quite silence the baying of the griffins and manticores howling at the edge of the desert, so they must be brought promptly to heel.

Relativism is the progeny of those three distant ancestors whose genesis I promised we would trace: voluntarism, nominalism, and individualism.

Voluntarism

I N 2012, DURING A CHARISMATIC CHRISTIAN HEAL-
ing service in front of a live studio audience, Canadian televangelist
Todd Bentley kicked an old lady in the head. It was no accident. He
did it, he said, because God had told him to. "Why was the Holy Spirit not
moving in this place?" he wondered. Why was nobody being healed? The
answer came to him from an inner voice: it was because he had not kicked
that lady in the head.[1]

Such bizarre actions taken in the name of God are, alas, not unprecedented. One could equally cite the medieval crusaders' cries of "Deus vult!"
as they decided to make suicidal charges against the militarily superior Moors,
as portrayed in Ridley Scott's 2005 epic drama, *The Kingdom of Heaven*. Or,
for that matter, the Islamic suicide bomber who believes Allah truly wills
the indiscriminate death of infidel and Muslim alike, if they do not hold
exactly the right doctrine.

Popular culture gives a fair portrait of modern secular attitudes towards
religious believers. The portrayal of clergy in particular is telling. There are
basically five types. First, there is the "comedy vicar," as seen in *Father Ted*
or the *Vicar of Dibley* on Irish and British television. Second, there is the
wild-eyed preacher of cultist flicks and Westerns like the 2007 *There Will
be Blood*. Third, there is the exorcist, most obviously exemplified by the
eponymous Hollywood movie. Fourth, there is the corrupt official, often
typified as a venal, fat, and faithless bishop with a whiff of flamboyantly
coded homosexuality, such as those in *Robin Hood Prince of Thieves* or the
aforementioned *Kingdom of Heaven*. Finally, a more recent addition to this
motley cast is the pedophile priest. What these five types teach, particularly
to the young, is that Christianity is at best silly and irrational, and at worst
sinister, self-serving, and sexually disordered. Christians are then neatly

---

1 *Daily Mail*, "Tattooed preacher who 'cures' cancer by kicking people in the face
banned from entering the UK," August 25, 2012. https://www.dailymail.co.uk/news/
article-2193573/Todd-Bentley-Tattooed-preacher-cures-cancer-kicking-people-face-banned-
entering-UK.html.

divided into two camps and so conquered. First, the genuine ones who, probably because of some internal psychological deficiency with sexual implications, abandon adult reason to believe in the childish fancy of a supreme being who loves and favors them. These are the merely silly and irrational. The second camp comprises those who calculatingly abuse the irrationality and credulity of the former to further their own nefarious and deviant ends, financial, political, or sexual. All of this hinges on the willingness of gullible people to obey slavishly the diktats of an inner voice they call "God."

These assumptions are not limited to the popular sphere. Unlike in the US, God is strictly off-topic in UK politics. Prime Minister Tony Blair's adviser Alistair Campbell reputedly advised the press that in Government, "we don't do God." When Tim Farron, a Christian Member of Parliament, later became leader of the Liberal Democrat Party, he was grilled by television and radio interviewers on his faith. He was interrogated on almost inquisitorial lines on whether he prayed to help him make decisions, with a clear implication that to do so would render him unfit for public office: as though prayer self-evidently meant, as for Todd Bentley, a divine voice speaking in one's head. What God wants may not be what the people want, and the latter must come first. This went so far that Farron eventually resigned, his views on human sexuality deemed too regressive for a modern politician. [2]

The world of the arts, too, has moved a long way from Raphael and his fresco of the great theistic philosophers of the world. As learned a literary professor as John Carey in his frankly depressing 2005 extended essay on aesthetics, *What Good are the Arts?*, dismisses God from consideration in the first chapter. [3] Carey's book is entertaining but only likely to convince if you already agree with his opening gambit: namely, that beauty is solely in the eye of the beholder and has no transcendent value. Within pages, he dismisses the Platonic idea of beauty that has informed millennia of speculation and debate among pagans, Christians, Muslims, and Jews, among others, cutting the question down to the dimensions of the voluntarism we are about to explore: beauty as the arbitrary taste of an unprovable divine being. The idea that beauty might be woven into the fabric of being itself as an expression, not of the divine will, but of the divine nature, goes unconsidered. Any such speculation, he says, just comes down to God's inscrutable

---

2 *Church Times*, "Tim Farron quits Lib Dem leadership to remain a 'faithful Christian'," June 15, 2017. https://www.churchtimes.co.uk/articles/2017/16-june/news/uk/farron-quits-lib-dem-leadership-for-reasons-of-faithfulness-to-bible.

3 John Carey, *What Good Are the Arts?* (Oxford: Oxford University Press, 2006).

"taste" versus our own. What follows from this rejection is a predictable "Mozart versus Banksy" sort of diatribe, in which the author concludes that only the literary arts are really worthy of our attention, because only they are written in words and as such are readily comprehensible. Anything else is mere opinion. God is understood as some speculative being who, if he exists at all, is no more than one willing agent among many. Divine revelation in sacred scriptures is no different than voices in one's head, and far from guaranteeing truth. We have our opinions, and God has his.

In the West, God has ended up defined primarily in terms of will. Where the Platonic conception of God established divine goodness as the divine nature, it is now more widely understood as the outworking of his free decision, even (and especially) when his existence and his decisions are disputed or denied. For Platonic theologians, God is the Good, the Beautiful, and the True; in the modern Western understanding, if God is at all, he dictates what is good, beautiful, and true. His will transcends all.

The God of modernity is the God of free will. This is the God so readily attacked by the despisers of religion, cultured or otherwise. Yet they cannot be blamed for his advent, for many Christian theologians have for centuries now proposed such a view of God. The God Western atheists reject is the God not only of popular belief, but of much second-millennium theology, fighting on battle lines drawn long before by Al-Ghazali and Averroes.

John Duns Scotus (1266 – 1308), a Franciscan friar and late contemporary of Aquinas, made the first step in this direction. He is, alas and unfairly, perhaps most famous for the conical "dunce" cap of the Victorian classroom imbecile, an unfitting device for the one whom the Church named the "Subtle Doctor." Scotus started with a question of language.

For Platonists like Dionysius, God is the Good by definition, insofar as we can define God at all. That anything exists at all is simply because God is good, and it is in his nature to create. Therefore, insofar as something is, it is good; evil is a deficiency of being, of reality and therefore of goodness. This is tempered with the Aristotelian observation that what we mean by the "good" in a creature is the degree to which it fulfils its capacity for being what it really is. A good octopus or chimpanzee is good in a different way from a good person. For that matter, a good doctor is good in a different way from a good husband. Nonetheless, the word "good" has some common value. It does not mean something completely different in each sense that we use it; nor does it mean exactly the same thing.

As we have seen, St Thomas Aquinas explained this use of language by the term *analogy*: remember the bull and its urine? He realized that we could not use words like "good" univocally, in precisely the same way in every instance, nor equivocally, in such a different way that the word would cease to have any meaning. If this is true even among created beings, surely it is all the more so between created beings and God. To call God "good" and to call my dog "good" when it fetches a stick are to say something at once similar and yet radically different about God and my dog. This is even so when I speak of God as good and Socrates or St Theresa of Calcutta as good. God's goodness utterly transcends our own. Yet there is some commonality that makes sense of using the same word "good" in each of these cases. There is some conceptual overlap. We are speaking analogically.

As with goodness, so with being: to speak of my dog as having being or indeed just as "being," and to speak of God as Being, is not to say that God is "another" being like my dog. It is not even to say that God is the Supreme Being, since that still leaves God in the same category as a stone, St Paul, and Socrates. Aquinas is enough of a Platonist and Dionysian to recognize that God cannot possibly "exist" within this order of beings. But where Dionysius followed Plotinus in resolutely insisting that God is beyond being, and therefore foremost to be named as the Good, Aquinas insists that we can at least speak *analogously* of our being and God as Being.

Scotus thought Aquinas was right to describe God primarily as Being, but wrong to say that created being is only *analogous* to divine Being. If the word "being" is to have any meaning, he thought, then it must mean exactly the same of God as it does of us. After all, while we cannot be certain about the nature of God, we can at least be sure that God *is*, which is to say he has being just as we do. The word "being" must be used univocally of both God and us to have meaning. So, Scotus moved from treating God as Being itself, or the Act of Being, to God as *infinite* being, in contradistinction to our merely finite being. This does not necessarily lead to the conclusion that God is simply *a* being among others, and I am wary of accusing Duns Scotus of anything so simple. Not for nothing has he been dubbed the Subtle Doctor, and his writings on this, as on everything, are highly technical and abstruse. His writings make Aquinas's look easy. Nonetheless, he at the very least set the train of scholastic thought off in a direction which, in Professor John Milbank's words, "idolized God" as one (albeit infinite) being among many and so "set us on the intellectual course to modernity."[4]

Sharing the Platonic insistence that being is the consequence of God as the Good which itself is beyond being, Dionysius had preserved both

---

4 John Milbank, "On Theological Transgression," in *The Future of Love: Essays in Political Theology* (Cascade: Eugene, OR, 2009).

God's transcendence and immanence. To be is to derive from, share in, and ultimately return to God as a manifestation of his goodness. Beings are individuated manifestations of God's presence, and so God is immanent in being. Yet at the same time God as cause of being is differentiated from being itself. In Dionysius's words, it is as "the divinity *beyond* Being" that God is "the Being of all things."[5] To be is, in Platonic understanding, precisely *not* to be God. God is "no one thing among beings."[6] He is, nonetheless, "*all* beings" to the extent that "he is Being to beings."[7] While not "Being" in himself, God manifests beings as the outworking of his goodness. God is simultaneously beyond all being and present to all beings as their cause.

The ironic consequence of placing God and creatures in the same category of "being" is that it makes them other from one another. By their very similarity they are made different. God becomes in one sense as different from a man as a man is from a monkey or an accordion; and in another sense, because He is infinite, even more so. The transcendence of God is asserted at the expense of his immanence. Scotus's insistence on the univocity of being between God and creatures heralded the transition from this older Platonic theology of *participation* of beings in God to a theology that opposes creation to creator as other beings, like and so differentiable. Where God had been the indivisible One beyond being in whom the multiplicity of beings "lived and moved and had their being," God was starting to look like one supreme and ultimately alien entity among others. He was differentiated, not by his unique status as the cause of all being, whom Augustine could describe as simultaneously "higher than my uttermost heights and deeper than my most intimate depths,"[8] but by his infinitude.

This contributes to Scotus's theology of *voluntarism*. *Voluntas* is the Latin word for "will." For Platonists, including Aquinas, beings had participated in God as unfoldings of the Good. God was now seen as entirely external to the created order, and by extension, so was his goodness. Instead of goodness being defined as the divine nature, and the created order as an expression of this divine nature, divine goodness started to mean something quite different: in effect, an imposition of whatever God, as the most powerful being, willed it to be.

Take the Ten Commandments. Following Scotus's logic these were given by God simply because he wanted to. Scotus himself applied this logic only

---

5   *Celestial Hierarchy* 1.4, 177D.

6   *Divine Names* 1.3, 589C.

7   *Divine Names* 5.4, 817D.

8   *Interior intimo meo et superior summo meo*, *Confessions* 3.6.11.

to the latter five commandments, which treat of the moral duty to one's neighbors. God might for instance have commanded us to commit adultery rather than not to. The first five he took to be consistent with the nature of God and therefore immutable. But for some, Scotus's logic stopped short. William of Ockham (1287–1347), Scotus's late contemporary and a fellow Franciscan, thought that the Subtle Doctor was being inconsistent. If Scotus were right, then surely God could equally have willed the direct opposite of any of the Commandments, even those first five. He *might* have willed that we hate the Lord our God with all our heart and all our mind and all our strength, make idols, and worship other gods before Him. Otherwise we compromise the freedom of God implicit in his status as supreme, infinite being. God's commandments against idolatry or adultery are not good in themselves, reflections of the divine nature. They are good because God says so. "Everything other than God is good," Ockham echoed Al-Ghazali, "because it is willed by God, and not vice versa."[9] Where the Platonist saw the divine intellect and the divine will as harmonious, Ockham drove a wedge between them. So, if God had told us to hate our neighbor or kick old ladies in the head, that would be good for the same reason: because God says so.

Already in late medieval theology, God as unfathomable mind of Goodness, as light beyond light and Being-beyond-being, was starting to be displaced by *a* god, the supreme being, defined in terms of absolute alterity and sovereign will — emphases that would unfold and emerge in different intensities over the several centuries leading to modernity, and sow the seed of many of today's problems. For if God kept us in check only because his was the strongest will and the greatest power, who takes over when we no longer believe in him?

The answer: whoever has the strongest army.

---

9   John Duns Scotus, *Ordinatio* III, dist. 19.

NOMINALISM

DESPITE THE WIDENING GAP BETWEEN THEOLogy and philosophy, Dionysius's Platonic vision of the cosmic harmony was never completely erased from the Western consciousness. There is more than one story of the West, however loudly one may shout down the others. The Renaissance brought a renewed interest in Proclus and the wider classical inheritance. Some of those drawn to Platonism were students of the occult, a pursuit that in some cases has unjustly damaged the reputation of their scholarship in later centuries. The Plotinian strand of Platonism continued to exercise more of an influence on English theology than on Catholic and Reformed mainland Europe, exemplified by such well known Anglican divines as Richard Hooker, George Herbert, and Lancelot Andrewes. Descartes and Spinoza were indubitably Platonic and heralded the Enlightenment, but as it progressed, Platonism flourished more as a minority report in the works of theologians, poets, and novelists than of philosophers "proper." Some were notable workers in all three of these fields, notably Samuel Taylor Coleridge and his peers known collectively as the "Cambridge Platonists"—to the embarrassment, I am told by an insider, of many in the thoroughly analytical Faculty of Philosophy at Cambridge University today. Now, as then, Platonism was not entirely respectable.

In the twentieth century, J. R. R. Tolkien, C. S. Lewis, Dorothy L. Sayers, and the unjustly neglected Charles Williams formed the loose literary circle known as the Inklings, united by a commitment to restore the Platonic sense of wonder to the world. Both Tolkien's Middle-Earth and Lewis's Narnia are worlds mythically sung into existence. The heroes who populate their worlds represent aspects of biblical characters engaged in a Platonic quest for unity through Christian acts of self-giving love. The Inklings wanted to inspire their readers with a vision of a cosmos brimming with meaning. In a world stripped of significance, they were trying to recapture the understanding of an enchanted world, every aspect of which revealed something of God.

The Inklings' call for a world of transcendent meaning was born of their medieval preoccupations and, while Tolkien denied it, their experience of the First World War must surely have had some part in prompting such a reaction to humanity's accelerating technological domination of the cosmos. In contrast, medieval Europe was oriented deliberately around symbols of transcendent good, Lothlórien-like havens, temporal conduits of eternal rest. Churches were at the heart of our settlements, their towers and spires pointing upwards to show that all our life was focused on and guided by that which is beyond our naming and making. Their beauty was uplifted by the piercing arrow of the Gothic arch and cascaded down from vaulted ceilings, a Platonic aesthetic deliberately intended to lift up the soul with the eyes toward that height beyond existence from which all potential flows down into actuality.

Spatially, the churches acted as literal waypoints punctuating the landscape for the traveler, who first from afar might spy the village tower or the cathedral spire. Once within, one could orient oneself from the churches' dedications: St Peter's in the east, by association with heaven and his keys to its gates; St Stephen just outside the walls, since that is where he was martyred; St Giles nearby, safe refuge for lepers; St Bartholomew's for the sick or injured pilgrim; St Ann's for soothing drafts from her holy wells. By both the spires and names of churches, wanderers found their way, whether topographical or spiritual. [1]

The sacred space of our older land was not confined within church walls. The guilds of work and trade, law, medicine, and learning, fed into the churches as the Church fed them, in Tolkien's terms, with the life-giving *lembas* bread and the *miruvor* of her sacraments. Their buildings grew to echo the shape of the churches, their architectural forms proclaiming a common language, articulating their common source and common aim in the common good.

Even the space between the churches and the civic buildings, homes, and shopfronts was marked by a signpost of the transcendent: the market cross. The routing of transcendent values from the marketplace is a modern innovation that would confuse our European forebears in the medieval village, or the ancient Agora or Forum. But now the public square is disenchanted, traded "goods" are good in name alone, stripped of any transcendent value, their value bestowed by the utilitarian metric of nominalist brokers. Nothing has enduring value. Money is the measure of all things.

Not only has space been stripped of its markers. Time too has been razed like the forest of Isengard. It can be measured only by counting the rings

---

1   Martin Palmer, *Sacred Land: Decoding the Hidden History of Britain* (London: Little, Brown, 2012).

on its dead stumps. When the elves lived among us, we marked the passage of time annually with Christian feasts, weekly with Sunday observance, daily with the Mass and Hours. On festivals and saints' days we shared our common story with plays, songs, games, foods and drinks, unique to their season. The atrophied stumps of Christmas, St Valentine's Day, and Easter are all that remain of that woodland, with Hallowe'en, twisted into a morbid bacchanal of transience, overshadowing all. The life-giving fruits of time have been desiccated, shredded, shrink-wrapped, and shelved. The traditional foods, once markers of the season, arrive so prematurely that much of them, unwanted and untimely ripped, end up in supermarket dumpsters. All the signposts have been turned toward profit, our only common destination now.

The signposts of words — and especially names — are important in the works of the Inklings, a theme continued by the great fantasy author, Ursula Le Guin. Her *Earthsea* trilogy tells the story of a young apprentice magician who unlocks the magical potential of things by learning their true names. These names are not mere tokens assigned by humans as a convenient code for navigating around reality, but are essential and inherent keys to their identity. *Earthsea* is a world of just that Christian-Platonic confluence we found in Dionysius, where beings are spoken or even sung into existence. This is not to suggest that there really is some primal Enochian language of the angels spoken by God, as though he were a being with a larynx. Rather, it is a layer of metaphor by which we come to intuit the Parmenidean maxim that things are insofar as they are intelligible.

The magical language of *Earthsea* is quite contrary to modern Western notions of language and thought, and our assumption that names are merely given by us to identify an essentially external material world ultimately separate from mental concepts. The efforts of the Inklings and Le Guin have been diluted into mere entertainment, notably in the spectacular films of the *Lord of the Rings*, from which the screenwriters have either excised metaphysical and biblical references, or more likely, simply never noticed them in the first place. This is surprisingly true even of the Japanese Studio Ghibli's rendition of *Earthsea*, whose writers are usually far more attuned to the mythopoeic, especially in *Spirited Away*, replete with its Shinto allusions. Even in Japan, it seems, the modern Western mindset has taken hold. To find where this mindset came from, we will need to return where we left our Late Franciscans, John Duns Scotus and William of Ockham.

In the Dionysian worldview, every being is an unfolding of God's presence. This means that we can justly "name" God by reference to anything in existence. God bears all names, because every being pre-exists enfolded, as it were, in the mind of God.[2] Yet Dionysius radically qualifies this by saying that just as we affirm all beings as names of God, we must equally deny them of him, because while immanent in being, God is simultaneously utterly beyond being. This is no mere or mystical paradox. If God were a being, then both his transcendence and immanence would be compromised: he would be one being among many, and so not transcendently beyond them; but also separate from all other beings, and so not immanent in them. It is only because God is beyond being that he can be present to all beings, rather than merely separate from them. God's transcendence preserves his immanence, and so everything that exists becomes an icon of his ineffable presence.

In the late Middle Ages, Western philosophy started drifting away from this iconic insight into the world and started the steady progress towards our modern regard for being as bare matter. Following the finger of their master on Raphael's fresco, Platonists had sought truth from the top down, seeking unity with the mind of Christ in contemplative faith so that they might understand the cosmos truly. The new Aristotelians, and particularly the acolytes of Averroes, were convinced that the only access to truth was, rather, from their master's downturned palm. It would be found not in extra-sensory, non-discursive meditation on the dizzying heights of universals, but on the microscopic examination of beings in their particularity. Even Aquinas, we saw, had controversially repeated the Aristotelian dictum that all knowledge is derived from sensory perception.

Scotus picked up Averroes' empiricist thread from where Aquinas had left off. Formally, Scotus distanced himself from "that accursed Averroes."[3] He was particularly concerned, as was Al-Ghazali, to avoid any inference of necessity to God's creation of the world, and thus to protect the freedom and sovereignty of the divine will which Averroes seemed to contradict. The picture is complicated by his continued commitment, with Aquinas, to the reality of the Platonic-Aristotelian Forms, a position known as "realism." Nonetheless, both Avicenna's and Averroes' shift of gravity from the universal to the particular and their renewed focus on sense-perception, which Aquinas himself had embraced, would evolve by way of Scotus into a very different way of looking at the world.

Scotus's move towards understanding God primarily in terms of will was magnified and intensified by his fellow Franciscan successor, William of Ockham. Ockham refined Scotus' doctrines of the univocity of being

2   *Divine Names* I.6, 596A.

3   *Quaestiones in Lib. IV Sententiarum* (*Ordinatio*) Dist. 43, 1.2.

and voluntarism into a far more atomized understanding of reality. In a move reminiscent of Al-Ghazali, Ockham posited that God, as the highest being, keeps all other beings in completely separate, individual existence, by what he called *potentia Dei absoluta*, the absolute power of God. [4] There is no common bond of being between beings, no existential relationship between them at all: the only relationship beings have in common is that they are all projections of God's power.

For Ockham, then, the definition of things — what Dionysius called "names" — were not revelations of the mind of God from which they unfolded, but arbitrary codes imposed on a reality essentially separate from God. The cosmos was stripped of divine presence, leaving it a blank canvas onto which names and meaning would be imposed by sheer force of will. Things no longer have meaning because they are divine self-revelation, insights into the Intellect or mind of God, but only as expressions of his sovereign, indisputable, and loving will. The universal categories embodied by Platonic forms were not, after all, real in their own right, but only as *nomina mentalia*, "mental names." [5] This "nominalism" was not original to Ockham — it had been posited by the great Peter Abelard before him — but his pervasive influence in later intellectual history has served to identify his name above all with the doctrine.

To understand why Ockham wanted to make this shift, it helps to know something of his life and time. In dark centuries of plague, heresy, and the threat of obliteration by the Mongol forces at the gates of Christendom, the inherent goodness of the created order was hard to see. Burgeoning amid such misery, Franciscan spirituality stressed the loving will of God made manifest in the Crucifixion. On the Cross, God had known the suffering and pain known by the people the Friars served. In the Incarnation, He had lived among the poor, leprous, and incontinent — and loved them. Amid such suffering, that love looked more like a contradiction of the natural order than a perfection of it. The world on the other hand looked far less obviously like an unfolding of the divine mind. It might, more conceivably, be a neutral testing ground for love devised by the divine will. Nominalism conveniently abstracted the cosmos from God's nature, disenchanted reality, and made it into this neutral zone for the use of creatures in their exercise of obedience to God's loving will.

For the Realist, being coheres with intelligibility, breaking down the barrier between thought and object, mind and matter. Mental apprehensions

---

4 *Quodlibeta* VI, q.vi.
5 Ockham, *Ordinatio* I.d.2.q.6.

of objects are constitutive of the objects themselves, and however hazy such apprehensions may be, they nonetheless share to some degree in the true and real idea of those objects. For the nominalist, this is not so. The mind is only one reality utterly separate from all others. Matter has no essential intimacy with mind or thought. Thoughts are, rather, the imposition by a conscious being on another being, whether its object is conscious or not. This implies that there is no fundamental truth to be discerned in beings: the truest "name" of any being is that which is ascribed to it by the most dominant will. For Ockham, as a Christian Friar, this was God. Things are such because God, as most powerful, makes them so. So, for Ockham, the names and nature of God are not revealed in the created "effects" that unfold from him. Rather, his self-revelation and indeed the entire act of creation itself are acts of his will. Where creation and revelation were seen as part of a unified, iconic unfolding of the divine mind, creatures began to look more like atomized instantiations of the divine will.

What we see here is the start, in earnest, of a wholesale replacement of the older metaphysics of participation with one of isolation, and mind with will. The possibility of knowing God at all became more challenging to defend. If even intelligent beings are not considered such by merit of their participation in the higher, divine intelligence, our potential to know the mind of God becomes something like the potential for an ant to know the mind of Albert Einstein, but magnified in distance to an infinite degree. One might go so far as to say that it makes us more like ants in relation to God than like God's children. He, like Dr Manhattan in Alan Moore's *Watchmen*, becomes an alien intelligence of inscrutable will, looking at us like cogs in some vast machine. The seeds of eighteenth-century Deism are sown here. William Paley thought that the apparently mechanical nature of the universe pointed to a deliberate, willing designer. But if creation does not participate in the creator, then beyond that basic insight that a creator "exists," nothing more specific about the creator can necessarily be perceived through his or her or its work. At best, we might just about perceive some trace of the creator's handiwork like an artist's brushstrokes or the fingerprints of a maker in clay; but as John Calvin would counsel at the Reformation, our unparticipated, separate, fallen, and infinitely inferior intellect might be mistaken even in those deductions. Reason is all we have, but sundered from its source, even it cannot be trusted. Hence, all tradition is to be rejected unless directly demonstrable in the divine revelation of Holy Scripture, which becomes our only reliable oracle of the Divine Will. The only way we might understand anything of God is if

He, as the supreme willing being, wants us to. The Protestant antitheses of revelation versus reason, faith versus works, and scripture versus tradition all owe something to the influence of the Late Franciscans. There can be, *pace* Thomas Aquinas, no natural law or natural theology, because even intelligent creatures are not participants in the creative order of the divine mind. We cannot discern his will in his nature as loving gift through the gifts of being we receive. We can only seek his will, and only through his pronouncements of it. Obedience is changed from a sublimation of the intellect into a submission of the will.

All the above comes with the caveat of oversimplification. The Late Franciscans were no doubt more subtle than many of their later interpreters, and far more subtle than I. Nonetheless, the picture of God as tyrant emblazoned in the mind of sceptics by pop-atheists like Philip Pullman owes something to the nominalist and voluntarist shift which the late Franciscans set in motion: the triumph of Averroistic Aristotelian epistemology over the Neoplatonic synthesis of Plato's and Aristotle's metaphysics. No longer is God a singer calling melodies into being, creative play, and harmony; he is a taskmaster making playthings for his unknowable pleasure and barking orders at them through the firmament; no longer an artist painting images resplendent with his own inner light, but a draughtsman delineating implacable laws; no longer the transcendent rays that penetrate all being to give life, growth, and sight, but a metaphysical lantern that shines on whom it wills; not one in the sense of indivisible unity of all but in the strict numerical sense of one and other; not the verb of giving but the noun of giver.

The implications for modernity are manifold. In a post-truth world instilled for centuries with voluntaristic assumptions, reality is to be defined by the strongest will. Nominalism grants permission for this redefinition, since nothing has any intrinsic meaning: the world becomes a no-man's-land, passively awaiting human exploitation. Any continuity between nature and culture, let alone the divine and the created, is irrevocably severed. People can be declared subhuman, terminated on a whim, or bought and sold as resources. Some are born to sweet delight, some are born to endless night, and there's nothing you can do about it but pray and obey, or resist, and make your own truth.

INDIVIDUALISM

Nihil est unum et idem in utroque.
"Nothing is one and the same in any two different things."
— William of Ockham, *Ordinatio* I.d.2.q.6

THOUGH THERE IS A RISK IN ATTRIBUTING THE
views of characters in a novel to their author, Houellebecq's various
protagonists share such a common mold that it is hard not to discern
something of the creator in his creatures. Invariably male, middle-aged,
single, and disappointed in his professional and personal life, the Houel-
lebecqian hero craves the stability his fathers enjoyed: hearth and home,
a faithful marriage, a respected place in society, at times religion, maybe
even actual belief in God. He mourns the loss of all these elements of social
stability modernity has taken away, even while availing himself addictively
of their replacements: a bachelor pad, easy sex, money, a conscience clear
because it is empty.

A common thread of longing runs through Houellebecq's works for
what looks much like the Platonic universe of old, yet he seems unable to
bring himself to believe in it. What Houellebecq seems to want to believe
is something like this, an almost metaphysical internal retort against the
title of another book, *Atomized*:

> The lover hears his lover's voice over mountains and oceans; over
> mountains and oceans a mother hears the cry of her child. Love
> binds, and it binds forever. Good binds, while evil unravels. Sep-
> aration is another word for evil; it is also another word for deceit.
> All that exists is a magnificent interweaving, vast and reciprocal. [1]

Yet Houellebecq's attitude towards religion, surely the most consistent source
of metaphysical speculation, is ambiguous. To recap *Submission*, part ode
to and part parody of Islam, the growing Muslim immigrant middle class
of France takes charge, effectively making Islam the state religion. The

---

[1] Michel Houellebecq, "No Title," in *Atomized* (Westminster, London: Penguin, 2001).

protagonist can continue in his career at the Sorbonne if he converts. This prompts him into a foray into his nation's native Catholicism, which has always been there but to which he has never had cause to give much thought. A visit to a monastery yields nothing but a little fond nostalgia for what is clearly a spiritually spent force. Submission to the newly dominant creed will afford certain perks, not least polygamy. It offers far greater stability, certainly, than the collapsed rubble of modernity in which he had been raised. In pursuit of order, he converts.

Houellebecq's more antithetical stance toward religion can be read in his engagement with the works of Howard Phillips Lovecraft. Lovecraft's 1920s horror sci-fi was in his lifetime considered little more than pulp fiction, yet one of Houellebecq's earliest published works is devoted to him. Its title, *Lovecraft: Against the World, Against Life*, gives some sense of the nihilism behind it.[2] In recent decades, the Cthulhu Mythos he created has enjoyed a renaissance among fantasy writers of every hue, influencing the likes of Neil Gaiman, Alan Moore, Caitlin O'Kiernan, and China Miéville with its unremitting vision of a universe populated by uncaring, inscrutable, and hostile gods. Cthulhu is only one of the Great Old Ones who exercise their will on the universe, to ends our meager intellects cannot hope to divine. For those foolhardy souls who try to pry into their mysteries, only madness awaits. In this universe Houellebecq discerns a new mythology for modernity comparable to the world of Homeric epic. He notes how Lovecraft's texts have pervaded youth culture through video games, comics, tabletop roleplaying games, and even rock music — to such an extent that many enthusiasts are "initiated" into the Mythos without ever intending to read his "canon." Lovecraft's frighteningly seductive world is "a supreme antidote against all forms of realism,"[3] including religions, those "sugar-coated illusions made obsolete by the progress of science."[4] Good and evil are mere "Victorian fictions. All that exists is egotism: cold, intact and radiant." This is a strictly materialist mythos: Lovecraft's gods are all beings within the universe. There is nothing at all beyond. Humanity is trapped in a cosmic warzone between cruel and monstrous intelligences, destined to be crushed by them or assimilated to their enslaved hordes of mindless, creeping things. The compulsion of this vision lies in the shudder as we apprehend our absolute insignificance.

---

2   French edition first published in 1991. Now available in English translation, Michel Houellebecq, *Lovecraft: Against the World, Against Life* (London: Orion, 2008).

3   Ibid., 37.

4   Ibid., 40.

Some critics see Houellebecq as a charlatan, others as a prophet. Perhaps, though, the way he navigates between his desire for a metaphysics of love and his fear of a nihilistic, Lovecraftian universe, makes him one of the few novelists truly grappling with the great intellectual problem of the West. Others have taken for granted the nominalist world of Ockham and descended into a kind of parochialism, limiting themselves to their own experience. We see this in the arguments over cultural appropriation, as the bounds of acceptable writing continue to constrict tighter and tighter: for if one's own sensory perceptions are the only means to knowledge, one cannot dare imagine oneself in the role of anybody else. A white Anglo-Saxon male must write only from the perspective of a white Anglo-Saxon male. Only gay actors may play gay roles. Imagination is out of bounds. How, with such constraints, could one even begin to write about matters of cosmic import under such limitations? One cannot: what is beyond "lived experience" is taboo.

Houellebecq adopts this limitation himself, but only in order to break it. He writes his protagonists, almost always, as fairly transparent avatars of himself. Other perspectives are relegated to secondary roles or bit parts, and at times his protagonist (if not the author himself) is guilty of making lazy racial stereotypes. Yet in every case they are both a part of Ockham and Lovecraft's nihilistic world, individuals divided and conquered by more powerful forces — and they resent it, seeking something to bind and unite them with other nations, other races, the other sex, even God. Houellebecq is the rare modern writer who still remembers enough of the old Platonic universe to recognize the tension between it and the universe of Lovecraftian indifference to which Ockham was unwitting midwife.

The growth of this universe to its present grotesque enormity took centuries. Following the voluntarism of Scotus and Ockham, the Reformation fixated on God's sovereignty and the absolute primacy of his revealed will. Luther despised Aristotle so much that he reputedly made a bonfire of St Thomas Aquinas's writings. Calvin, reading Augustine through the new lens of nominalism, would come to see human reason as so utterly corrupted by the Fall that it could in no way discern, let alone participate in, the mind of God. The mind's eye could see nothing unless directly opened by the grace of God:

> Augustine, in speaking of this inability of human reason to under-
> stand the things of God, says that he deems the grace of illumi-
> nation not less necessary to the mind than the light of the sun to
> the eye (Augustine, de Peccat. Merit. et Remiss. lib. 2 cap. 5). And, not

content with this, he modifies his expression, adding that we open
our eyes to behold the light, whereas the mental eye remains shut,
until it is opened by the Lord.[5]

This eye-opening grace was so obliterated by the Fall that now it can be
imbued by God only by a free act of his will:

> For as an eye, either dimmed by age or weakened by any other
> cause, sees nothing distinctly without the aid of glasses, so (such
> is our imbecility) if Scripture does not direct us in our inquiries
> after God, we immediately turn vain in our imaginations. . . .
> Justly does Augustine complain that God is insulted whenever any
> higher reason than his will is demanded.[6]

All that was left was submission of the lesser wills to the greatest. And
naturally, this will extended to the smashing of images and icons, since it
was a gross error to assume that merely created things could in any way
mediate the utterly other divine. Protestants tended towards moralism, as
they came to see right action as discernment of and obedience to God's
law, and the Good simply as whatever God wills, regardless of reason. Since
nature did not participate in God, his will could be known only through
his direct revelations. Hence the doctrine of *sola scriptura*: by Scripture alone
could God's will be known.

The Reformation, however, would segue into the age of the Enlightenment. The works of the Reformers would be subjected to just such skepticism as they had deployed against the medieval Schoolmen. The scriptures
themselves would not escape such critical scholarship. So the very basis even
of discerning God's will, supposedly so stable, came into question. Not that
it had gone entirely unquestioned before. Certain doctrines, which Calvin
thought were incontrovertibly grounded in the Bible, seemed far less con-
vincing to some of his Protestant successors. Doctrines, for instance, like the
Trinity. A plethora of sects began to emerge, each applying the Reformers'
maxim of *sola scriptura* and coming to quite different conclusions about
exactly what is was that God willed. At the far frontiers of Babel, one might
hear cautious voices suggesting that God's will cannot be known at all, and
could be safely ignored.

The wedge that had gradually been driven in between faith and reason
over the centuries was now opening the fissure wider than ever, but it would
be a mistake to label the Enlightenment as a straightforward triumph of the

---

5 Calvin, *Institutes* II.2.25.
6 *Institutes* I.14.1.

latter over the former. In his essay "Truth and Freedom,"[7] Pope Benedict discerns two different currents.

Benedict describes the first current of the Enlightenment as the "Anglo-Saxon," oriented towards human rights and constitutional democracy as the means of providing freedom. This he sees as a political settlement, opposed to the absolute power of the monarch or the state over individuals; but importantly, it is based on a transcendent reality. The idea of human rights and liberty depends on the truth that there is inherent value to life, and indeed to the world. It thereby assumes a natural, inherent orientation of reality towards goodness in something like the Platonic-Aristotelian sense.

The other, more radical, current he attributes to the Franco-Swiss philosopher Jean-Jacques Rousseau (1712 – 1778). In this strand of Enlightenment thought the natural human is a pure and free individual, essentially good, who is molded and corrupted by the impositions of an artificially contrived "society." All social influence is then perceived as a barrier to be overcome, a restraint on the fundamentally good nature of the solitary individual. Rousseau speculated that children were born as pure blank slates, which would only later be corrupted. Left to be free to their nature, humans would be gentle and innocent, could not help but love one another, would need no money, would have no rulers, would be in harmony with the rest of nature, would enjoy perfect health and would live naked, completely sexually unrestrained. It is only culture, and especially Christian culture, which has imposed the constraints on an otherwise good human nature and so leads to evil, suffering, inequality, and injustice. Somewhere out in the wilds untouched by Western civilization, he thought, there must be a tribe of "noble savages" who lived just like this.

Not only does Rousseau's ideal of a naturally good human society not exist, anywhere, but he was utterly incapable of living it himself. He had five children and sent them all to orphanages. They were just another obstacle to his freedom, and why should he listen to "culture" dictating that he had any responsibility for their upbringing?

In one stroke Rousseau cut off nature from culture. To be truly natural is to be spontaneous and utterly unfettered, in absolute freedom. Reason and all its contracts, including all morality, gender, sexuality, and social expectation, are merely "cultural" and so can and should be cast off. Rousseau's successors took the further step of questioning whether God even

---

7   In Benedict XVI, *The Essential Pope Benedict XVI: His Central Writings and Speeches*, ed. John F Thornton and Susan B Varenne (New York: Harper Collins, 2007).

"existed" at all, for by now it was obvious that only things which "exist" can be real. Gone was the sense that there is a source of existence we might understand through its effects, and which through scripture and reason together we might come to discern as the God revealed in Jesus Christ. Since God was a being, his reality was as demonstrable or otherwise as the reality of a coffee cup or a unicorn. Either the all-powerful being exists or it does not, and that is the end of it. To those who concluded that he did not, lay unimagined vistas of freedom. The freedom, for instance, of the Marquis de Sade (1740 – 1814), that epitome of the Rousseauvian strand of the Enlightenment, to abuse children and degrade women; and the free violence of the French Revolution, to which Rousseau's thought directly led.

The "Rights of Man" were declared in 1789. In the early days of the French Revolution, it was closer to Benedict's "Anglo-Saxon" model in its determination to establish liberty, equality, and freedom through the over-throwing of a tyrannical and oppressive regime. But tellingly, a new secular calendar was also instituted, dismissing the birth of Christ as an irrelevance, and starting again at year one. All Christian festivals were erased.

Three years later, thousands of Christians were being slaughtered. When the Jacobins took control in 1793, they were determined to eliminate the faith by violence, believing that science must replace religion. They insti-gated the Reign of Terror by the end of which 250,000 people were exe-cuted, including children. Extermination camps were set up in La Vendée, where people tried to cling to the faith. In a hideous foreshadowing of Rousseau's later heirs, ovens were used, along with poison, mass shootings and drownings. John Marsh's *The Liberal Delusion*[8] gives greater detail, more sickening than I wish to recount here. Suffice it to cite some words from General Westermann, who was responsible for the atrocities in the Vendée, in his report back to his masters in Paris:

> There is no more Vendée. It died with its wives and its children by our free sabers. . . . I crushed the children under the feet of the horses, massacred the women. . . . I do not have a single prisoner to reproach me. I have exterminated them all. . . . Mercy is not a revolutionary sentiment.

Later, in the 1870s, there was a new Jacobin-inspired uprising. Seventy clergy were slaughtered. Following the events from Russia, Dostoyevsky wrote, "It's the same old Rousseau and the dream of recreating the world

---

8   John Marsh, *The Liberal Delusion* (Bury St Edmonds: Arena Books, 2012).

anew through reason and knowledge."[9] He could not know then that his own country would soon be party to worse atrocities still, and under the same philosophical inspiration. The new ideology of Marxism, too, claimed that it would usher in a new order of undreamt-of freedom for all.

The Jacobins devised their own catechism which maintained that "a child is like soft wax capable of receiving any imprint one wishes." Chairman Mao justified brainwashing his people with the *bon mot*, "It is on a blank sheet of paper that the most beautiful poems are written." Behind the French Revolution, Marxism, and Nazism lies a common pedagogical methodology inherited directly from Rousseau. It is the idea of the child's mind as a blank slate or empty vessel waiting to be filled with whatever adults want to fill it with.

The influence of Rousseau's blank slate theory persists in many presuppositions of postmodernity too. This rests on his assertion that culture is distinct from nature, and that even this nature has no metaphysical grounding in any transcendent order. Goodness, truth, and beauty are *just* cultural constructs defined at will, with no reality in nature. Yet this godless, antimetaphysical society is an audacious experiment. Until now the separation of nature from culture has been alien to any known society on earth. Not only humans but animals have societies, as we know through observing the behavior of species ranging from monkeys to elephants and dolphins, or even ants. We would never dream of saying that animal cultures are somehow distinct from their nature. Animals are cultural by nature: even social by nature. Only humans, insist the heirs of Rousseau, are different — and this is by virtue of the separation between the intellect and the will that began with the Late Franciscans. Society becomes just an imposition, a limit on my freedom. We write things off as being only *social* constructs: gender, marriage, and social hierarchy among them. That is to say they are not part of our *nature*, which in the end is subject to determination only by the gloriously emancipated, unfettered, isolated, individual *will*.

The deficiency of Rousseau's thought, and so ultimately of ours, is born of a deficient understanding of God. Heir to the voluntarist assumptions that began in earnest with Duns Scotus, Rousseau understood God primarily in terms of the exercise of power by his own free will: in other words, as merely *a* god. This effectively makes "God" just a superior and more powerful version of ourselves, and us humans a pagan polytheistic pantheon of gods in our own right. Eliminate the "great big God" of the children's hymn, and we are free to pursue our own individual agendas. To

---

9 Cited in Marsh, *The Liberal Delusion*.

be godlike for Rousseau meant to exercise untrammeled will oneself. What Rousseau wanted, as it seems many moderns want, was to be a god himself, dependent on nothing and no-one.

This hypothetical Rousseauvian god has little to do with the Trinitarian God revealed in earlier Christian tradition. The divinity in which we participate as iconic image-bearers is not some Lovecraftian autarch in the sky, Richard Dawkins' idiotic spaghetti monster, one great god among gods, but is by nature three persons in union. God is at heart communal, and in sharing his image, we are fundamentally and naturally social, communally oriented creatures. Christ in his Incarnation and Crucifixion reveals the image of a God who is intrinsically oriented towards the other, not imprisoned in an isolated selfhood, but being self by the gift of self: God, in short, as kenosis.

Separate the divine Good from the created order of Being, and not just the human mind but the entire world, plant, animal, human, and even the air and water, becomes a blank slate, a resource to be exploited by the dominant will. There are advantages to this. The willingness to experiment fearlessly and trust the evidence of our senses has led to great advances in medicine and technology. But penicillin and refrigerators have come hand-in-hand with thalidomide, DDT, and nuclear weapons. Our strident belief in the possibility of redefining everything according to its utility to us has led to racialism, empire, slavery, war, and environmental devastation. All of these are the motley fruits of Western progress.

Progress is perhaps the most enduring myth propagated in Western schools today: namely, the notion that we can naturally assume that the past was inferior, and that we are moving inexorably towards a better future. Dresden, Auschwitz, and Hiroshima were just the unfortunate side-effects of testing certain hypotheses now happily debunked. An important component of this myth is the notion that because religious observance is declining in the more technologically advanced countries of Western Europe and America, this must be a sign of the inferiority of religion. Implicit in this is the assumption that religious decline has happened naturally, as an inevitable matter of course, rather than being engineered socially. By religion, we should note, secularists tend to mean Western Christianity, which they associate (not unfairly) with voluntarism; but where their invective becomes decidedly less fair is in categorizing all religion in history and throughout the world by this strictly intra-Western, intra-modern paradigm. Religion so defined as unquestioning obedience to an arbitrary divine will helpfully plays into Rousseau's narrative of autonomy and individuation, and props up the deeper myth that materialism (by which I mean the philosophical rejection of any non-material reality) is the sole strictly neutral viewpoint from which all others may be objectively judged.

Like the myth of relativism as neutrality, the myth of progress stems from a particular Western European tradition, and in particular from Hegel's insistence that human development follows a trajectory from primitive Eastern thought towards the heights of modern Western superiority. Even now, the very Western liberal commentators who berate traditional world views for their intolerance tend also to maintain that they are the true defenders of diversity and respect for minority positions. The reality is that just as European Christians imposed their worldview on foreign nations by persuasion or coercion, economic promise, or the threat of arms, so Western liberals seek to do the same. And their postmodern successors try to do the same to their compatriots at home, but by lawsuits, pressure groups, de-platforming, social media pogroms, and the inquisitorial officers of Diversity and Inclusion departments. An observation Edmund Burke made on the intellectuals behind the French Revolution in his day is no less applicable to certain pedagogues of today's American and British universities: "In the groves of their academy, at the end of every vista, you see nothing but the gallows."[10]

Secular attitudes towards Christian Africa are instructive. Once upon a time, Europeans berated Africans for engaging in homosexuality; nowadays, Europeans berate Africans for condemning it, and are affronted that they no longer obey. In liberal Christian circles I have often heard clergy quietly making snide comments about the Church being "held to ransom" over sexuality by African bishops, often comparing them to "tribal chieftains." These are the very people who harangue conservatives on Twitter for racism. Regardless of one's position on the issues of sexuality, the hubristic assumption of inherent Western superiority is the issue here. Belittling those whom one wishes to persuade and writing them off as primitive bigots is unlikely to win hearts and minds, as the bellicose attitude of the West towards Islamic countries amply testifies. If only Muslims and Africans knew better, the rhetoric implies, they would be just like us.

Apart from concealing racism under a rather diaphanous veil, the myth of progress also depends on a false narrative about the relationship between science and religion which foments around the evolutionary theory of Charles Darwin. Suffice it to say here that the majority of scientists who

---

10 Edmund Burke, *Reflections on the Revolution in France*, ed. J. G. A. Pocock (Indianapolis: Hackett, 1987) 66–67.

accepted Darwin's findings in his time were themselves practicing and devout Christians. The eminently readable *Making Sense of Evolution: Darwin, God, and the Drama of Life* by John Haught gives full details.[11] Here, I want to expose the misleading narrative that religion until Darwinism was "fundamentalist," and that his science has in some way liberated humanity from superstitious error. In reality, fundamentalism and relativism are really two sides of one equally devalued coin.

If fundamentalism is taken to mean a literal reading of the Bible as inerrant history, then this was certainly not the position most Christians held in the time of Darwin, nor is it is the position they hold today. It originated in early twentieth-century America, and for better reasons than today's cultured despisers of religion might think: as a reaction to the bad science of social Darwinism. Despite the efforts of some of his later disciples, Richard Dawkins and Jerry Coyne among them, Darwin himself had not intended his evolutionary theory to become the sole hermeneutic for understanding reality. He certainly had not expected it to offer an ideal model for human society. "Survival of the fittest" was not intended as a program for social engineering. Yet it did not take long for scientists to establish, through techniques respected in their day but now debunked, the evolutionary superiority of some people over others. Notably, in the United States, the scientific orthodoxy of the day led to the stratification of different races. Measurements of the cranium and, later, highly culturally specific IQ tests were applied to show the evolutionary superiority of the "white" over the darker-skinned peoples. So scientific reason was applied to promote slavery and empire.

Although these scientific theories have now been superseded by later evidence, they were highly influential at the time. Christian fundamentalism was a horrified response to a scientific assault on human dignity completely at odds with the notion of all people being made equally in the image of God. Presented with the apparently incontestable weight of scientific "proof," these Christians decided all they could do was discard it. Taking to its extreme the Protestant doctrine of *sola scriptura*, the idea that Scripture alone is necessary for salvation, they declared that the Bible was verbally inerrant and that any knowledge that did not conform to it was simply false. They fought one absolute with another. Christianity was reduced to biblicism, science to scientism: the ideas that the Bible or science provide the sole means to truth.

---

11   Haught, John F, *Making Sense of Evolution: Darwin, God, and the Drama of Life* (Louisville, KY: Westminster John Knox Press, 2010).

Neither biblical nor scientific fundamentalism have served humanity well. The biblicist defense did not stand up to the rationalist onslaught. Well into the middle of the twentieth century, evolutionary theory was still being used to justify the elimination of genetic deficiencies from the human race. The Nazis are the obvious example, but moderate left-wing intellectual organizations such as the Fabians firmly supported eugenicists' proposals to abort children with disabilities and sterilize their parents.[12] Marie Stopes, who founded the UK's leading provider of abortions that bears her name, was an anti Semite and admirer of Hitler who wished to create a super-race and disowned her son for marrying a short-sighted woman.[13] In the UK, fetuses with Down's Syndrome are routinely terminated. In poorer parts of the world, it is overwhelmingly girls who are aborted, simply for being girls. The disabled and girls are deemed too much of a burden to their families and to society. This tends to be overlooked by popular Western discourse, which wants to portray abortion as a societal good and a sign of progress. Abortion is, notably, an incontestable nostrum of critical theorists, despite their professed resistance to any absolute moral norms.

Against that Western discourse, Quranic fundamentalism is as much a late-nineteenth-century phenomenon as Protestant biblical fundamentalism and scientism. The Western pursuit of empire that had once been waged under the banner of Christianity was now flying the flag of scientific and genetic superiority instead. Western generals and diplomats began dividing up tribal Arab lands and imposing the obviously "superior" Western model of the nation state, literally drawing the lines on the map. This set up the conflict between secularist and theocratic movements that still devastates the region to this day, and has made religious freedoms far more fragile than they were even just a hundred years ago.

Both scientific and biblical fundamentalism rely on the idea of an absolute and unchallengeable authority behind them. On this shallow foundation each builds its own huge, casuistical edifice through the exercise of reason divorced from any connection to transcendent goodness or truth. Each forges its own truth by sheer strength of will. In this, both scientism and fundamentalism are heir to the philosophical heritage of Scotus, Ockham, and the Reformers — albeit in a debased form that does not do full justice to any of those thinkers. Postmodernism has the dubious added privilege

---

12 https://www.newstatesman.com/society/2010/12/british-eugenics-disabled.
13 https://www.dailymail.co.uk/femail/article-2649024/Monster-mother-A-birth-control-pioneer-revered-parenting-guru-But-Marie-Stopes-treated-son-died-week-abominable-cruelty.html.

of Rousseau's lineage in its genetic makeup.

The boundless scope of fantasy and science fiction can offer an illuminating window into our society's collective fears and desires. The last hundred years have left us with a choice of two different fantasy universes. The one that has come to dominate Western thought is broadly speaking that of Lovecraft and more recently the *Game of Thrones*: a disenchanted war zone without commonality or unity, where "nothing is one and the same in any two different things," so hostile powers must compete for territory and strive to plant their flags. The other, as we mentioned before, is that Platonic world of the Inklings and Ursula Le Guin, a magical realm born of song and made for playful, harmonious creativity, where all things participate in one another to some degree, and in God immediately and absolutely. In the first, beings are individuals, vying for power; in the second, voices united in a cosmic hymn of praise. The cosmos is either warzone or theophany.

Like most of us in countries influenced by the West, Houellebecq straddles both worlds. Beneath the horrific exterior of an apparently Lovecraftian universe, he gestures towards a human freedom that rests not in our abilities to conquer and destroy one another, but to love another. To those who would object that the latter can only ever be a fantasy world, we reply that not only did the greatest minds of Greek antiquity and the first millennium of Latin philosophy subscribe to it, but it is far closer also to the older philosophical positions throughout the world — and not only the Abrahamic religions, but even certain traditions of the nontheistic East. So, the lost path to a re-enchanted world takes us at last off the edge of the Silk Road, over the sea to medieval Kyoto and the rising Buddhist schools of Japan.

How I Met Shinran

THIRTEENTH-CENTURY JAPAN MAY NOT SEEM VERY promising territory for a philosophical rapprochement with Christianity. Other than a passing reference to an East Syriac physician traveling to Japan in AD 739 to help Emperor Shomu plan a hospital, there is no evidence of East Syriac Christianity exercising any influence in Japan.[1] Yet despite its prided status as an island nation, Japan was not yet in quite the splendid isolation it would later enjoy. Buddhism itself was a Chinese import, and as we have seen, Buddhists interacted with Christians all along the Silk Road. So it was that a specifically Chinese development of Buddhism grew popular in Japan. This "Pure Land" Buddhism was eventually refined by a thirteenth-century monk called Shinran into his True Pure Land School or *Jodo Shinshu*, called "Shin Buddhism" for short.

Shin Buddhism focuses on devotion to a particular manifestation of the Buddha under the name of Amida. Shinran emphasizes three key doctrinal points:

1. Amida as the compassionate manifestation of rationally inconceivable Buddha-reality.
2. The need for complete reliance on Amida's Vow for salvation from the cycle of death and rebirth.
3. The *nembutsu* — grateful recitation of Amida's Name for the gift of liberation.

Already you may detect some at least cosmetic similarities to Christian teachings, and scholars have mused over whether there might have been some historical influence along the Silk Road. While that remains a possibility, there is no hard textual evidence for a direct connection between the two. Nor is such a direct historical connection between Christian Platonism and Buddhism strictly necessary. As we look into the origins of Shinran's thought, we will find that it is perfectly consonant with historical developments within Buddhism.

---

1 Baum and Winkler, *The Church of the East: A Concise History*, 65.

Shinran's teachings do not sit in radical, reformist opposition to the Buddhist teaching that came before them. Nor, however, can their differences be diluted by a convenient narrative of conformity. Shinran offers new insights in his native Buddhist tradition which are nonetheless developments of entirely Buddhist themes. A variety of motives underlies attempts either to differentiate it radically from mainstream Buddhism by attributing its development to alien influences, or to harmonize it so seamlessly with other schools of Buddhism that its differences are eroded or explained away.

Conventional Western scholarship has made connections between Shinran's Buddhism and the thought of the Protestant Reformers, particularly in regard to the priority he appears to place on "faith" over works. Some Shin Buddhists have accepted such comparisons more or less happily, while others have fiercely contested them. Having exposed the origins and motives behind both these conciliatory and oppositional agendas, I will point to a deeper, older harmony between Shinran's Buddhism and the older sacramental philosophy of the Christian Platonists, exemplified in general more by traditional Catholic and Orthodox doctrine than by the Protestant thought with which Shinran is so often compared.

First, let me explain how I met Shinran in the first place, and why I feel called to bring him to wider attention in the West than he has hitherto enjoyed.

Conventions of Western modernity demand a complete separation of the personal from the intellectual, as though any alignment of head and heart were cause for suspicion. It is only fairly recently that the use of the first-person pronoun has shed its air of disrepute in academic journals. This results inevitably in convoluted and absurd passive constructions, as scholars engage in all sorts of verbal contortions to avoid any implication of personal interest in their research. The reader is not supposed to divine the motivations of the writer, supposedly irrelevant as they are to the objective matter at hand.

Such schizophrenia was unknown to the ancients. The matter of their lives was woven inextricably into the work of their minds. We might discern doctrine in a biography of Plotinus, a letter from Shinran to his wife, a reference to the spiritual experience of Dionysius's albeit pseudonymous bishop. The modern, Westernized mind is trained to extract objectives truth from subjective data. The early twentieth-century biblical scholar Adolf von Harnack (1851 – 1930) is one great exemplar of the method called "demythologization." It was he who began in earnest the quest for the historical Jesus, the man hidden behind the myths of Church and scripture. Through critical scholarship he and his school thought they could dissect the Bible with the precision of a Victorian vivisectionist, excising its component parts and laying them out in logical array. Yet, having stripped away such credulous accretions around the person of Christ as miracles and assertions of divinity, the man he found at the end of the scalpel bore an uncanny resemblance to its bearer. The historical Jesus, it turned out, was not God in human flesh after all. He was a Victorian German liberal who had traveled through time in the disguise of a first-century Middle Eastern Jew. God bore the image of von Harnack!

Similar scalpels have been brought to bear on Dionysius, Shinran, Plotinus, Proclus, Iamblichus, and all the rest, with much the same result: whatever organs the surgeon considers unnecessary are thrown into the incinerator like burst appendices, and in the end all skulls grin alike. Victorian and early twentieth-century scholars dismissed elements of the supernatural in their subjects' thought as signs of intellectual weakness and obstacles to the real, objective truth. But in this, they failed to see that rather than mere disposable vehicles of truth, the mythological and supernatural worldview of these ancients is essential to their communication. So, too, their biographies: not merely for psychological purposes, but because in their cases they understand their lives as governed by forces not subject to their will or even their reason. Was Abelard's thought untouched by the fiery love that joined him to Heloise? Do we profess to understand his thought more clearly in abstraction from the passion of his affair that we know so manifestly drove it?

Likewise, my own motives in studying Shinran and Dionysius, in making the editorial decision to compare the two, and to promote what I have learnt from them, are not merely incidental to my work. I do not see why the reader should have to decipher those motives as it were between the lines. So, I mean to explain a little about how I met Shinran, in circumstances that surmount the wall convention would erect between my academic interests, and my personal and spiritual life.

I first met Shinran in Bristol, where I was reading for a research degree under the Catholic professor of Theology, Gavin D'Costa. My interest was in twentieth-century Catholic theology of nature and grace and its implications for Christian engagement with other religions, especially Buddhism; my chosen lens, the apparent antithesis of Karl Rahner and Hans Urs von Balthasar. This pair is popularly taken as representing, respectively, the more liberal *aggiornamento* and the more conservative *ressourcement* strands of thinking that contributed to the Second Vatican Council. Rahner draws more on Kant and subsequent secular philosophical disciplines in his thought than

Balthasar, whose method is to return more to the Church Fathers. In the course of these investigations however I was led to their older contemporary, the great Jesuit theologian and student of the Fathers, Henri de Lubac. To my surprise and delight I discovered that de Lubac had written two entire books on a decidedly niche kind of Buddhism (niche outside Japan, at least): Shinran's True Pure Land school. At Bristol I also discovered that my teacher of Buddhism, Professor Paul Williams, had converted to Roman Catholicism after 25 years of adherence to Buddhism partly as a response to his reading of Shinran.

This is where we need to breach the wall. For my motives cannot be said here to be purely academic. Nor am I convinced my studies would have benefitted from such disinterest. The reasons I wanted to take this research degree in the first place were expressly personal and spiritual. I was in my mid-twenties and had only recently come to faith, by a route one could rightly call circuitous.

Brought up in a non-churchgoing and basically non-religious household, I had grown to despise religion in general, and Christianity with a particular venom. That, at least, is the tale I usually tell, because it is easier not to mention that I flirted with liberal Judaism in my early teenage years, enjoyed Religious Studies classes, and took especial pleasure in reading Plato in the Greek classes I took in Sixth Form (what North American readers would call "Senior High"). Nor is it perhaps entirely incidental that I was taught both Latin and Greek by my school chaplain, the Reverend Ronald Darroch, a vastly intelligent low churchman of the old-fashioned kind whom I deeply admired, even if I professed disdain for his religion. He chain-smoked Hamlet cigars and poured me cold Lapsang while he taught me one-to-one in his apartment, all unthinkable in these safeguarding-conscious days. Probably rightly so, though I think it a shame that teachers can no longer offer such kindness and hospitality to their students as I enjoyed without arousing suspicion.

So, the seeds of religion, you might say, were secretly sown; but at that time I was still mired in the fruitless soil of secular materialism. I went up to read Classics at St Andrews, Scotland's oldest university. Though founded in 1411 by papal bull, the Reformation had done away with all that. John Knox had long since torn down the cathedral stone by stone and, by 1997 when I arrived, the Scottish humanism of the cultured despisers of religion flourished still. Victorian classicists, clinical dissectors of ancient texts, had practically made their subject the enemy of religion, and treated theologians with contempt. For centuries, classicists had made humans the subject of their study, as evidenced by the traditional title of their discipline in the older universities: Classics is properly called litterae humaniores at Oxford, and the study of Latin at St Andrews once rejoiced in the simple name of "humanity." Yet unlike their medieval and renaissance forebears who had thus christened the discipline, twentieth-century classicists understood humanity in strict isolation from God. I was happy to join that tradition, and did so with gusto, tirelessly denouncing the oppressive superstitions of yore, whether in the Debating Society or around the table of the smoke-filled Cellar Bar at Aikman's. I was, as Mr Darroch had once described me, a "militant heathen," and probably something of a bore with it. I protested too much.

It was in Japan that the wall began to crack. After graduation, I had served for a year as an elected student union sabbatical officer, but then, yearning for further shores and an escape from the claustrophobia of office life, I applied for an English teaching post on the Japanese Government's Japan English Teaching (or "JET") Program. Again, my express motives need a little qualification. I have neglected to mention that in Scotland I had taken up the martial art of Aikido, and indeed taken to it with such fervor that a friend accused me of religion, a charge I hotly denied. Does it matter, I wonder, that my friend was a priest's son? The trouble with providence is that once one believes it, one starts seeing signs of it everywhere. Yet I cannot deny that there was something in the meditative pursuit of the almost magical freedom of movement I was learning in Aikido which drove me to Japan to train more and seek more deeply the roots of peace it had started to unearth in me.

Aikido is part of the story of my movement towards Christian faith, and somewhat ironically with it, towards Shinran. After a year as a decidedly lefty student sabbatical politician, I was out in the Orient "looking for myself" through Aikido training while teaching English to make a living. A living embodiment of the gap-year cliché, I was "finding myself" in Asia and practicing martial arts with a Buddhist monk. Sorry to dispel any Mr Miyagi scenarios, but no cars were waxed in the process. Takahashi Sensei, one of the Aikido practitioners I met training in the Prefectural Dojo in Kochi City, was anything but a cliché. Aikido is a relatively soft martial arts form, but he practiced hard and dirty techniques, ramming me down to the floor with a knock of the hip or a sudden sweep of the leg. For months I had no idea that he was a priest: his arms were like gnarled tree trunks, and he spoke with the sort of 20-a-day growl that might have adorned the yakuza boss of a 1970s Suzuki Seijun Tokyo gangster flick. But if Aikido had softened my heart, then visiting Takahashi Sensei's temple opened my mind.

Takahashi never really spoke much at all on the mats, let alone in English, but when I asked my naive questions at the temple, he talked about the mutually dependent co-arising of beings and the plenitudinous emptiness he perceived at the heart of existence. With deep reserves of learning which his gruff exterior hid from view, he easily exposed the chinks in the fortress of atheist materialism I had built around myself for so many years. As with my school chaplain, I was forced to recognize that there were people far more learned, intelligent, and wise than myself who held well-grounded beliefs in the supernatural. Puncturing my youthful hubris, the revelation finally dawned: if I could respect such convictions in a Buddhist, then why not in a Christian too?

Thereafter I started to haunt Buddhist temples and Shinto shrines, suspiciously sniffing out the stillness that drew me to them. But there was one final and conclusive factor in my conversion: the young woman who would become my wife. If Mr Darroch and others had sown the seeds, Aikido had softened the ground of my heart, and Takahashi Sensei and others had watered it, then Nao was the vehicle by which I would now say God gave me growth. Sometime after I met her, I had an intense experience of an inner, instant, and blinding spiritual light that finally knocked down the wretched wall within me.

Nao and I lived far apart, so I used to take the overnight ship and meet her half-way in Osaka. The Kinokuniya bookshop there served as our rendezvous. Despite its distance, it was the closest place to Kochi in those days with a decent selection of English-language books. Like a shy bachelor in a gas station, I found myself surreptitiously eyeing-up the top shelf. I was not looking for anything saucy. To my far greater shame, I wanted to buy a bible. I took home a King James version, and read it with newly opened eyes. While I was still wary of considering my experience of that inner light as having had anything to do with "God," I did at least learn the word to describe that timeless moment of light I had experienced as "Damascene."

Before it seems I have drifted into irrelevance, let me pick up the thread. Nao, it turned out, while not a Christian herself, had attended church faithfully for quite some time as a JYA student in the US. When we moved to the UK, it was she who encouraged me to go with her to church. Yet unlike me, she came from a household that already had a strong religious devotion: to Shin Buddhism.

I had no real awareness of my wife's family's True Pure Land school beyond the name of Shinran until, like poacher turned gamekeeper, I changed my academic direction from Classics to Theology. I was working, again rather unexpectedly, as a schoolmaster teaching Latin and Greek in Exeter Cathedral School in the UK. Through the pleasurable duty of escorting the choristers to Evensong, and thanks to my own explorations of a local Anglo-Catholic church, I finally submitted to baptism. Wanting to bring together my spiritual awakening in Japan, and all that had contributed towards it, with the Christian faith of which I was now at last convinced, I applied to Bristol to study under Professor of Catholic Theology, Gavin D'Costa. The convergence of my wife's family faith, de Lubac's books on Buddhism, and Professor Williams's journey from Buddhism to Catholicism led me to want to read Shinran for myself. And so I did, some years later when I brought him, together with my old Platonic interests, into my PhD studies at Cambridge — as well as studying classical Japanese so that I could, as best as possible, read his work in the original language.

Takahashi Sensei taught me that there comes a time where points of apparent coincidence converge so densely, and in such number, that it becomes less logical to attribute them to chance than to providence. Rather than isolated dots, they appear to be the intersections of crossing threads, like knots in a net. If the net I have woven still seems too loose, perhaps one final knot will help to draw it in.

While I was writing my PhD thesis, my wife and I went back to Japan, as we do most years, to visit her parents. We were going through some boxes that had belonged to her sister. In one box we found an old 1990s word processor with a disk still inserted. To our surprise, it still worked: and on the disk, we found Nao's older sister's unfinished undergraduate thesis. The topic was Shinran and Christianity. To some extent, I hope that I am completing her unfinished work.

My cards are on the table. I mean to introduce Shinran's thought to Christian readers, not out of some liberal concern to demythologize or relativize the two religions, or to suggest that Buddhism and Christianity are ultimately "the same." Rather, the study of Shinran is part of the strange path that led me inadvertently to the Christian faith, and I consider my witness to this an aspect of my vocation. I have found through my studies of Shinran and Dionysius an account of the providential love that sunders the wall between faith and reason and satisfies both heart and mind. The Buddhist and the Christian alike discern a person of compassionate love beyond being, yet who sustains all beings; beyond comprehension, yet who offers to lighten the eyes of souls even as blind and darkened as my own.

WHY THE WEST HASN'T HEARD OF SHIN BUDDHISM

Y OU CAN BUY A STATUE OF THE BUDDHA AT YOUR
local garden center. Buddhism is hardly a *terra incognita* in the West.
Suzuki Daisetz[1] (1870–1966), the great exponent of Zen in the
English language, inspired the Beat generation and introduced generations
of twentieth-century Westerners to Buddhist thought, and thanks to his
efforts books on Zen predominate on the shelves of Western bookshops'
religion sections. The cultural influence of Zen on Japan is second to none.
But in terms of committed adherence, Zen is far more popular in North
America and Europe than in its homeland. Only some 2% of the Japanese
count themselves Zen Buddhists, about the same population as Christians.
Compare this with the roughly 60% of Japanese who belong to the various
Pure Land schools,[2] and you may wonder why we have heard so much
about Zen and so little about them.

Western interests in "Eastern spirituality" from the turn of the twentieth
century account for this to a great extent, and they have not changed much
since. In the languorous *fin de siècle* cafés of Vienna and Paris, spiritualists,
theosophists, and occultists sought relief from the ennui of lumpen Christianity. Influenced by the sophisticated philosophy of Schopenhauer and the
perennialism of William James and Rudolf Steiner, when they looked East
they wanted to find something exotic that would confirm their prejudices
against the dualism, dogmatism, and exclusivism of Christianity. In Zen,
with its embrace of paradox, relativization or rejection of outward ritual,
radical monism, suspicion of doctrine, and professed atheism, they thought
they had found just what they sought: a path of personal spiritual awakening, liberated from Western mores. Pure Land teachers on the other hand
stressed something far more mundane, far less exalted: a kind of "faith"

---

1   Note that throughout this book, when I refer to Japanese writers, I will follow the
Japanese custom of writing surnames before given names.
2   Robert S. Ellwood, *Introducing Japanese Religion* (London: Routledge, 2008), 236.

in the saving power of a personalized Buddha, Amida. For sophisticated Western tastes, such fideism had far too strong a whiff about it of Christianity. Amida Buddha offering the faithful a place in his Pure Land seemed to replicate exactly the dualism between God in heaven and humanity on earth which they found so objectionable. Pure Land Buddhism could only be at best some kind of folk-religious hick cousin to such a refined spirituality as Zen: an exoteric religion for the masses, to be despised by the esoteric cognoscenti.

Not that Christians were very sympathetic to Pure Land Buddhism themselves. When the Jesuit missionaries first arrived in Japan, its apparent proximity to their own religion made them suspicious. They took what seemed its reliance on "faith" as evidence that the "devil of Lutheranism" had beaten them to the mission field.[3] In the twentieth century, Karl Barth was equally dismissive. Although Barth deemed Pure Land Buddhism "the most adequate and comprehensive and illuminating heathen parallel to Christianity," this led him to reject it all the more forcibly, as a warning to those who might fall into the trap of thinking that natural religion could proclaim God's grace.[4] It is the name of Jesus, not of Amida, which saves.

Suzuki's own presentation of Pure Land Buddhism also helps explain why Westerners have not much bothered with it. Though sympathetic, he tends to present it as substantially not all that different from Zen. The differences, he explains, are merely *upāya*, conventional truths or different means of expressing one truth, like the proverbial "finger pointing at the moon." Any apparent dualism between Amida and sentient beings was precisely that: apparent only.

Suzuki's presentation of Pure Land Buddhism was not an intentional act of deception or appropriation. Japanese Pure Land scholars of his time were equally keen to show the continuity of their own tradition with Buddhism in general, including Zen. The Meiji period of 1868 – 1912 heralded three strong forces for them to oppose: Christian missions, Western science, and the state-sponsored cultus of imperial Shinto. For almost three centuries Japan had been closed to all foreign influence. Now, forcibly reopened by Admiral Perry, it came into the ambiguous new relationship with Western colonial powers. This continues to inform its attitude of simultaneous admiration and resentment towards the West in general, and the US in particular,

---

3   Galen Amstutz, *Interpreting Amida: History and Orientalism in the Study of Pure Land Buddhism* (New York: State University of New York Press, 1997), 45.
4   Karl Barth, *Church Dogmatics*, Volume 1, Part 2 (New York: Continuum International Publishing Group, 2004), 430 – 42.

to this day. After over two hundred years of banishment, Christians were exercising religious freedom, building schools and hospitals, and winning converts. Trade with Westerners brought medical and military scientific advancements, but as Muslims were seeing around the same time in Egypt and the Middle East, it carried the risk of chatteldom. Closer to home, the Japanese had seen such neighbors as Hong Kong, Singapore, and the Philippines recently succumb to Western empires. Japan responded by militarizing. In order to avert foreign concerns about proper freedoms of religion, the Government established Shinto as a "non-religion," compulsory for all, which would define and unite Japanese identity around the veneration of the Emperor.[5] Confronted with the religious revivals of Christianity and now Shinto, Buddhist schools could not afford to be divided. Yet they also needed to respond to the new scientific (that is, Western materialist) spirit of the age and its disdain for the supernatural. Seeing how Protestant Christianity had so largely accommodated itself to the Enlightenment mindset, they adopted its tactics, impressed by the demythologizing biblical criticism of Adolf von Harnack and the German Religious Studies School. References to the miraculous and otherworldly in Buddhism were already being downplayed by the time Suzuki packaged Japanese Buddhism for the Western market.

The new orthodoxy proclaimed that in the end all the old sectarian differences between the Buddhist schools were really only cosmetic. All Buddhism supposedly professed non-dualism in the same way. But this elision of difference proved costly to Buddhists of the True Pure Land School, who proclaim reliance on Amida Buddha as the sole means of enlightenment. For centuries the two largest True Pure Land temples in Kyoto had explicitly denounced strict non-dualism as heresy. The Higashi Honganji in 1695 and Nishi Honganji in 1778 affirmed that the believer is *other* than Amida Buddha, and that the salvific practice of calling on the Name of the Amida Buddha is entirely powered by the Buddha, not by the practitioner himself.[6] The traditional emphasis was on what Shinran calls "other-power" (*tariki*): the Buddha is "other," and it is by the Buddha's gift alone that sentient beings can reach enlightenment.

The other-power doctrine of True Pure Land Buddhism was a deliberate rejection of the Zen teaching of "self-power" (*jiriki*), the idea that we have

---

5 James C. Dobbins, *Letters of the Nun Eshinni: Images of Pure Land Buddhism in Medieval Japan* (Honolulu: University of Hawai'i Press, 2004), 109.

6 James C. Dobbins, "The Concept of Heresy in Jōdo Shinshū," *Transactions of the International Conference of Orientalists in Japan* (Kokusai Tōhō Gakusha Kaigi Kiyō) 25 (1980): 33–46.

within us the means to achieve enlightenment by meditation, and equally a rejection of any sort of combination of self-power and other-power. Yet in an attempt to harmonize their specific school of Buddhism with that of the Japanese mainstream in solidarity against Shinto, Christianity, and Western modernity, reforming True Pure Land scholars and clerics such as Nonomura Naotaro (1870–1946) and Sōga Ryōjin (1875–1971) started teaching that there was no duality between Amida Buddha and sentient beings, and that self-power and other-power were only different expressions of the same non-dualistic truth; but not without controversy: they were forced to resign their clerical orders and teaching positions at True Pure Land universities. In the end, though, their approach came to dominate the field. Much as Western preoccupations wrote Platonic philosophy out of the post-Averroes history of Islamic thought, the new generation of scholars now worked to soften the distinctiveness of Pure Land Buddhism. This is partly why, outside specialist circles, Shinran is about as well-known as Suhrawardi or Ibn 'Arabi.

The Pure Land propensity towards dualism might make it seem an odd choice in my search for a non-dualistic point of metaphysical consensus among religious philosophies. Yet it is exactly the True Pure Land school's unique philosophical positioning within Buddhism that makes the comparison so fruitful. Western thought is often characterized as dualistic, thanks to its nominalist emphases and the severance of mind from body typified by Descartes. Buddhists have historically criticized Christianity for its dualism between God and creation. Yet as we have established, the Eastern Platonic tradition of Dionysius is a far less obviously dualistic, pre-modern understanding of that relationship. Buddhism on the other hand is generally understood as strictly non-dualistic, particularly in the Mahāyāna branch to which Pure Land Buddhism belongs. Yet the True Pure Land school nuances that position considerably with its insistence that sentient beings rely on the other-power of Amida Buddha. We may not establish any direct historical influences between Pure Land and mono-theistic thought, but these two traditions do push out to the extremes of their own philosophical limits: True Pure Land to the edge of Buddhist "non-dualism" and Dionysian thought to the edge of Christian "dualism." So, they nevertheless reach out across continents and centuries to touch one another and make creative contact.

As a Christian, I do not intend to pronounce either way on whether True Pure Land Buddhism should or should not be non-dualistic: that is a matter for True Pure Land Buddhists themselves to decide. What I do mean to do is establish how historical self-understandings of the True Pure Land tradition can help Christians understand the relationship between God and the world, and indeed to understand Buddhism more subtly. If these reflections help Buddhists to consider differently what they perceive as the dualistic flaws of Christianity, then all the better. I also hope to contribute to the ongoing apologia for True Pure Land Buddhism against those Western Buddhists who even now dismiss it as "folk religion" or those Western Christians who see it as "Lutheranism lite." I am not going to argue that Pure Land thought is in essence the same as all other Buddhism with only some cosmetic differences, still less that it is Protestantism without Jesus, but to display its specific intellectual riches as a unique tradition. This, I hope, will also inform the mission, which I set out at the beginning of this book, to encourage inter-religious solidarity against the atomizing forces of modernity, but without sacrificing the particularity of our own respective traditions.

And so it is time, at last, to journey to our final destination, thirteenth-century Kyoto, and there to meet Shinran.

NOT JUST A
JAPANESE LUTHER

"Decomposing bodies too horrible to behold" were piled up along the Kamo River in such number that "there was not even room for horses and cattle to pass." So the chronicler Kamo no Chomei describes the state of his city, ravaged by war, famine, fire, and earthquakes. Far from the serenity for which it is now reputed, the Kyoto of Shinran's time (1173–1263), the Kamakura period, was so precarious that "all felt as uncertain as drifting clouds."[1]

Like Christians in Europe grasping for theodicies in times of plague, Buddhist religious leaders in such uncertain times needed to explain how such horrors had come to pass. They had for some time diagnosed the suffering of their times as the symptom of a wider spiritual malaise. The *Lotus and Diamond Sutras* had predicted that human receptivity to the teaching of the historical Buddha, Śākyamuni, would one day diminish beyond repair, leading to *mappō*, the "last Dharma age." The poverty of medieval Kyoto persuaded Buddhist scholars there that this age was now fully upon them, and was brought into relief by the spiritual poverty of so many all-too-worldly and bawdy monks. Humanity had fallen away from the Buddha to such an extent that full understanding of his teaching was impossible by our own efforts, and religious practice could no longer ensure enlightenment.

It was in this fervid religious environment that three of Japan's greatest religious leaders were born, each responding to the state of *mappō* in his own particular way. All three hailed from the same monastery on Mount Hiei, overlooking Kyoto. The ancient Tendai school into which they were ordained taught a range of spiritual disciplines and texts for the attainment of enlightenment. Each of the three leaders would take one of these disciplines and make it the focal point of his new Kamakura-period school.

Dōgen (1200–1253), a keen meditator, determined to resist *mappō* by returning to the pristine teachings of Śākyamuni Buddha. He therefore

---

1 Kamo no Chomei, Hojoki, tr. Donald Keene (Pawlet, VT: Banyan, 1976), 8–10.

traveled west to China in hope of finding a teacher of the ancient, authentic path. There he encountered the Chan school, radical in its simplicity, which claimed there was nothing more or less to the Buddha's authentic teaching than sitting. This was the tradition he brought back to Japan as Zen, establishing new monasteries but also effecting a surge in lay spiritual practice.

Nichiren (1222 – 1282) and his eponymous school may be less well-known in the West than Dōgen, but many will have heard of the *Lotus Sutra*. This, he claimed, was the key to Śākyamuni's authentic teaching, and promoted it exclusively: during the Dharma-ending age, one's own meditative efforts counted for nothing, and recitation of this *sutra* alone would suffice for enlightenment. Monks of his school are readily identified by the unique drums they carry to aid in rhythmic chanting. Nichiren Buddhism remains well established in Japan, but is better known abroad for its more evangelical offshoot, the Sōka Gakkai, characterized by the rapid communal chanting of the first verse of the *Lotus Sutra* and its adherents' testimonies of worldly success and happiness.

The third of these great fathers of Kamakura Buddhism was Hōnen (1133 – 1212), founder of the Pure Land school (Jōdō-shū). Like Nichiren and Dōgen, he agreed that the age of True Dharma (shōbō) had passed. Like Nichiren and unlike Dōgen, he maintained that human spiritual efforts could no longer yield enlightenment. But unlike either of them, he insisted that since Śākyamuni's age had finally passed, humans must look to another Buddha to rely on: now, he said, it was the age of Amida, the Japanese name for Amitābha, Buddha of infinite wisdom and light.

A distinguishing feature of Mahāyāna Buddhism is its doctrine of the *bodhisattva*, sometimes translated as "Buddhist saint." This is not entirely inaccurate, and would be misleading if we imagined anything like the conventional Christian understanding of a cloud of witnesses surrounding Christ in heaven. Rather, bodhisattvas are beings of such rare holiness as to have achieved nirvana and yet postponed it for the sake of guiding others. Readers more familiar with Abrahamic traditions at this point need to remind themselves that nirvana is not a heaven or even a state of being — rather, it indicates having escaped from the cycle of death and rebirth, called *samsara*. Bodhisattvas have achieved that escape, but stay behind in the samsaric round of existence to guide other sentient beings.

In the vast expanse of Buddhist cosmology, such bodhisattvas — through having accrued vast spiritual merit — are said to have become fully enlightened Buddhas who established their own particular spiritual realms or "lands" for the salvation of suffering beings. From these lands, they bequeath to others the karmic merit they have earned over myriad lifetimes of selfless practice and virtue. In the Theravadin tradition, now most active in South East Asia, the role of the laity was mostly limited to providing for the monks with a view to being reincarnated as such a monk in a later life. The bodhisattva ideal opened up new devotional possibilities for a more rapid cessation of the cycle of samsara. While monks engaged in intensive meditative visualizations of these Buddhas, the laity could still play their part by the simpler practice of reciting the Buddha's name. A widespread aspiration developed, particularly among the laity, to pay devotion to bodhisattvas in the hope of being reborn in their lands. There they would learn the Dharma directly from the Buddha, thus accelerating, without impediment, their own karmic progress towards nirvana.

It is in this context that the specific teachings about the Pure Land of Amida Buddha emerged. Devotion to Amida had been well-established as one of several spiritual exercises in the Tendai school in Japan for around two hundred years, a fact attested by the sudden surge in the number of statues of him around the tenth century. Outside Japan, though, Pure Land practice boasted an older lineage still. The original Amitābha sutras were composed in northwest India around 100 BC, and there are references in Sanskrit literature to Pure Land practice around that time. However, as Buddhists were driven out of India, Pure Land devotion would develop fully only in East Asia, almost exclusively within the Mahāyāna traditions.

Pure Land practice was never uncontroversial. A manuscript called the *Mahāyāna-saṃgraha*, now extant only in Chinese and Tibetan but ascribed to the fifth-century Indian scholar Asaṅga, criticized Pure Land practitioners for relegating Śākyamuni to secondary status beneath Amitābha. The fact that this point needed arguing shows just how popular such devotion had already become. Yet the Pure Land practice had the reputation of being an inferior one — the "easy way" for the less committed laity rather than the hard path of the meditating monk. It was a path to nirvana that obviated the need to work for one's own liberation and instead allowed the practitioner to rely on the karmic merit and compassion of Amida Buddha.

The key to Amida Buddha's popularity can be found in one of the core scriptures of the Pure Land tradition, the *Larger Sukhāvatīvyūha Sutra*,[2] a text dating probably from the second century and still extant in Sanskrit as well as Chinese translations. In this sutra, the Buddha tells his disciple,

---

2 Available in English translation: Hisao Inagaki, *The Three Pure Land Sutras* (Berkeley, CA: Numata Center for Buddhist Translation and Research, 2003).

Ananda, the story of a king who renounced his throne to become a monk, taking the name *Dharmakara* (literally "Dharma Store" or Hōzō in Japanese). Dharmakara attains buddhahood and so becomes Amitābha, after practicing for the five eons that were necessary to establish his forty-eight vows for the sake of sentient beings throughout the cosmos.

The eighteenth of these vows is so important to Pure Land tradition that it is called the Primal Vow:

> If, after I have attained buddhahood, sentient beings in the ten directions who have sincere minds, serene faith, and a desire to be born in my country, should not be born there even with ten recitations of my name, may I not attain perfect enlightenment. [3]

In the context of the Buddhist tradition, this was a revolutionary approach to liberation: Amida Buddha's own perfect buddhahood is in a mutually dependent relationship with all those who call upon his name for their own buddhahood. To call on his name is to gain birth in his Land and access to the karmic merit of buddhahood that he has attained, entirely at his gift. The practitioner does not need to spend several lifetimes in grueling meditation. All that was needed was the recitation of the name, a practice the Japanese called *nembutsu*. Even ten recitations of the *nembutsu*, spoken with sincerity, serenity, and trust, would be enough to guarantee birth in the Pure Land. Amida Buddha had staked his buddhahood on it.

For the diseased and impoverished medieval layman of Kyoto, the promise of birth in even a metaphorical land where suffering would cease was seductive enough, but all the more so given the easy means of getting there. So, was Pure Land devotion, after all, a kind of second-rate folk Buddhism?

Hōnen thought not. He spoke from experience, having devoted himself for years to the many spiritual methods taught on Mount Hiei. He found himself getting nowhere, until he devoted himself exclusively to the simple practice of the *nembutsu*.

Only by calling on the name of Amida and relying on the Buddha's other-power could Hōnen, in his own spiritual poverty, hope to receive enlightenment and so escape the cycle of death, rebirth, and suffering. From his own experience, he concluded that this was the universal practice that would save all such "foolish beings" as himself from their prison of *mappō*. Henceforth, total reliance on Amida by the trusting recitation of his holy name would be the only cure.

---

3 Hisao Inagaki, *A Dictionary of Japanese Buddhist Terms*, 5th ed. (Berkeley, CA: Stone Bridge Press, 2007), 109.

The word "only" caused trouble. Hōnen had moved from offering his practice as just one among many, an easy route for the spiritually weak laity, to a policy of "exclusive nembutsu" for everyone, lay or clergy. The implication that all other practices were null and void invited the consternation of his fellow Tendai monks, who appealed to the authorities. This resulted in the suppression of Hōnen's activities in 1207. He was defrocked and exiled from Kyoto, along with his promising disciple, Shinran (1173 – 1263). In 1211, they were offered the chance to recant and receive pardon. Hōnen accepted these terms and was able to resume his priestly vocation. [4]

Shinran refused. His unbending devotion to the *nembutsu* gave rise to the fourth of the great Kamakura schools of Buddhism. Splitting off from Hōnen's Pure Land school, the Jōdō-shū, Shinran founded the True Pure Land school, Jōdō-shinshū, often just called "Shin Buddhism." This was destined to become the most popular form of Buddhism in Japan to the present day.

Shinran let his hair grow a little and adopted the nickname Gutoku, meaning "stubble-headed fool." The stubble implied that he was neither a bald bonze, since he had been cast out of orders, nor yet entirely a layman with a full head of hair. By this stage he had with Hōnen's blessing already broken the Buddhist clerical tradition of celibacy, marrying Eshinni (b. 1182) and fathering several children. By marrying, he was practicing what he preached: that the *nembutsu* promised enlightenment for any practitioner, not privileging the clerical state over the lay. So in life as much as in his teaching Shinran set out a way for both men and women to attain enlightenment in their everyday lives.

Hōnen had taught that because self-power had been made redundant by the waning of the Dharma age, recitation of the *nembutsu* was exclusively necessary to bring enlightenment. Amida's Primal Vow stipulated that even just ten sound recitations would guarantee rebirth in his Pure Land, but since one could never know which of the ten one chanted were really efficacious, Hōnen urged his followers to repeat the chant as often as they could.

Shinran took Hōnen's teaching to the logical extreme. He argued that this repeated recitation itself could become an act of self-power, just another doomed attempt to effect one's own enlightenment by self-willed spiritual exercises. So, he argued, only *one* recitation of the *nembutsu* in one's entire lifetime was strictly necessary — as long as it was said with truly "deep entrusting" or *shinjin*. Often this is translated as "faith," but in its most literal interpretation it means a "true heart." However inadequate we may

---

4 For detailed discussion, see Richard John Bowring, The Religious Traditions of Japan, 500 – 1600 (Cambridge University Press, 2005), 248 ff.

be, anyone who has said the name just once with *shinjin* would receive the promise of Birth into Amida's Pure Land, the promise of immediate enlightenment — without the need for several further reincarnations to become eventually a monk, and then several more before going to the Pure Land, and more yet before that final severance of karmic ties known as nirvana. The promise of nirvana was instant and, some of Shinran's followers would argue, irreversible.[5] Further recitations of the *nembutsu* thereafter were still to be said, but out of gratitude to Amida for his benevolence:

> I praise Amida's wisdom and virtue
> So that beings with mature conditions throughout the
> ten quarters may hear.
> Let those who have already realized shinjin
> Constantly respond in gratitude to the Buddha's benevolence.[6]

Rebirth in the Pure Land had historically been understood as a chance to accrue, after one's death, pure karma from the Buddha's realm of utmost happiness (*sukhāvatī*, literally "adorned with bliss"), and so to reduce the number of further cycles of death and rebirth one would have to endure. Shinran, however, saw it differently. For him, Amida's Pure Land was synonymous with nirvana. Shinran taught that a single *nembutsu* recited with *shinjin* would give the devotee the assurance, in this life, of attaining nirvana without fail at the time of death (known as the state of "non-retrogression"). This is liberation, the extinguishing of the karmic ties that bind beings to samsara.

Christian readers will see here why the Jesuits thought that " the devil of Lutheranism"[7] had beaten them to Japan's shores, and why Protestant scholars have been so keen to draw parallels with Shinran's religious developments. Luther's declaration of salvation by faith alone looks rather like

---

5   Whether or not one attains Birth in this lifetime remains controversial between the Nishi (West) and Higashi (East) Honganji, the head temples in Kyoto of the two main schools of True Pure Land Buddhism. The former tends to maintain that Birth happens at the moment of death, the latter makes a distinction between Birth in the mind of *shinjin* in this lifetime, and Birth beyond the confines of the body at the moment the body dies. Higashi Honganji scholars tend to argue that Shinran was therefore not concerned with the afterlife because this was already taken care of by Amida when we attain *shinjin* in this life (with thanks to Dr Michael Conway of Ōtani University, Kyoto, for this clarification).

6   *Hymns of the Pure Land* 50, in Shinran, *The Collected Works of Shinran*, ed. Dennis Hirota (Kyoto: Jodo Shinshu Hongwanji-Ha, 1997).

7   Amstutz, *Interpreting Amida: History and Orientalism in the Study of Pure Land Buddhism*, 45.

shinjin, and his call for a priesthood of all believers resembles the status of "Gutoku" Shinran — someone who is "neither monk nor layman." Shinran's advocacy of exclusive *nembutsu* practice has something in common with the Lutheran appeal to simplicity, including the simplification of religion. Both opposed monastic corruption and breached clerical celibacy. Both set up an apparent opposition between the absolute salvific power of a transcendent other, whether God's grace or Amida's benevolence, and the fruitless works of humans. There are Reformation parallels beyond Luther too. Echoes of Calvin's "absolute depravity," the radical reading of Augustine's doctrine of original sin by which the French lawyer declared all humanity totally reprobate, might be discerned in the duality of the Pure Land of the Buddha versus the fallen world of *mappō*. Shinran also shares with Luther something similar to the sense of being *simul justus et peccator*, "at once a sinner and justified" — going as far as to make the extraordinary claim that it is precisely *because* we are evil that we receive the Buddha's compassion: "If the good person is saved, how much more the evil one!"[8]

Such comparisons have been made by Christian and Buddhist scholars alike, and far more deeply than at this cosmetic level. However, in making them, we risk transferring the concepts and assumptions of one religion directly onto another and so misreading it. Worse, Christians risk patronizing Buddhists by telling them that deep down they really believe the same thing as we do. We have to avoid both the Scylla of interpreting True Pure Land Buddhism through the lens of Western post-Reformation Christianity, and the Charybdis of making it conform to our idea of what Buddhism should be, pre-conditioned by interactions between Japan and the West in the nineteenth and twentieth centuries. Whether we crash into the clashing rocks or get sucked into the whirlpool, we can end up shipwrecked by Westernized readings of an ancient Japanese Buddhist tradition. So let us strap ourselves to the mast and listen for a moment to the sirens, all the better to avoid their lures later on.

---

8   Shinran, *Tannishō* 3.

DUALISTIC BUDDHISM?

I HAVE ALLUDED ALREADY AND AT LENGTH TO THE danger of trying to extract a pure philosophical doctrine uncontaminated by the biographical detail or superstitious baggage of ancient thinkers. One cannot make such an incision without puncturing the spleen. Yet Shinran is as often subjected to such butchery as any medieval Christian thinker has been.

If Abelard is only half himself without his Heloise, then so is Shinran without his Eshinni. They married on the advice of his master Hōnen, breaking the tradition of Buddhist clerical celibacy. Their letters speak intimately of the spiritual milieu they shared. To attempt to sift those nuggets to which moderns would ascribe philosophical value from their more spiritual or supernatural soil reflects our preoccupations more than Shinran's. It risks remolding the thirteenth-century priest in our own twenty-first-century secular image.

In their letters, Shinran and Eshinni paint their world in unmistakably dualistic shades.[1] There are clear references to a spiritual realm discrete from the material, common to Shinto thought in Shinran's time. Worse still for those who wish Shinran to conform to modern, demythologized renditions of Buddhism so popular among Westerners tired of Christian credulity, Shinran insists that Hōnen was an incarnation of the bodhisattva Seishi (Skt. Mahāsthāmaprāpta), and Eshinni thought her husband was an incarnation of Kanon (Avalokiteśvara), the bodhisattva of compassion whose name now honors a Japanese camera and computer peripheral company. Shinran was no more a skeptical, proto-Enlightenment Averroes than he was a Buddhist Luther.

But however wary we should be of ignoring Shinran's personal and spiritual milieu, we must also watch out for the equal and opposite risk of over-conflating his biography with his intellectual work. We will find that, in fact, while Shinran's thought is not straightforwardly monistic, neither is it by any means as straightforwardly dualistic as his letters to Eshinni might

---

1   Dobbins, *Letters of the Nun Eshinni*.

suggest. It is precisely this nuanced middle way between strict dualism and strict monism that makes him so interesting to Christian theological tradition, which from the beginning has faced similar problems in its attempts to reconcile the idea of God as absolutely, transcendently other and yet at the same time intimately present to all beings at all times: the God, as St Augustine put it, who is "higher than my highest height and deeper than my innermost being."[2]

Modern Shin Buddhist scholars tend to promote the twentieth-century reading of Shinran as conforming in all essentials with the more mainstream non-dualistic philosophy of the Mahāyāna expounded by the second-century Indian philosopher Nāgārjuna. All Buddhists concur that the Buddha's spiritual awakening started with his discernment of the First Noble Truth: to exist is to suffer. So, suffering is perpetuated by the wearisome cycle of birth, ageing, sickness, death, and rebirth from which the Buddha taught we could escape by entering nirvana. It is not a heaven, nor even a state of being, but precisely the extinguishing of one's rebirth in the relentless cycle of samsara. From these teachings of the Buddha, Nāgārjuna formulated his "Middle Way" or Māhdyamika teaching. Neither samsara nor nirvana, he taught, has any intrinsic or fundamental existence in a conventional sense. Rather, the ultimate truth of both is emptiness, *śūnyatā*. The alternative errors either side of the Middle Way would be either to slip into annihilationism, where we say that nothing exists after death, or eternalism, where we live forever as an individual and hence, according to Buddhist teaching, must perforce continue to suffer as a conditioned being. Since both nirvana and samsara are ultimately emptiness, they are in the end identical. Enlightenment is the realization of this truth. Conversely, by Nāgārjuna's account, maintaining any dualism between nirvana and samsara is an obstacle to enlightenment.

Despite modern Shin scholars defending their school's founder within the bounds of this Māhdyamaka teaching, it remains a matter of historical record that Shinran and his followers were historically accused of dualism and that, for centuries, the True Pure Land school declared non-dualism a heresy — though precisely what "non-dualism" means in Pure Land thought is admittedly contentious.[3]

The first apparent dualism in Shinran's thought is the opposition between the impure world of *mappō* and the Pure Land of Amida Buddha, equating the latter to nirvana. The historic appeal of Shinran's teaching was precisely

---

2 *Deus interior intimo meo et superior summo,* Augustine *Confessions* 3.6.11.

3 Mitsuyuki Ishida, *Ianjin* (Kyōto: Hōzōkan, 1951) offers a comprehensive study of the concept of "heresy," *ianjin,* in Shin Buddhism.

in its offer of an escape from the impure land of earthquakes, fires, poverty, and corruption. There would seem to be no room in Nāgārjuna's Middle Way for such alterity. Yet the medieval Japanese dualism between the natural and supernatural, evident in Shinran and Eshinni's letters, may have been exactly what provided such fertile ground for the development of his thought. Pure Land teaching offered an alternative to a world riven by famine, disease, natural disaster, and poverty. The Pure Land sutras conjured a jewel-clad heaven of indescribable beauty, and it offered it to lay people who could not afford to give up family and home to enter Buddhist orders, all too aware of their inadequacy to attain enlightenment by their own means. To be told that the Pure Land and this world are "in no way other" would make sense if one were trained in the subtleties of Buddhist philosophy, but to uneducated peasants for whom this world was a brutal and decidedly unhappy place, it offered little comfort. The Pure Land Shinran depicts is one which at least appears to be radically different. Nor was Shinran averse to making references to the *kami*, the spirits honored in the Shinto shrines of Japan's older and lasting pagan tradition which, unlike European paganism, was never suppressed by the later and more literary religion but lived on side-by-side with Buddhism. Accordingly, Shinran quite naturally aligned the Shinto division between the supernatural and the natural with the Buddhist teaching of *mappō*.

Secondly, Zen Buddhists have historically criticized Shinran's thought for its apparent dualism between the self-power (*jiriki*) which they profess and the other-power (*tariki*) of Amida Buddha on which the Shin Buddhist is exhorted to rely. The Zen master Hakuin (1686 – 1769) summarized his school's critique in a supplement to his magnum opus, the *Orategama*, which defined Zen as a path of radical self-salvation without room for "otherness," and rejecting devotion to Amida as an inferior practice for those incapable of Zen's meditative exertions. For Hakuin, nirvana means "seeing into oneself" rather than rebirth into any Pure Land. More recent Zen scholars, such as D. T. Suzuki and Abe Masao (1915 – 2006), have reduced the difference to a matter of *upāya* or "expedient means," merely a different expression of the same truth. This is certainly more conciliatory than Hakuin's approach, but still leaves the aftertaste that True Pure Land doctrine would be better if it had been expressed with the clarity of Zen monism.

These two apparent dualisms are linked by a third, which has a more ethical character: "Even a good person attains Birth [in the Pure Land], so it goes without saying that an evil person will." This famous dictum from the *Tannishō*, a short account of Shinran's teachings by his disciple

Yuien-bo, can easily be misconstrued. Its import is quite the opposite of conventional wisdom. Nor does it at first sight accord with mainstream Buddhist teaching. Surely those good Buddhists who have forged positive karmic bonds by lives well lived are the ones for whom birth in the Pure Land "goes without saying"—so is not the salvation of the wicked more questionable? Given the ubiquitous sense of "fallenness" in medieval Kyoto, it may not be surprising to find in both Shinran and his master Hōnen's thought an emphasis on the unworthiness and inability of sentient beings to attain enlightenment. Yet Shinran goes so far as to profess that Amida's Vow is precisely for the sake of evil people. The healthy have no need of a physician. Those incapable of recognizing their incapacity to save themselves are those for whom it will be hardest to benefit from the Vow. One recalls a certain camel and the eye of a needle.

On a research visit to Ryukoku University in Kyoto, connected to the temple of Higashi Honganji, I met Professor Mark Blum of Berkeley, who was working on a translation of the Nirvana Sutra. He found in this scripture the basis for the emphasis on the salvation of the wicked in the thought of Shinran, whose use of this sutra, Professor Blum told me, is unusually extensive among proponents of the Pure Land tradition. In one of the more controversial passages of his magnum opus, the True Teaching, Practice and Realization of the Pure Land Way (Kyōgyōshinshō), Shinran relates various tales from the sutra to drive home the point that Amida shows particular beneficence towards the evil. He recounts the tale of a villainous King, Ajātaśatru, who usurps the throne by killing his own father but nonetheless receives Amida's compassion.[4] More striking still is the story of the historic Buddha's evil cousin Devadatta. He plays a part in the previous story of Ajātaśatru, encouraging the patricidal plot, but worse, wishes even to kill the Buddha himself. This earns him the status of an icchantika, one who, having so defiled his karmic roots of goodness that it is impossible for him to attain nirvana, is condemned to eternal rebirths in the lower regions. In him, the Buddha says, there is no shinjin at all. Yet despite Devadatta being utterly reprobate, the Buddha exonerates him.

Professor Blum found Shinran's choice of source for the tale of Devadatta particularly interesting, because it is told rather differently in the Lotus Sutra, which his master Hōnen cited and which was, generally, a far more prevalent scripture in Mahāyāna Buddhist thought. Devadatta is exonerated in this version too, but in this case it is only because he undertook meritorious acts in the past; in other words, he had good karma. So by deliberately

---

4   Kyogyoshinsho 3.115f, in Shinran, The Collected Works of Shinran.

choosing the more obscure version in the *Nirvana Sutra* it seems that Shinran is — typically — going further than his master Hōnen. He rejects even the notion of securing salvation by virtue of one's past karmic merit. His choice of text is a graphic and extended metaphor on the need for utter reliance on Amida's karmic treasure trove alone: so, if the good realize birth, how much more so the evil! Those who know their own wickedness and unworthiness are the prime beneficiaries of Amida's compassion. They attain birth in his Pure Land and, with it, buddhahood. The antithesis of self-power versus other-power could not be starker.[5]

Far from straightforwardly conforming to typical Mahāyāna non-dualism, the subsequent True Pure Land tradition radically reinterpreted traditional Buddhist beliefs and practices that relied on the efficacy of any self-power. The status of the *Tannishō*, being after all a posthumous record of Shinran's teaching, is disputed among the various True Pure Land schools, but is highly regarded in the Higashi Honganji or Otani tradition, one of the two largest branches. In it, Shinran purportedly laments eight prevalent wrong beliefs, among them the notion that studying sutras can guarantee Birth in the Pure Land, that the "good practice" of the *nembutsu* itself ensures Birth rather than reliance on Amida, that the *nembutsu* eliminates evil karma, and that temple offerings contribute towards becoming Buddha. He thus relegates the academic work of the monk, anathematizes the non-exclusive *nembutsu* practice of his former Tendai colleagues, and jeopardizes the monasteries' traditional earnings from the collection plate. Nothing we mortals do in this impure land during the age of *mappō* can contribute at all to our liberation from samsara, and our personal goodness or evil is of no account whatsoever in face of the compassionate transference of unlimited karmic merit by Amida Buddha. Entrusting is all.

By the eighteenth century both of the main schools of Shin Buddhism — the Kyoto-based Higashi (East) and Nishi Honganji (West) temples of the Primal Vow — had declared it heresy to proclaim that Amida and the believer are "not other," or that the *nembutsu* is a composite of self- and other-power.[6] Such non-dualistic ideas were seen as obstacles to true *shinjin*, reliance on Amida Buddha. Shinran's worldview contained undeniable dualistic emphases. So why did the nineteenth-century Shin Buddhist establishment work so hard to elide them?

---

5   Mark Laurence Blum, *The Origins and Development of Pure Land Buddhism* (Oxford: Oxford University Press, 2002).

6   Dobbins, "The Concept of Heresy in Jōdo Shinshū," 42.

Beyond Dualism
and Non-dualism

TSUKIJI HONGANJI, IN THE SAME DISTRICT AS THE
enormous and eponymous Tokyo fish market, looks nothing like a
Japanese Buddhist temple. Built in the 1930s, its architectural mélange
of Indian and European influences bears witness to the ambitions of its
Shin Buddhist founders from the Nishi Honganji school.

Its headquarter's temple in the former capital of Kyoto, rebuilt in the
seventeenth century, reflects the Japanese aesthetic ideals of that time: despite
its vast scale, the unnailed wooden beams and tatami matting and open face
to the open gravel courtyard in which it stands make the Nishi Honganji
a typically Japanese rendition of the impermanence of things, in harmony
with the passing tides of nature. Its daughter temple in the new capital of
Tokyo is of a different order entirely. There is nothing impermanent about
it. The old wooden ways may do for those with the delicate temperaments
of the quaint and quietist Kyotoite, but a temple for the thrusting seat of a
new empire with international ambitions needed to be set in stone. Uniting
elements of East and West, it would serve not only the local Japanese, but
send chaplaincy missions to serve the increasing numbers of faithful who
lived and served overseas.

Later, Tsukiji Honganji would cater also to English-speaking immigrants
and ex-pats in Tokyo. After all, if the Christian missionaries could build their
stone churches on Japanese land, not to mention the Asian countries they
had conquered, why should Buddhists not do the same? Shin Buddhism,
too, offered a message of universal scope. It was only natural that it should
adopt the dress of the times.

Go to an English service in Tsukiji Honganji, and one may be surprised
to find an organ and hymn books in the chapel. For there, as in the Honganji's temples in the USA, Buddhism has taken on a distinctly Protestant face.
Many of the hymns are new Buddhist words simply set to old Protestant
tunes. Titles such as "the Reverend" and even "bishop" have been adopted

for the Shin Buddhist clergy. This was the kind of inculturated religion that would appeal to the Western-dominated world order of its time.

It should not be surprising then if people began to wonder whether any real difference of content lay behind the similarity of form between Shin Buddhism and liberal Protestantism. There have been Western converts who seem to see Shin Buddhism as a modern answer to Christianity, without the inconvenience of the Incarnation or miracles. Likewise, there have been Japanese Shin Buddhists keen to distance Shinran's teachings from the perceived errors of the Christian West.

Once, at Tsukiji Honganji in 2010, I heard an English-language sermon on just this theme by the eminent Shin apologist Rev Haseo Daien. It was a sermon rather than an academic lecture, but Rev Haseo explained how the main problem with Christianity, which differentiates it from Buddhism, is the dualism it imposes between a creator God and the world of created beings.

It is true that the strict dualism between God and creature which Western Christians have professed in recent centuries has yielded many of the negative consequences of secular modernity. Using the concept "being" univocally, we alienated God from beings, and beings from one another. This led to the voluntaristic conflict between the divine will and human wills, and between one human will and another. Reality came to be seen as a conflicted space open to definition by the strongest will, segueing neatly into nominalism: things are what we name them. We have come to see reality as grounded in conflict, whether with God, one another, or the world. We see fit to redefine the world's land, flora and fauna, and even humans as "resources," and so arrive at the utilitarian understanding of "good" as meaning whatever is "good for" the majority will, achieved by the threat or exercise of power. Untempered dualism has led, in short, to a replacement of harmonious participation among beings with conflict. Historically, we have seen the results of such dualism in the exercise of empire, technological mastery of the world and its concomitant pollution, in the resources committed to perfecting ingenious and efficient machines for killing people in the shortest time and greatest possible number, and in the many attempts to redefine morality from scratch by revolutionary socialists, fascists, communists and libertarians.

But if Buddhism is so averse to such dualism, how did Japan become one of the most notoriously brutal imperial powers in the twentieth century, among its many competitors for that title? Western education about the Pacific War portrays Japan as the aggressor, particularly in relation to her supposedly unanticipated assault on American territory. This is unsurprising, given the dominance of the US in post-War Japan Studies, yet in an age where we deem the pre-emptive strike a lawful military doctrine, it seems somewhat disingenuous to say the least to denigrate Japan for the same tactic. There is no space here to engage in a revision of the history of the Pacific War, but it should suffice to recall that European nations and America had both expanded considerably in Pacific Asia for several decades, colonizing city states like Singapore, Macao, and Hong Kong, and islands like Hawai'i, all the while establishing decidedly one-sided trade agreements with grudging and erstwhile sovereign nations.[1]

Japan did not want to go the way Hawai'i or the Philippines had gone under the US, or Hong Kong and Singapore under the British. Hence their establishment of the "Great East Asia Co-prosperity Sphere." The actual treatment of nations "welcomed" into this union betray it as a rather cynical tribute to Western imperialism and a cover for Japan's own territorial ambitions: essentially, Japanese annexation of Korea and Taiwan. Still, the work of a Shin Buddhist philosopher called Tanabe Hajime shows that despite its regrettable execution, the idea itself should not be so readily dismissed. In On the Logic of Co-prosperity Spheres, Tanabe insists that the Japanese Imperial policy perverted the authentic logic of the Co-prosperity Sphere. Although its military implementation was brutal, as an intellectual concept it was a rallying cry against Western imperialism in Pacific Asia.

Tanabe was part of a loose group of philosophers inspired by Buddhist and Western thought, known to posterity as the "Kyoto School." Reviled for decades by the neo-Marxist mainstream of Japanese academia as collaborators with the military regime, these thinkers are now being reviewed in a more dispassionate light and their contribution to world philosophy rightly recognized. In this they are comparable to Heidegger, who influenced their thought, notwithstanding the tarnished reputation he gained through his murky relationship to Nazism. Yet there is a growing awareness that the Kyoto School was in many cases highly critical of the regime; in some cases to the extent that they were forcibly silenced and even imprisoned for their protests against it. In their as yet untranslated The Standpoint of World History and Japan, four of the Kyoto School's principal exponents explicitly rejected racially-based nationalism, whether that of their fellow Japanese or of the American and European nations who surveyed their lands with imperial ambitions. For doing so, they were proscribed by the military government.

---

1   For a full and nuanced discussion, see David Williams, Defending Japan's Pacific War: The Kyoto School Philosophers and Post-White Power (London: Routledge Curzon, 2004).

The progenitor of this Kyoto School was Nishida Kitarō (1870 – 1945). Reared on Zen and broader Mahāyāna thought, he also engaged in a comprehensive study of Western philosophy. He found himself confronted with a Hegelian worldview which declared that intellectual history began in the East and ended in the West: that the Greeks appropriated all that was of value in the Orient and that this was further refined in later Europe, such that European philosophy could comprehend Eastern, but not the other way around. We can see this as the West's philosophical parallel to its militaristic expansion, according to which the East would find its consummation only once subjected to the civilizing influence of the West.

Nishida subscribed to Hegel's philosophy of history, but rejected his Eurocentric conclusion. Like Heidegger, Nishida discerned an obsession with Being in Western thought and found it wanting. Even where the West conceived of "non-being," Nishida believed it did so only in opposition to Being, and therefore as *something* in its own right. His Buddhist thought, on the other hand, conceived of an absolute nothingness (*zettai-mu*) that transcends the categories of Being and non-being and subverts the distinction between the two.

Nishida and his Pure Land Buddhist protégé Tanabe wanted to unfold this Japanese philosophy in the language of the Western philosophical tradition. They saw themselves as uniquely placed to do so as inheritors of Eastern traditions spreading from India through China and Korea to their own islands. At the same time they were well-versed in the Western thought that had been imported at the dawn of the Meiji era (1868 – 1912), when Japan was finally (and forcibly) re-opened to outside trade and influence after almost three centuries of isolation. Japan's location on the intellectual frontier was mirrored by its military-political frontier against increasing European and American expansion.

Nishida's and Tanabe's visions of Absolute Nothingness diverged to the point where they ended up communicating with each other only by elliptical and uncomplimentary references in print. Both conceived of Absolute Nothingness in terms of self-emptying. Nishida located Absolute Nothingness in terms of "place" (*basho*), opposing self-emptying to Western notions of "substance." Tanabe, influenced by the Pure Land thought of Shinran, conceived of it more in terms of "praxis" (*jissen*), the active *working* of nothingness as self-emptying love. The difference reflects Nishida's more static Zen monism versus the more kinetic relationship between Amida and sentient being of Tanabe's Shin influences. Tanabe's philosophy resonates with the Platonic unfolding of reality from the self-giving One, and especially with

Dionysius's reading of "theurgy," God's self-emptying love working though ritual practice. Nonetheless, while they differed in their understanding of how Absolute Nothingness manifests itself, Nishida and Tanabe shared the aim of reconciling Eastern and Western philosophy from a deeper basis that transcends the distinction between Being and non-being. Rather than the wisdom of the East finding its apogee in the West, Hegel's linear evolution would, then, become a pendulum swinging back to where it had come from.

Although he was himself a Zen Buddhist, Nishida's most esteemed disciple was the Shin Buddhist Nishitani Keiji. He faced a different problem. Despite the perceived Western bias towards ontology, Nishitani recognized the danger of its own nascent nihilism, as heralded by Nietzsche. He traced the advent of nihilism in the radical opposition of "nothingness" against the God whom Christian theology had made into "Being," but who had been latterly abandoned in the face of scientific progress. The disavowal of Being as a fundamental category left neither the fertile Emptiness of Buddhism nor the plenitude of the super-existent God, but just a hollow nihility that drained life of any purpose, or to put it more precisely, deprived it of any purpose.[2] This European slide into meaninglessness was being spread through the world both by force of arms and cultural dominance. Nishitani effectively reversed Hegel's history of progress, arguing that the West needed to move towards the Eastern, Buddhist ideal, but that it could do so only by way of its own Christian premises. Scientism would lead only to nihilism. Nishitani moved from Nishida's Absolute Nothingness to what he called a "standpoint of Emptiness," where Emptiness referred to the Mahāyāna concept of śūnyatā. Nishitani sought to overcome nihilism by passing through it to an Emptiness in which a fundamental, infinite plenitude is revealed.[3] Again, true to his Shin Buddhist roots, he wanted to move away from the static, almost reified, monistic noun of "nothingness" towards śūnyatā as a more vital process of "emptying." Everything must be dynamically emptied. Even the hollow nihility of our being must itself be emptied and converted into the Emptiness of an open expanse. Analogous to Dionysian kenosis, Being is the self-negation of Absolute Nothingness.

Would that philosophy had triumphed over arms! While the mid-twentieth-century Japanese philosophical attempts to qualify the hegemony of Western thought failed to win the day, the parallel military offensive in the Pacific War partially achieved its objective. European colonization

---

2 Keiji Nishitani, *Religion and Nothingness*, ed. Jan van Bragt (Berkeley and Los Angeles: University of California Press, 1982), 124.

3 Nishitani, 138.

of the East has largely receded, and sovereignty has been restored to its nations — or claimed by China. Yet despite substantial military withdrawal from the East, the West continues economic and intellectual expansion worldwide. Even China, the great economic rival of the West, is governed by the fundamentally Western, materialist ideology of Communism. Meaning is mechanically stripped from the world to the detriment of the environment, interpersonal relationships, human psychology, and peace (both within and between nations). The danger of global homogenization threatens to crush the very ideas that might save the world from the ideological impasse between the Supreme Being and sterile nihilism.

Despite the Kyoto School's efforts, its contemporary successor Professor Ueda Shizuteru (b. 1926) claims that in the face of such global technocracy "philosophy is almost powerless."[4] Yet this is by no means conclusive. The cracks in Western assumptions of cultural superiority and universality that were opened by the Pacific War, and wedged out by America's defeat in Vietnam, are breaking into new and ever more violent fissures — September 11, 2001 being one of the most momentous from the American perspective. A European-originated post-Christendom continues to assert its political will through military might, intellectual domination of the scientific method, and economic superiority. Yet the ability of either the New World or the Old to continue to dominate any of these fields is increasingly questionable. America and Europe are militarily overcommitted and impotent in the realm of terrorist warfare; our intellectual commitment to scientific technocracy continues to blight the world as much as heal it, holding the poison in one hand and the antidote in the other, refusing to discern any meaning to life beyond the relentless prolongation thereof. Yet the days of Western economic mastery seem numbered. We have little idea of the wider cultural effects this will entail. Quite suddenly, the rest of the world may find it no longer needs to articulate itself in terms acceptable to American and European sensibilities. The fragile mask of reason that contrives to disguise post-Christian elements of Western law and culture (including, for example, human rights) as rational universals, will be broken to reveal their limited cultural specificity and the sterile bankruptcy of spent power which is all that really underlies them. Having neutered with European nihilism the foreign philosophies that might offer a credible shared metaphysics, our own cherished mores will fall victim to the same.

---

4   Shizuteru Ueda, "Contributions to Dialogue with the Kyoto School," in *Japanese and Continental Philosophy: Conversations with the Kyoto School*, ed. Bret W. Davis, Brian Schroeder, and Jason M. Wirth (Bloomington, IN: Indiana University Press, 2011), 19–33.

Japan was one of the few Pacific nations to resist colonization. Contrary to the dismissive attitude of certain *bien pensants* towards Japan, by economic and former military might she has resisted Western ascendancy more successfully than any other non-white majority nation. Japan has adopted foreign learning more or less on its own terms. This is as true of its assimilation of Confucianism and Buddhism in the sixth century as of Western learning and technology in the nineteenth and twentieth. Japan is uniquely placed in Asia to generate an intellectual milieu that could accommodate the best of Western wisdom without being overawed by the brute power of the worst of it. The Kyoto School achieved this, and the world would benefit from its insights, which promised to transfigure the dead end of materialist nihilism into creative and spiritual life. The difficulty, as Ueda hinted, is that philosophy's voice is washed away in the tempest of vacuous activity engendered by technological "progress."

However, if 9 / 11 has shown us anything, it is that religion's voice is rising above the storm. In this case it did so in a terrifyingly violent and evil way. Its instigators doubtless hoped to stoke a clash of civilizations, a violent reaction against the Muslim world that would force their otherwise peaceful co-religionists into equally violent counteraction. It is a tactic of which Lenin would have been proud. To some extent, and especially through online "communities" of the like-minded or vulnerable, they succeeded. On the other hand, mosques and churches around the world have resisted the bombers' call to crusade and entered into more fruitful dialogue and understanding of each other. But discontent with the hegemony of Western political norms is by no means restricted to Muslims or to the Middle East, nor even to "rogue states" such as North Korea. Since the Meiji Restoration of 1868, Japan has striven to prove her superiority to those nations who condemned her as uncivilized, and Buddhism has played a significant role in this. Zen representation at the World's Parliament of Religions in 1893, for example, "was a strategic statement in the discourse of Buddhist nationalism" meant to counter Western assumptions of superiority "in standards of intellectual, artistic, and material achievement."[5] Yet, since the occupation of Japan by the U. S. following the Second World War, Japan has been blighted by an altogether Western polity of Right versus Left, with the Right tending towards nationalism and the Left towards even greater compromise with Western political ideologies.

Many Christian churches and Buddhist schools, particularly that of the

---

5   Judith Snodgrass, *Presenting Japanese Buddhism to the West: Orientalism, Occidentalism, and the Columbian Exposition* (Chapel Hill: University of North Carolina Press, 2003), 20.

True Pure Land School, have sided intellectually and politically with the Left: indeed, the Shin cleric Unno Taitetsu has even described Shinran as a "forebear of modern Marxism."[6] Yet neither of these positions, Left or Right, reflects the Kyoto School's nuanced balance of resistance to nihilistic Western materialism and appreciation of the more ancient Western philosophical and cultural merits.

It is worth reflecting on the political temper of Christianity in Japan, which remains a small minority religion, claiming only 2% of the population, despite over a century of open evangelization. One reason for this may be that it seems such a foreign religion. Buddhism was also once foreign, but more or less readily assimilated itself with prevalent native religious practices. Go to a Christian church in Japan, however, and one is instantly confronted with its European bias. Its architecture, its music, the dress of its clergy and its liturgy, are directly transposed from Western archetypes with barely any attempt at inculturation. The only difference between an English or American church and most Japanese ones is the language. Everything else, even down to the hymns, is an exact replica. This utter lack of Japanese form is naturally mirrored in the content of the churches' various theologies, which are direct European-American imports with little Japanese input. More recently it has been heavily influenced by the Marxist-influenced school of Liberation Theology. The churches' teaching often emphasizes Christianity's utter difference from Buddhism and antipathy towards Shinto, especially in the role the Emperor plays in the integralism of Shinto worship with the State. Little wonder that so few Japanese find a home in such a patently Western Christian environment, one that discourages them from participation in the common rites and festivals of their national and familial culture.

Christian churches in Japan should ask themselves whether they are not in fact collaborators with the spread of homogenizing nihilism throughout the non-Western world. Does their cosmetic rejection of native Japanese art, architecture, and music not mask a more fundamental dismissal of centuries of Japanese thought? If so, even the little missionary success they still enjoy is grounded in the fundamentally unchristian imperialism of Enlightenment modernity and its voluntaristic, nominalist assumptions. It has little to do with the older metaphysics of participation and coinherence.

Christians believe that Christianity genuinely has something to offer to all people, yet all too often the way we spread the faith crushes what

---

6   Mark Unno, "Shin Buddhist Social Thought in Modern Japan," in *Engaged Pure Land Buddhism: The Challenges Facing Jodo Shinshu in the Contemporary World*, ed. Kenneth K. Tanaka and Eisho Nasu (Berkeley, CA: WisdomOcean Publications, 1998), 78.

makes those people who they are. The use of Western music, whether Evangelical pop-hymnody or more classical Western melodies, as the exclusive
medium of evangelization yokes the Church to the consumerist machine
that flattens world cultures into a bland homogeneity: the spread of the
religion becomes a measure of "success" to be achieved by the novelty of
its appeal to the market. In other words, it plays exactly the same divisive
power game as any corporation in secular modernity. This is not love of
neighbor, nor is it seeing the face of Christ in others. It is, rather, twisting
neighbors' faces until they match one's own, like the surgically modified,
blonde-dyed, blue-lensed Japanese models on a Tokyo advertising billboard.
This is not just an aesthetic matter — as if anything were "just" aesthetic.
Form masks content, and in this case, where the mask does not fit, the face
is tortured into conformity.

Religion, albeit for the wrong reasons, may be the only philosophical
outlet that the secular West now takes seriously as it keeps trying, even in
its death throes, to homogenize the world. It takes it seriously because it
is afraid of it. Nonetheless, Christians have a duty to engage more deeply
with other religious philosophies — both the older Platonic philosophy of
the West itself, shared with Islam and Judaism, and the philosophies that
developed further afield. Judging by Japan's example, this duty is com-
pounded by the Gospel imperative to spread the Good News to all peoples,
since ignorance of local thought has proven disastrous in the mission field.
The challenge for Christians now, though, is to spread the Good News
without making it Bad News. Idle, uncritical complicity with nihilistic
politico-philosophical forces will not help.

Western thinkers will not much longer be afforded the cultural capital
of their philosophical and religious outlooks, which they have erstwhile
enjoyed. Western Christians in particular will have to apply themselves to
a far more rigorous exploration of philosophies that did not originate in
Europe. This will become more difficult as the advocates of those philosophies come to realize they no longer need to submit their thought in a
form (or even a language) suited for a Western-educated audience.

The Kyoto School lived on the military and philosophical borders between
Asia and the West. Yet its thinkers did not fall into the error of either
the American or Japanese exceptionalists who believed their nation alone
should dominate. They did not unilaterally advocate the superiority of
Asian thought, but attempted in their characteristically Japanese way to
synthesize their own tradition with the best elements of foreign philosophy
and religion. As the global dominance of Europe and America diminishes,

it would pay Western thinkers to give due honor, at last, to a philosophical school that sought to bridge the theological and philosophical impasse between East and West.

This is why, in the end, it matters to Christians whether Shinran's thought is dualistic or not: first, because unmodified dualism can have disastrous consequences; and second, because Shinran's subtle navigation between the poles of dualism and monism left a lively wake that Christians and Buddhists can follow together. It gives us ways of understanding the problems in our own tradition and responding to them, not by syncretism or dilution but by looking into the depths of our own philosophical tradition and finding common concerns.

I once went to a seminar on Tokyo centered around the idea of "Shin Buddhist Theology." To anyone acquainted with Buddhism, this is a highly contentious phrase: for since the Buddha himself maintained that talking about God or gods was fruitless, and Buddhists would largely avow themselves atheists, what can Buddhists have to do with "theology," which literally means "God-talk"? We will see that the "god" Buddhists conventionally dismiss is very far from the concept of "God" in Dionysian thought. Whether or not we use the term "theology," I hope this suffices to establish that, insofar as both Shinran and Dionysius are engaged in the question of immanence and transcendence, the relationship between the natural and supernatural, or dualism and non-dualism, they are undertaking comparable quests. This is not to say they are "pursuing different paths up the same mountain," or that they are examining the "same thing," since either of those descriptions makes two modern presumptions that both would reject: first, a privileged objectivity that allows us to see the "mountain" from afar, as though we were not on the mountain ourselves but hovering above it in a virtual helicopter; and second, the notion that either God or Buddha is in any sense a "thing" that might be made the object of study. Rather, we are walking on paths that often cross and sometimes join together for a while. The destination is open for discussion, but we cannot talk unless we walk together.

We do not need to relativize our philosophy, our metaphysics, or our theology. Nor do we need to build a transcultural hybrid of East and West, like Tsukiji Honganji with its Indian roof, Greek columns, and American hymn books. The Areopagite way does not lead to a vision of beings cemented into eternal and static conformity, but to a dynamic unfolding of all from the infinite plenitude of divine self-emptying. We should seek out wisdom in the gaps between our differences rather than merely trying to fill them all in.

Being, Naming, Acting

A man that looks on glass,
On it may stay his eye;
Or if he please thee, through it pass,
And then the heav'n espy.
— George Herbert, *The Elixir*

WE HAVE MET DIONYSIUS AND TRACED THE influence of his Platonic thought down the Silk Road. We have sailed off the continent to Japan, and there met Shinran, founder of the Shin or True Pure Land school of Buddhism. Along the way we have seen how Platonism in its broadest sense can offer the West, and particularly Western Christians, an alternative to secular materialism and a metaphysics that allows more meaningful interaction with the wider, mostly religious, philosophies of the world. Now it is time to put the theory into action. The remainder of the book brings together distant sages from Syria and Kyoto, addressing the problems I have categorized as nominalism, voluntarism, and individualism. Together, Dionysius and Shinran will help us to ask three questions.

First, what is it *to be*? Are we torn between the two poles of either submitting to the inscrutable will of an all-powerful Supreme Being, or of admitting that Nietzsche was right, and there is nothing beyond this material realm? Dionysius and Shinran offer other possibilities. Dionysius's Christlike God beyond being who reveals himself by emptying himself into beings overlaps conceptually with Shinran's understanding of Amida Buddha as the inconceivable light that permeates and grants vision of all reality. Both point towards Nishitani's understanding of being as dynamically unfolding from an infinite plenitude of self-emptying love.

Second, what are we doing when we *name*? Are we atomized individuals who impose mental constructs onto an otherwise meaningless universe, who merely happen to consent to a system of codified grunts and gestures in order to make ourselves understood? Do we make meaning, or discover it? For Shinran, the Name of Amida Buddha is not merely a handy sign pointing towards reality, but is indivisible from reality itself; and for Dionysius, beings intrinsically yield meaning: in a way, all things "name" God. In neither case are these names amenable to discursive reasoning because true reality is beyond this kind of knowledge. Language at its most profound takes us beyond mere description, by means of which we discriminate among things by our analysis of their differences, and leads us into a wordless song of praise, wherein we find that we participate in the cosmic and celestial harmony of reality in its fullness. Shinran and Dionysius invite us into an enchanted world replete with meaning.

Third, what is it to *act*? Is reality a warzone of individuals offering victory only to the strongest will? Or worse, are we subject to the inscrutable machinations of insane, Lovecraftian deities? Neither Dionysius's God nor Shinran's Amida are in any sense rivals to sentient beings. In Dionysian liturgical teaching of "theurgy" and Shinran's *nembutsu* we will find something approaching a common sacramental principle. The true self is found only when our false self is relinquished and the other-power of the self-emptying One begins to act through us. True liberty is found not in the assertion of unfettered will but in offering ourselves in profound trust to the flow of self-emptying creativity that constitutes reality, and so always into relationship with others. Through the veils of being that name it, true reality reveals itself as an inconceivable self-emptying for the sake of the world. Love bids us, names us, and sings us, so that through the mirror of kindred creatures we may see.

BEING:
WISDOM EMPTIES HERSELF

With you is the fountain of Life; in your Light shall we see light.
— Psalm 35

Here a fountain is one thing, light another: there not so. For that
which is the Fountain, the same is also Light: and whatever you
will call it, for it is not what you call it: for you cannot find a fit
name: for it remains not in one name.
— St Augustine, *Commentary on the Psalms*

"WHAT IS BUDDHA?" IS A REASONABLE QUES-
tion, but no more straightforward than to ask, "what is
God?"
Perhaps it is best to start with what Buddha is not. Buddha is not a
god. The problem some Buddhists, especially Western ones, have with Shin
Buddhism is that it does make Amida Buddha look rather like a god, even
a personal savior. Hence the accusations of metaphysical dualism. As Christianity can appear to oppose God in heaven to his creation on earth, so
Shin Buddhism can appear to have Amida Buddha in the Pure Land seem
remote to foolish sentient beings of this impure world. It looks like being,
or existence, is divided in two.

So, is Shinran in fact a closet theist, his Amida a helpfully demythologized
version of the ontologically other God of Christianity? One sometimes gets
the sense from reading the work of Western converts that Shin Buddhism is
basically Christianity with all the awkward supernatural elements taken out.
But Buddhist scholar Tokunaga Michio (b. 1941) would reply to the question
with an adamant "no." Professor Emeritus of Kyoto Women's university, he
spent several years at Harvard University and engages particularly in Shin
Buddhist apologetics for English-language readers. In one such article,[1]

---

1 Michio Tokunaga, "Amida as an Ultimate Point of Reference," *Muryoko*, 1992, http://
www.nembutsu.info/tokuamid.htm.

he writes that the great divide is between the "reification of God" versus the "formless form" of Amida. God's eternity and uncreatedness stand in duality against the created order of time and space. Amida, on the other hand, is the non-dualistic manifestation of both being and unconditioned eternity. Amida's Primal Vow shows that Buddha and sentient beings are in mutual dependence, whereas Christian thought expresses a dualism in which creatures depend on God as creator. Shin Buddhism and Christianity therefore offer rival and incompatible accounts of Being.

The God to which Professor Tokunaga objects bears a close resemblance to the God of John Duns Scotus's successors and much modern Christianity. Scotus taught that the word "being" must be applied univocally to both God and creatures. They are different examples from within the same overarching category. However strong our relationship, this leaves us as separate from God as we are from any other being. God and the rest of being are in dualistic opposition. Voluntarism fits well with this metaphysical differentiation. God's supremacy over other beings is the expression of his having the strongest will and greatest power. The role of created beings, then, is to submit to the will of the uncreated and supreme being.

That Tokunaga should see the Christian God as this utterly transcendent supreme being who rules by sovereign and inscrutable will is unsurprising given his Japanese context. This is the pretty much the God whom European Protestant missionaries brought with them in the nineteenth century when they expanded their empires to the East, from India to Singapore. After the Second World War, Japan's primary experience of Christianity was through the broadly Protestant United States. The US had occupied Japan, and what's more, the majority of Shin Buddhists outside Japan lived as ex-pats in the United States. So, of course, Shin Buddhist-Christian dialogue is likely to be dominated by Protestant concerns.

Shin Buddhism always had to defend its ostensibly dualistic position on the relationship between Buddha and sentient beings. There is some truth to Karl Barth's concerns that the apparent proximity of Shinran's Amida Buddha to the God of Reformed Christianity actually conceals fundamental differences and risks confusing incompatible philosophical and theological differences. Shin Buddhists protest against simplistic identifications of the Christian God and Amida Buddha because they want to affirm their Buddhist orthodoxy and avoid the reputation of being a kind of Christianity-lite for skeptical Westerners. However, the God against which Tokunaga protests is not the only Christian understanding of God. It is not the oldest Christian understanding of God. The cosmetic similarity between Shinran and the Protestant Reformers has the unfortunate effect of obscuring a potentially fruitful source of comparison and conceptual overlap: the God whom Dionysius professed, along with the greater part of the Church both West and East until the late medieval Aristotelian turn — or more properly, Avicennan and Averroistic turn — led to the widespread adoption in Latin Christendom of nominalism and the eventual scission of faith from reason.

The God that many Buddhists reject looks far more like *a* god than *the* God beyond being proclaimed by Dionysius and the older tradition of the Christian Church. But God is not a god. This is fundamental to Dionysius's metaphysics. For his master in the pagan Platonic tradition, Proclus, there was certainly a multitude of gods: but God the Father was not one of them. The One and the Good was not just one more among Proclus's myriad divinities. God is not one *of* anything. He is simply One, not in the sense of being countable on a single finger, but in the sense of transcending any kind of multiplicity. Immeasurable and unboundable, God is necessary for the existence of beings, but in no wise a being himself.

The origin, goal, and sustainer of being, but himself beyond being, God is not in duality with the cosmos. God is not another being within the cosmos, and so cannot be dualistically other to it. Nor, though, is God monistically identical with the cosmos. To crush a rock or tread on a snail is not to destroy a "part" of God, because God is without division and so without parts. Rather, the cosmos is the expression of the mind of God, spoken — perhaps, better, sung — into being, and returning to itself. All that exists is a theophany, a shining forth of divine light.

It is easy to jump to conclusions about what other people mean by the words they are using, especially when those words are given color and texture by miraculous tales and parables, the outer signs of inner and less palpable truths. If Christians can disagree profoundly about who and what God "is," then Christians studying Buddhism need to take even greater care to understand what Shinran means when he talks about Amida Buddha. My preconceptions of Buddha may be as misleading as Buddhist preconceptions about God.

School textbooks tell us that Buddhists see this world as one of sheer illusion and Buddha as the only reality. This, I am afraid, is as much a simplification as certain Buddhist (and, for that matter, atheist) notions of the Christian God as supreme being who creates and acts by the exercise of sheer, arbitrary will. Neither does justice to the varieties of expression within the other's tradition. This is the danger of Religious Studies as a discipline: it is susceptible to the Western encyclopedic tendency to categorize, differentiate, and define in sweeping and easily comprehensible terms. It looks for general characteristics that can help to explain anthropological differences and similarities between peoples. This is not the way of the Areopagite. Dionysius is a native in both Christian and Platonist tradition, inhabiting the particular Iamblichean-Proclean locale of the more easterly stream. So too must we avoid comparing a general Christianity with a general Buddhism, neither of which actually exists. We need to be specific, to spend some time in one neighborhood and really learn its ways. This is why I bring the specifically Dionysian idea of God to the locality of Shinran's thought. Instead of shouting out the question "What is the Buddha?" and expecting the entire Buddhist world to reply in terms that we can understand, we go quietly to one Buddhist school, the True Pure Land school of Shinran, and learn his local dialect as best we can to ask him a more specific question: "Who is Amida Buddha?"

AMIDA BUDDHA

"Amida" is the Japanese phoneticization of the Chinese form of the original Sanskrit names *Amitābha* and *Amitāyus*. Shinran himself translates the former Name as *fukashigi kō*, "Immeasurable Light," and cites sutras describing Amida as "the form of light called *Tathāgata* of unhindered light filling the ten quarters."[2] Light here signifies, as it does in Platonic and Christian thought, wisdom and awakening. The "ten quarters" refers to the entire span of the spiritual cosmos: this light penetrates all reality. As in Proclus's metaphor of the sun, the question of being cannot be untangled from the question of intelligibility.

Precisely what it is that illumines beings is expressed in the word *Tathāgata*, a title of the Buddha. Rendered by the Japanese *nyōrai*, it is often appended to Amida's name. It means one who has both "come from" and "returned to" Suchness or *tathatā*, which is a notion that we need to unpack to grasp something of the significance of Amida's Name.

Buddhist thought is in general wary of the sort of thing Western philosophy would describe as "ontology." The notion of "being" is all too close to the error of eternalism, suggesting that there is some "thing" unchanging and absolute. Nirvana, as unconditioned, is unchanging, but is surely not a thing, or a being. *Tathatā*, Suchness, means things as they really are: which is to say, transient and empty (*śūnyatā*) of their own-being (*svabhāva*). When we consider samsara and nirvana from the perspective of emptiness, we come to realize that they are neither the same nor identical.

2 *Notes on Essentials of Faith Alone in Shinran* (in *The Collected Works of Shinran*), 461.

Amida Buddha is the light that illumines sentient beings so they can perceive Suchness. The Name of Amida, Shinran writes, is not an *upāya*, a disposable "means" that can be abandoned upon enlightenment. Let this serve as a caution against applying nominalistic assumptions to Buddhism. We may be tempted to see Amida as "just" a name, bequeathed by humans onto an external reality. Yet Shinran maintains that this is not so. The Name itself is constitutive of reality. The Name is the Light that manifests Suchness.

In Mahāyāna thought, everything in existence is a manifestation of the Dharmakāya (or Dharma-Body) which, in its immanent aspect, is called the "Buddha-nature" (Tathāgatagarbha). Yet this Buddha-nature itself is subject to different nuances within Buddhism. It ranges from the idea that all beings have an embryonic Buddha within them and are wombs of the Buddha, to the idea that Buddha is the core or essence of all things. A brief comparison between Dōgen's Zen perspective will help us understand Shinran's more clearly.

When Dōgen brought Zen from China to Japan in 1227, a firmly monist understanding of Suchness came with it. This was the inheritance of a Chinese scripture called *The Awakening of Faith in the Mahāyāna*, which portrays reality as the unfolding of the "One Mind," a unifying substrate beneath both nirvana and samsara. Dōgen refined this into the monistic idea that the world of observable phenomena in which we live, in all its mutability and transience, is itself this "One Mind." It is not enough to say, with Nāgārjuna, that nirvana and samsara are "not other" — for Dōgen, they are absolutely one and the same. There is only the Buddha-nature that pervades all things. All beings are already, and have always been, Buddha, and thus always enlightened: it's just that they are ignorant of this fact. Hence the Zen focus on meditation and, in the Rinzai tradition, the breaking down of discriminative intellection by the paradoxical riddles called *kōan*. One must abandon the dualistic opposition of self-versus-other, and see that there is only Buddha. Even to distinguish between sitting in meditation and doing other things, or to conceive of a purpose for sitting other than the sitting itself, is to fall into the error of dualism. To eat when you eat and walk when you walk: this is enlightenment.

There is beauty in the radical simplicity of the Zen tradition, but Shinran sees things quite differently. Remember that his answer to the terrors of *mappō*, the calamitous end of the Dharma Age, was to see that we do not have the internal resources for our own enlightenment. Instead, as we might by now predict, he identifies the Buddha-nature with Amida. He agrees with Dōgen that sentient beings are always and already enlightened. Yet for Shinran, this is not because of their own merit or even karmic capacity. It is only because of Amida's compassion shining through the cosmos. Suchness cannot be perceived through our own meditative efforts, however strenuous, however simple. For Dōgen, we are fundamentally Buddha and as such fundamentally good, hence the efficacy of self-power, which is none other than the Buddha's power. For Shinran, however, we are *bonbu*, "foolish beings," our actions conditioned by previous lives of karmic evil, empty of truth and reality.

While for Dōgen, nirvana and samsara are united in the Buddha-nature without distinction, for Shinran the two must always remain distinct even in their unity. Inconceivable Suchness is made manifest in the light of Amida; all beings utterly depend on Amida's Vow and exist in a relationship of simultaneous alterity and unity with the Buddha, who is at once utterly transcendent and compassionately immanent in them.

Students of Augustine and Calvin will see parallels here. Both doubted the human capacity for goodness. Augustine was up against Pelagius, who taught that since we are made in God's image we are capable of achieving salvation by our own innate goodness. There is something like Dōgen's understanding of the universal Buddha nature here. Yet Augustine thought this risked making Christ's sacrifice on the Cross redundant. If we could save ourselves, what was the point of the Incarnation, Passion, Crucifixion, and Resurrection? He concluded that the image of God in us, while originally good, was marred by the Fall to such an extent that it could be redeemed only by divine grace.

Calvin took this further. He saw the image of God as not just marred but utterly broken, such that there is almost no innate goodness within humanity at all. Even that which remains is deceptive unless restored by divine grace. This teaching of "complete depravity" might look rather like Shinran's understanding of humans as *bonbu*, foolish beings bereft of karmic merit. But this is where the parallels start to break down. Calvin's commitment to voluntarism was such that he downplayed Augustine's teaching on the Church and sacraments as sources of grace. The created order, detached as separate "being" from God, did not mediate his goodness. It might indicate his goodness, as the brushstrokes in a painting reveal something about the painter, but even so, the painting and the painter are ultimately different things. There is quite a difference between the world as the unfolding of the divine mind, and the world as a blank canvas on which God imposes meaning by acts of will. Moreover, Calvin considered our reason so far fallen that we could recognize those strokes only after we have been granted divine grace through faith awakened by Scripture. This grace was distributed purely by the divine will, salvation granted to whomever God elected, and damnation to those he did not. This rests on a metaphysical divide between God and (other) beings quite alien to the intimate relationship between Amida Buddha as source of light and the Suchness that "perfumes" all beings, according to The Awakening of Faith in the Mahāyāna. So, while Shinran's account of human nature and our inability to save ourselves may seem cosmetically similar to Reformation anthropology, the similarity is undercut by his very different metaphysical and epistemological considerations, which are surprisingly closer to the more sacramental kind of Christianity we find in Dionysius.

Shinran understands Suchness as a movement of salvific reality implicit in the Name of Amida. This resists a straightforward duality between the Buddha and sentient beings, but neither does it collapse the two into monism. Here we see a parallel with the broadly Platonic treatment of beings and their source in God as beyond-being. The Platonic, Dionysian God is "One" not in a monistic sense of absolute identity with beings, as in Dōgen's oneness of beings with Buddha-nature, nor as one among many beings and therefore in alterity to them, but in the sense of indivisibility and simultaneous presence to all beings as their source of being — and so, of intelligibility.

THE UNKNOWABLE SOURCE

In his May address of 2006, Pope Benedict proclaimed Dionysius a potential mediator between Western and Eastern philosophies.[3] He had in mind the apophatic strand of Dionysian thought: that negative "way of unknowing" we explored earlier. But in Platonism the question of knowing cannot be separated from the question of being. Something similar can be said of Shin Buddhism. For the Areopagite, being is defined by intelligibility; for the Buddhist, being cannot be separated from perception.

Dionysius's apophatic way is based on the Platonic premise that to be is to be intelligible. This means that if God is beyond being, God is beyond rational knowing. Amida, as the "personification" of Suchness, is also inconceivable despite being the "true and real." There is an apophatic side to Shinran's thought, as to Dionysius's, because insofar as Amida is Suchness, the self-revealing insight into things as they really are, Amida cannot be

---

3 Published in Benedict XVI, The Fathers, Vol. II (Huntingdon, IN: Our Sunday Visitor, 2009) and Great Christian Thinkers: From the Early Church through the Middle Ages (London: SPCK, 2011), 130–33.

grasped by mere calculative thinking (*hakarai*) but can be encountered directly in the realization of *shinjin*, which is the arising of the Buddha's mind within us.

Shinran writes that Amida as Suchness is without color or form: "the mind cannot grasp it nor words describe it."[4] It is not just that Amida is incomprehensible because his is an incomparably higher intellect than ours: this would be to categorize Buddha in terms of intellect, to make him measurable and comparable to sentient beings, and so to fall into the post-Scotist trap of placing him in duality against others. Like the Platonic One, Buddha is inaccessible to thought; not by comparison to anything else but in itself. Shinran uses the word *fushigi*, a Japanese translation of the Sanskrit *acintya*, which means "inconceivable" but also "unthinkable" or "beyond thinking." Echoing those words of St Paul at the Areopagus in which Dionysius placed such stock, to "know" the truth of reality which is beyond being one must participate in the universal act of "unknowing." In the next chapter, we will find out how Shinran and Dionysius respectively articulate the act of unknowing as we unfold their practices of "naming" and "acting" in the *nembutsu* and *theurgy*.

Yet there is also a cataphatic side to Shinran, as there is to Dionysius. We are not abandoned to absolute ignorance. Despite being beyond conceptual or "calculative" thinking, Amida is himself the light of wisdom that illumines sentient beings. Shinran and his followers can and do speak of him in intelligible terms — which after all are the only terms we have. These enable us to understand Amida's emergence from the formless realm of Suchness in the form of his Vow to save all beings.

Here Shinran refines the Mahāyāna non-dualism of samsara and nirvana. There is throughout his writing a cataphatic sense that the reality of samsara in which we live and suffer is not merely something to be escaped from into blissful nirvana, but is itself the vehicle of salvation and illumination. His turning point from the older way, which he calls the "Path of Sages," was the realization both of his own inadequacy to achieve enlightenment, and further of his own downright evil:

> Lacking even a modicum of love and compassion,
> How could I hope to benefit sentient beings?
> Were it not for the ship of Amida's Vow,
> How could I cross the ocean of painful existence?[5]

---

4   Notes on *Essentials of Faith Alone* in Shinran, *The Collected Works of Shinran*, 461.
5   *Gutoku's Hymns of Lament and Reflection* 98 in Shinran.

The reason why in 1201 Shinran "took refuge in the Original Vow," as he wrote, was awareness of his own inadequacy to save himself. More than an expression of his own personal, psychological journey, humility is fundamental to Shinran's teaching on the nature of reality as a whole. Buddhists, like Platonists, reject the polarization of intelligibility and being. To be enlightened is most fully to be, because it is to see things as they really are. To know fully is to partake in the plenitude of the "true and real." Shinran's awareness that he cannot save himself through self-power is itself the working of other-power as actively present in Amida's Vow. Only when we are made to see that our reality as ordinary beings is to be "burdened with blind passions"[6] can we be liberated from the myopic delusion of self-sufficiency. This is as much an ontological as an epistemological claim, that reflects an understanding that the immeasurable light and life of Amida is the very vehicle of salvation.

Compare this with Dionysius's theophanic view of reality. Beings are not external objects being shone upon by a sun-like God other to them. Rather, God is the very light itself, the illuminating rays that inseparably give growth and light, being and intelligibility, to all things. But this light is hidden and clouded. Like the pillar of smoke by day and fire by night in which God manifested himself to the Israelites in the desert, this dazzling gloom transcends the duality of light and dark altogether. We see this in his prayer to the Trinity at the beginning of the Mystical Theology, where Dionysius stretches at the limits of language with a whole list of compounds of hyper, meaning "beyond":

> Trinity, beyond being, beyond divine, beyond Good, guide of Christians in divine wisdom: lead us beyond unknowing and illumination to the highest peak of the mystic scriptures, where lie hidden within the shadow-beyond-light of mystery-shrouding silence the simple, absolute, unchanging mysteries of theology, which in the utter dark illumine beyond illumination that which is utterly beyond manifestation, and infinitely fill beyond measure our unsighted minds with splendors beyond beautiful.[7]

For Dionysius, to call God "God" seems too much; even the Platonic identifications of the One as the Good and the Beautiful run close to idolatry. He has written an entire tract on the practice of knowing and unknowing the Divine Names, but here, at the outset of his next book, even to claim

---

6   Tannishō 3.
7   Mystical Theology 1, my translation.

to "unknow" God is extravagant: one must be led by the Trinity beyond unknowing, in fact beyond the binaries of knowing and unknowing, seeing and blindness, light and darkness, hiddenness and revelation, scripture and silence. Nonetheless, the revelations and manifestations and splendors are real. The apophatic and the cataphatic ways are complementary, not mutually exclusive.

We find a similar trend in Shinran. He also speaks of Amida in terms of both unknowability and knowability: respectively as the "Dharma-body as Suchness" (*hosshō hosshin*) and the "Dharma-body as Compassion" (*hōben hosshin*). The word *hōben* is a translation of *upāya*, understood as "saving means" in this context. Shinran insists that these two aspects of the one Dharma-body are *identical* in their essence, while differing in function. While the Dharma-body as Suchness has an ontological priority, without its complementary aspect of Dharma-body as Compassion sentient beings cannot be grasped and saved from the clutches of birth-and-death.

Despite its inconceivable nature, Shinran does venture to intimate something of the Suchness of Amida Buddha. He alludes to its "Oneness" (*ichinyō*)[8] and indwelling presence as the true essence of all "dharmas,"[9] which in this context does not mean just "teachings" but "things" as the constituents of phenomenal existence. He distinguishes the oneness of the Buddha's Suchness as "unconditioned" as opposed to its "conditioned" manifestation in things. There is no opposition here between metaphysical absolutes, like creator and creation — only the suggestion of an indivisible Oneness as true reality which both transcends and suffuses all things, utterly beyond everything that is finite and yet abiding in the heart of all that is.

The Buddhist idea that all beings are illumined by a non-dualistic "emptying" may seem alien to modern Christians. But three images of emptiness from Scripture may help us to make a connection: first, the empty nothingness from which God effects creation; second, the empty womb of the Blessed Virgin from which Christ is Incarnate; and third, the empty tomb from which Our Lord rises at the Resurrection. Creation, Incarnation, Resurrection: each image conjures a profound, immeasurable emptiness from which the fullness of life and wisdom spring. To know these doctrines, and especially the Incarnation and Resurrection, is not only to assent to certain historical events. Their historicity is essential to the faith: they are not mere metaphors, convenient names for a deeper reality, or disposable props to be thrown away after enlightenment. But

---

8 *Passages on the Pure Land Way*, in Shinran, *The Collected Works of Shinran*, 301.

9 Kyōgyōshinshō 4.17 in Shinran, 318.

the Christian faith consists in far more than intellectual cognition. It is, rather, an apprehension of their truths at a far deeper level in the heart. It is the sure and certain knowledge of salvation to which empirical reason alone can never attain: a supra-intellectual apprehension of the true reality of things; a knowing beyond unknowing; a rebirth through the plenitude of pregnant emptiness.

This helps us understand how, for Dionysius, our being as creatures is not in dualistic opposition to God as creator. The light that illumines, and the gift of being, are not other. The divine revelation or "theophany" is not the shining of divine light onto some external reality, as though God were giving form to some formless clay, or brushing his grace onto graceless matter. Rather, the theophany is the manifestation of God; his illumining is his self-emptying into being. Creation is constitutive of who and what God is as creative and creator. The hidden mysteries within him are not secrets for the chosen few, but everything, all beings. When the divine darkness shines out to fill sightless minds, the splendors of his divine Word are not mere images of some external reality but are constitutive of reality itself. Plotinus says that the One is nothing among things, and Proclus speaks of God as in all things, but none of them. Dionysius found this Platonic image of divine self-emptying plenitude realized historically in the kenosis or self-emptying of God in Christ: Incarnate, Crucified, and Risen. The God of Dionysius, straining words and comprehension, is the self-emptying reality beyond being whose nature is to render himself nothing in order that all things might be in and through him.

CREATION, EMANATION, ARISING

Dionysian theology helps us see that God need not be a reified and solely other "being." Professor Tokunaga's second criticism, that Amida and sentient beings are mutually dependent, is harder to answer. The orthodox Christian might well blanche at the suggestion that God is somehow "dependent" on creation in the way that Amida's Vow shows a mutual interdependence between God and sentient beings. As we noted above in the discussion of Shinran's teachings on the Vow, there is a remarkable spiritual process at work here: Suchness has only assumed the form of "Dharma-Body as Compassion" so that all beings may attain the same Buddhahood as Amida. For Shinran, Amida as the personal and saving manifestation of Suchness exists only because suffering sentient beings in need of emancipation exist. Christian theology on the other hand traditionally maintains that God is God regardless of his creatures (and thus essentially separate from them), and would remain God even if there were no beings. He could have "chosen" as it were not to create at all.

With the help of Dionysius's Platonic theology we can answer this charge without breaking from Christian orthodoxy. Christian Platonists have been accused of heresy for taking an "emanationist" view, understood as implying that it is in God's nature to generate or emanate being, rather than creating solely as the result of his free will. This would seem to limit divine freedom, making God something less than omnipotent, and so something less than God.

However, "emanation" is a complex and disputed term even within Platonic tradition. Plotinus devoted an entire tractate, *Ennead* 6.8, to the tension between the necessary generation of beings and the freedom of the divine will. Dionysius inherits this tradition. He builds on Plotinus's sense that being is generated from an overflowing of divine goodness. God creates because God is good, and creatures long to return to their source. Yet as we saw in our discussion of the Dionysian cosmos, more like Proclus than Plotinus, Dionysius understands that longing as two-way. God desires beings as well as beings desiring him. This is not because God lacks anything beings have, for every metaphysical "cause" prepossesses all its effects. God is not needy. Rather, following Proclus's departure from Plotinus, Dionysius understands God not only to produce but actually to *be* the beauty in all things. Beauty is that which awakens the desire for the Good. Therefore God is, for Dionysius, both the Good and the desire for the Good — that is, God is the desire for himself. This is a profound expression of the Christian revelation that God is love, as revealed in the relationship between Christ and the Father in the Holy Trinity, and expressed also in the strong sense of *eros*, a fire of longing rather than the gentler heat one might associate with *agape*. The reciprocal yearning between Father and Son overflows and spills out as life-giving Spirit. This divine love is not an adjunct to being, or a superimposition onto being as external stuff "outside" God, but is actually constitutive of being. Love is God manifest and present in being.

Divine love is not some static pool, but a living, active spring. It empties out with all the potency of the blood and water pouring from the side of the Crucified. Once we have broken away from the idea that God is a being or even "Being" itself in any static sense, and recognize him as more verb than noun, more action than subject or object, we can begin to see God as what he does rather than what he is. In the end, that is as much as we can hope for. It is impossible for us as beings to know the One who is beyond being as he is, but we can hope to glean something of him through his activity. Hard as it might be, we need to escape some of the images of God we have internalized from childhood. People often see him as something like a bewigged judge, a disciplinarian headteacher, or an absent father. This is often why we reject him, or perhaps worse, end up haunted by our own psychologically damaging projections. The Dionysian view would have us transcend these kinds of figures, and leave us with God as far more redolent of the "heart" or "mind of great compassion" (daijihishin), by which Shinran designates Amida Buddha.[10] God is not just compassionate: God is compassion, yearning so much that he empties himself into being.

This Dionysian universe is profoundly Platonic, but no less profoundly Christian and Christ-centered. Dionysius locates the origin of the entirety of being in the "emptying of self" of the ancient Christological hymn of Paul's Epistle to the Philippians 2:5–11. As for Plotinus, to be is to unfold from the mind of the One, so for Dionysius, to be is to participate in the mind which is in Christ. This is not merely a matter of emulating Christ (though there are worse questions than "What would Jesus do?"), but of joining in the divine self-emptying by which the mind of Christ was Incarnate in the person of Jesus. To be most fully is to be as God is, as far as we can: to be the complete emptying of self out of sheer goodness, which allows us to call God love and to make room for him in our hearts. It is to live as gift in the grammar of love, in which subject, verb, and object become one. To be oneself most fully is to lose one's self, to possess is to be possessed, to desire is to be desired.

God is, as far as definitions can allow, an emptiness, or perhaps better, the act of emptying. But this is not a hollow nothingness. Rather, it is what Douglas Hedley calls "the emphatic nothing of [the medieval Dionysian Platonist John Scotus Eriugena's] nihil per excellentiam: 'nothing' as paradoxical expression of finite language to capture the majesty and plenitude of true being."[11] Like the fecundity of the virgin womb or the empty tomb, Dionysius's God is empty, beyond being and non-being, precisely because he is self-emptying from a dimension of infinite plenitude. It is an emptiness of emptying, of motion rather than stasis. To describe this action Dionysius borrows a term from Proclus now familiar to us in quite different contexts: ecstasy. God is the One who in the literal sense of the word "stands outside" himself, and yet without ever truly moving or changing.[12] If pushed to define what God is, we might say God is what he does: erotic, ecstatic kenosis.

---

10 Tannishō 4.6.

11 The Iconic Imagination, p. 69.

12 Divine Names 4.13.

Only when we glimpse this, however darkly, can we address what is probably Dionysius's most notorious neologism for the description of the cosmos: *hierarchy*. "A place for everything, and everything in its place" is the bane of modern sensibilities, and maybe that is understandable, given the many centuries of the abuse of power and station we have witnessed. We think of hierarchies of class, race, or wealth as pyramidal structures that favor the few, but the modern notion of hierarchy as a power structure is not Dionysius's fault. As Dionysian scholar Eric Perl puts it, it has "nothing to do with domination and subservience, but only with love, the love of all things for one another which is the love of God in them all."[13] Absolutely everything that is, is the manifestation of divine love according to its capacity. For Dionysius, as for Proclus and Plotinus before him, God is not the apex of a pyramid of beings, with lower stages of being emanating from him, starting with the higher invisible realms of angels and ending up by way of animals and plants with insensate dust. Rather, we might see God as the center-point of concentric circles of reality, the still small voice in the whirlwind from which all things unfold and spiral without ever losing connection with him at their center. The center itself is not just infinitely small: it has no existence per se, but only in relation to the circles of which it is center. The One is, in the words of Proclus, "at once everywhere and nowhere."[14] God is beyond being and yet "central" to it, defining it, yet neither strictly inside nor outside it. God is not a being, but both transcends and permeates all beings as their generative origin, a sense we might clumsily occlude if we put this into simple terms of cause and effect.

Dionysius devotes an entire treatise to the *Celestial Hierarchy*. Angels and saints exist, invisibly, as intermediaries between the uncreated and incomprehensible Divinity and the visible, material realm. Yet their mediation is in no way a buffer to the immediate relationship between God and material beings. Our modern understanding of the word "hierarchy" as separating out levels of power is not what Dionysius, its inventor, intended. Rather, for him, it is hierarchy that guarantees the immediate presence of God in all things while simultaneously preserving his transcendence. What hierarchy, literally "holy order," means in Dionysius is the participation — *according to their capacity* — of all beings in God. Angels, saints, humans, giraffes, vines, and dirt all participate in God insofar as all are unfoldings of the divine mind. However, they all participate in different ways. This is where the hierarchy comes in. In an age that tends to equate hierarchy with injustice

---

13 Perl, *Theophany: The Neoplatonic Philosophy of Dionysius the Areopagite*, 77.
14 *Elements of Theology*, prop. 98.

this may be difficult to comprehend, but Dionysius sees it precisely as the guarantor of justice and hence goodness. I doubt many people think it unjust that a stone cannot think, or a mollusk not fly, despite the relative capacities of humans or birds. Hierarchy is the proportional existence of God in all things, and all things in one another. So, God can be known in every being. Every point on the line of a circle exists only in relation to the circle's invisible center and to every other point of the circle. The unity of the circle is guaranteed by the difference of each point on the line from all the others, and simultaneously united with all the others by their shared equidistance from the center. Without such differentiation and hence inequality there could be no being at all. Hierarchy is Dionysius's way of expressing how, in Proclus's terms, the One is "at once everywhere and nowhere," or as Plotinus put it, "all things are the One and are not the One."[15] God is the vanishing tensile point that holds all things in being. So, Proclus writes, "all things are in all things, but properly in each."[16]

Thanks to hierarchical ordering, all things exist in relationship to one another and, thereby, to God. Existence is possible only in relationship: no being is an island, man or otherwise. Such relationship implies a certain unity in otherness, and far from impeding equality is its guarantor. To return to the example of the Gothic arch, the equality of gravitational forces that sustains it in being, is guaranteed by the tension held in the capstone. To "equalize" the hierarchical imbalance of shapes and tensions in the arch would mean reducing it to rubble. Shifting from an architectural to an ornithological metaphor, we would not think a rock inferior to a duck because it cannot quack. Yet in the Dionysian cosmos the rock is no more "distant" from God than the duck. Both participate in divine love, not according to their power, but according to their proper nature and capacity. The "divine order," which is literally what "hierarchy" means, far from being divisive, guarantees that all things are in all things according to capacity.

God is immediately present in each and every thing because it is his nature to be so. Ultimately God would not be the God revealed in Jesus Christ if he did not create. But his creation is not an act of caprice. Rather, it is of God's nature to be creative. Plotinus argues in *Ennead* 6.8 that this does not constrain God, as though he were subject to some higher law compelling him to create. Rather, it reveals him *as* that very law, the super-existential principle of creation and illumination. God's Word is God, as the preface to the Fourth Gospel attests — perhaps if it were still read after every Mass

15   Plotinus, *Ennead* 5.2.225.
16   *Elements of Theology*, prop. 103.

as it was before the Second Vatican Council, its mystical significance might be better impressed in the minds of modern Christians. God is not subject to the Divine Word, the Logos by which creation was and still is spoken into being. He *is* the Divine Logos.

Nor is Amida "subject" to his Vow. Amida *is* the Vow in that it embodies his fundamental desire to save beings as revealed in his Name, which calls us to take refuge in it. On this Shinran is adamant. When a follower writes to him asking the relationship between the Name and the Vow, Shinran replies:

> I do not really understand how such a question as yours can arise, for although we speak of the Vow and the Name they are not two different things. There is no Name separate from the Vow and there is no Vow separate from the Name.[17]

Shinran portrays Amida no more as a static metaphysical absolute than as the God of Dionysius. The Dionysian God and Shinran's Amida embody a unifying dynamism that encapsulates all reality. We are left with the impression of a true reality, which is unknowable by bare reason, but which can be experienced as person and as gift; with a sense of the whole universe being grounded in a joyful, lively emptiness, a space that makes possible a teeming creativity. To be most fully is to see this space for what it is and to surrender to it in a spirit of both playfulness and reverence.

Shin Buddhists might also acknowledge that the supposedly "absolute" non-duality of the relationship between Amida and sentient beings is, at least, nuanced, perhaps even *weighted* towards Amida — comparable to the Christian logical priority given to God over creation. The very composition of the Vow, whatever the mutuality it suggests, implies a certain logical priority to the Buddha's benevolence over sentient beings' recognition and realization thereof. Shinran clearly distinguishes reliance on the Buddha from dependence on oneself: *jiriki,* "self-power," is to be rejected completely in favor of *tariki,* "other-power." This will become clear in the chapter on *Acting,* when we compare the *nembutsu* and theurgy and find in each a sacramental principle of reliance on, and participation in, the salvific mind beyond knowing and being.

Dionysius's self-emptying God beyond being, immediately present to all things, is far from the supreme being rejected by atheists or by Buddhists like Tokunaga. The relationship between God and creatures Dionysius portrays bears little resemblance to the voluntaristic God of power who dictates beings into existence. It is one of participation rather than emulation, and

---

17   *Lamp for the Latter Age,* in Shinran, *The Collected Works of Shinran.*

participation not in power but in self-gift. There is far more convergence between Dionysius's God and Shinran's Amida Buddha than between either of these and atheistic materialism. In both cases the conceptual is at least as real as the physical, and mind is logically prior to matter.

We will see how this priority unfolds more closely as we come to the question of how intelligible concepts relate to physical beings. We will enter back into that playful and open spirit of the children whom Jesus sets before his disciples as an example, remembering how to discern the meaning in the world rather than imposing our own on it, so that we might return to the Platonic innocence lauded by Wordsworth:

> There was a time when meadow, grove, and stream,
> The earth, and every common sight
> To me did seem
> Appareled in celestial light,
> The glory and the freshness of a dream.
>
> William Wordsworth,
"Intimations of Immortality,"
from Recollections of Early Childhood

NAMING
THE NAME

It is not easy to find any name that will readily fit such transcendent majesty. In fact, it is better just to say that this Trinity is the one God from whom are all things, through whom are all things, in whom are all things.

— St Augustine[1]

W E SPEND SO MUCH TIME TALKING. WHEN we are not talking, we fill the gap by watching, and sometimes even listening to, other people talking on our screens. We put the television on "just for company." As a parish priest I visited households where it is kept on all day, even while I was there to talk about funeral arrangements or wedding plans. Yet even the most ardent viewer will happily admit that most of what is said on the game shows, chat shows, and soaps is quite meaningless. Most of it in fact they won't really hear and won't remember. It is just there as a comfort blanket of noise. Anything to muffle the awful silence.

Few people will admit that they are actually afraid of silence. I wonder whether that is because we have never really encountered it. A few years ago, a British "reality TV" program invited some secular twenty-somethings to spend an extended retreat in a convent. Some of the contestants, if that is what they were, were absolutely terrified when they met real silence for the first time. In general, modernity offers unparalleled opportunities for its obliteration. Even when the TV is unplugged, the cellphone put away in the drawer, the stereo silenced, perhaps to go out for a quiet stroll or even just to try to sleep, the noise inside the head continues. The outer chatter may be subdued but the inner chatter gibbers on relentlessly. And on reflection, most of our inner dialogue, too, is inane. Thoughts suggest themselves in Tweet length. Our rewired minds begin to see all things of

1 Translated in Augustine and Edmund Hill, *Teaching Christianity: De Doctrina Christiana* (Hyde Park, NY: New City Press, 2007).

beauty as Instagram opportunities. Social occasions are exploited for max-
imal Facebook potential.

Silence is an acquired taste, and perhaps it has never been more difficult
to acquire than now; but like connoisseurs of fine wines or whiskies, those
who learn to love it will find their palate becomes attuned to a new world
of tastes and subtle distinctions. To switch metaphors, there are as many
kinds of silence as there are of snow.

There are the light and drifting kinds of silence that never settle and
that you know any minute will pass. The silence of a conversation that has
run its course. The silence of an awkward goodbye. The silences between
tracks on a CD.

There are the slushy, sleet-like silences, neither liquid nor quite solid,
ambiguous in meaning. The silence between a couple dining at a table
for two, born of a familiarity into which the observer might read either
intimacy or contempt. There are sudden blizzards of silence, like the gaps
between blasts of thunder. Sudden drifts of anticipation hastily cleared, but
the effects of which, good or ill, may linger. Silences of deceptive brevity
that in that moment seem eternal. The silence before the punchline of a
joke well told. The silence at the end of the symphony, that moment before
applause. The silence after words that cannot be unsaid: words like "I love
you" or "I leave you."

There are frosted silences that isolate a moment and hold it still and
glistening for slow inspection. The silence of a frozen leaf or corpse before
it thaws and decomposes. The silence of an empty house with its contents
left untouched for years. The silence of an Auschwitz shower room.

There are drifts of silence so deep they block your door and cover your
car, suffocating and stifling. The silence of the mute and muted. The silence
of a frightened witness. The silence of a journalist imprisoned and released,
afraid to speak. The silence of depression. The silence you heard when you
were dragged under the waves as a child and feared you would drown.

There is the salutary silence of the first snowfall to wake you from autum-
nal slumber, the blast of cold that concentrates your mind and makes you
hasten your step. The silence of refreshment, clarity, and focus. The silence
of absolute concentration on a task well done. The silence of a serious place
like a church, library, or dojo.

There is the silence of the snow on a mountaintop when the mist descends
and all you can see beneath your feet and before your face is white, a dazzling darkness and blinding glow. The sort of silence that drives you to your
knees in sheer awe. The silence of contrition after a confession well made.

The silence before the Cross in the Good Friday liturgy, gradually unveiled.

Then there are those thick, enduring silences, layer upon layer, in impenetrable, unfathomable drifts. Those greater Arctic silences spreading to the horizon and beyond, inviting and forbidding, that pierce the bone even when you gaze on them through the windows a fire-warmed room: simple, even simplifying in their beauty, yet preserving the shapes and contours of what lies beneath in a monochrome glow, at once veiling and outlining the distinction of all things. The silence of the grave. The telling silence of the empty tomb.

It is no surprise that we are so afraid of silence, especially as it points to that last and unknown greater silence. But for all its cold, it has its warmer moments too. The moments of play and rest which snow affords to skiers and to children. The silence of a sleeping child. The silence of a monastery can be like this, at times.

Jesus invited his followers, weary from their labors, to rest in him (Matthew 11:28–30), and called himself the Lord of the Sabbath (Matthew 12, Mark 2, Luke 6). He did not mean by this that he was Lord of the "day off." Rather, he was referring to the seventh day of rest by which Genesis refers to the culmination of God's creation. That creation is not yet finished. It is ongoing, and we are part of it. Yet its final goal, and so our final goal, is not a cacophony of urgent activity. It is the silence of divine rest, the unmovable simplicity and stillness that belongs to God alone: the silence of the Void from which God's Word spoke the infinite multiplicity of all things into creation; the silence of the Virgin Womb from which the infinite One himself entered into creation; and the silence of the empty tomb from which springs the perfecting water of infinite life.

Christians call the Bible God's word, and with good reason. Yet it is so only by analogy with God's Word with a capital "W": the divine *dabar* in Hebrew or *Logos* in Greek. This Word by which God spoke all things into being is the same Word who for a time came to dwell or "set up camp" among us, as the Greek of the Prologue to St John's Gospel puts it (John 1:14). By the return of Jesus, the Divine Word, to his Speaker at the glorious Ascension, we too are lifted up on the Way to eternal life.

This Word of God is not something that can be "spoken" in human words. God has no larynx. His Word cannot be contained by sounds. The Word of God is born of rest, of peace, the silence of *shalom*. Elijah hears it not in the clamor of the earthquake or the crackling of fire, but in the still, small voice of calm (1 Kings 19:12). God's Word calls us into being out of silence, and at the same time, silently, calls us to return to the silence from which we came. God's Word speaks in a silence richer than words, written not in ink but in the flesh and blood of Jesus Christ, in the action of breaking bread and pouring wine.

In the silence, we seek meaning. In particular, we seek our own meaning, and so our identity. Cars, airplanes, and online communication have made it possible to live further from our traditional communities of family, town, and even nation than ever before; and as it has become possible, so has it become economically advantageous or even necessary. People have had to become highly mobile to feed and house their families. This has eroded the older loyalties and sources of shared meaning that constituted our local identities. We know our neighbors less and, hidden from the disapproving eyes of older generations by the Gyges' rings of distant living and online anonymity, we can experiment with our identities however we please. Once, someone may have identified himself as the son or daughter of so-and-so, and been known readily enough by even such a limited designation, reflected in the patronymic surnames common to many cultures, from Atreides to Zlatkov. Now, though, with our newfound flexibility and distance, the question arises more pressingly for us than it did for older generations: who, exactly, am I?

The nominalist turn of modernity has trained us to think we can answer this question, as we answer all questions of meaning, by sheer assertion: by vocalization and verbosity. We understand language as our personal map of noises by which we can refer other people who happen to share the same series of grunts and gestures to all those external things that constitute reality. Anyone with the key — that is, anyone who has learned the same code — can understand what we are saying; but essentially, we impose our meaning of reality, subject to popular consensus. Names for things are arbitrary codes, secrets into which other people are invited to the degree their proficiency in the code we are using allows. From here we come to think that we can, and possibly even should, define ourselves. It is up to us to define who we are, in every particular. Nothing is given, nothing inherited: we name ourselves. We are our own maker.

Heidegger, among others, showed the limitations of seeing words as a map projected onto an external reality. Take the word "hammer." In a philosophy textbook the word "hammer" is going to be used to form logical propositions such as "the hammer is on the table," or "the hammer is made of rubber," or "a hammer is a tool for hitting nails." These can be empirically tested or disproven: they are either true or not. But, says Heidegger, this is not the primary use of the word "hammer." People did not start saying "hammer" so they could describe what or where hammers are, or even what they are used for. Most likely, if someone says to you, "hammer," what they mean is, "pass me the hammer." Possibly, if the hammer is falling from an open window on the proverbial fourteenth floor, they might be saying, "watch out for the hammer." In either case, the word "hammer" is a vocal substitute for pointing or gesturing at the hammer. It is not making any falsifiable claims about the hammer. The word is born from an action relating to an object. Both the action of pointing and the object of the hammer are themselves non-verbal. That is, they are silent. The word "hammer" is the vocalization of the silent.

Poetry offers another example of the limitations of a purely designatory understanding of language. Those limitations are especially apparent in translation. Novices in foreign languages often assume one language is pretty much substitutable for another: they're rival codes referring to the same "thing." Once they become more advanced, they will realize the limits of this approach even in prose, as they discover words that are untranslatable or carry very different nuances from their closest equivalent in the target language. Yet in poetry the gap between words begins to gape. Homer in English is not really Homer any more than Shakespeare in Sanskrit would really be Shakespeare — even between languages from the same Indo-European language family, too much is lost in translation. The gap widens even further if one is translating between, say, Indo-European languages, Semitic languages like Arabic and Hebrew, and the Ural-Altaic language of Japanese. When you get beyond hammers, you soon realize the language one speaks is not just mapping out a reality: it encompasses and engenders in those who speak and think in it a specific conception of what reality is. This is why Jews are expected to learn Hebrew and Muslims Arabic. There is a sense that their scriptures would not really *be* scripture after the distortion of translating them into a different register of reality.

For those who seek the meaning of themselves and the wider world, this leaves a problem. The existence of multiple languages, which is to say a potentially infinite range of conceptions of reality, makes any "objective" understanding of it seem impossible. It leaves our attempts at defining any kind of meaning at all looking arbitrary. We are left unable to define anything at all, even ourselves. All knowledge becomes questionable, the very frameworks that underpin our thoughts and assumptions inherited by the lottery of our place of birth. Even our sensory perceptions are rendered unreliable, mediated as they are by the grammar hardwired into our minds. And who wired them? Why, exactly those socializing communities of identity from which we learned our language, dialect, and accent: that is, our parents, towns and nations: all those influences from which modern people, inspired by the ideal of autonomy, seek further and further distance and dissolution.

The question of meaning is inevitably social. It is therefore inevitably noisy and verbose. Yet beneath this Babel of infinite languages rests the silent ocean from which all things came and to which all things will return. If we wish to follow the advice of the Delphic oracle and know ourselves, Platonists and Buddhists may agree that we will need first to learn the language of silence. For in silence we do not impose meaning but discover it. All our noise dulls us to the riches of its language.

CAELI ENARRANT

I look forward to the fourth day of each month. It brings, in the 1662 Book of Common Prayer from which I pray the daily office, Psalm 19, which begins:

> The heavens declare the glory of God: and the firmament sheweth his handy-work. One day telleth out another : and one night cer-tifieth another. There is neither speech nor language: but their voices are heard among them.

The Psalmist's picture of the skies themselves and the sun and moon silently praising God in their unceasing motions gives me the comfort that my daily round of prayer, nugatory and weak as it may be, is merely one voice in the harmony of a far greater hymnody.

The Benedicite is more explicit still. Taken from the deuterocanonical Song of the Children, you will find it printed halfway through Daniel 3 in Roman Catholic bibles, or otherwise separately in the Apocrypha. Set in the Prayer Book office of Matins as the alternative canticle to the Te Deum, that venerable hymn ascribed to Sts Ambrose and Augustine, the Benedicite was also used widely throughout the Western Church as a private prayer by priests after every mass until the reforms of the Second Vatican Council. Sadly, like the Te Deum, the Benedicite has fallen out of common use and familiarity especially to the laity. In Rome it has been confined to the Divine Office, which remains mostly the province of clergy and, in the modern Church of England liturgy, relegated to a rarely-chosen option at morning prayer. I say "sadly" because it expresses a worldview so very different from that of modernity — which may explain why it has fallen out of fashion. Like Psalm 19, the Benedicite speaks of a universe in which every aspect, visible and invisible, the living and the dead, the plants and animals, even the seasons, seas, and stones, sing to God an unending hymn of praise:

> O all ye Works of the Lord, bless the Lord: praise him, and magnify him for ever.

Our age is unlikely to take seriously the prospect even of angels singing, let alone, as the *Benedicite* continues, the "stars of heaven," "frost and cold," or "ice and snow." We may allow that the "fowls of the air" and even, albeit somewhat new-age-ily, the "whales" might sing, but surely not in order to "bless the Lord." Rare would be the pastor who numbered brute beasts and inanimate objects among the denizens of his choir stalls.

For early Christian theologians, whose intellectual language was not that of modern atomization but of a more Platonic participation, the biblical witness to the world singing God's praises made sense. We see this, for example, in St Augustine's commentary on Psalm 87. The psalmist sings of Babylon, famous for its repression of God's chosen people, returning to God's friendship via the heavenly city of Jerusalem, built on the foundations of Sion. Augustine relates the motif of "foundation" to Christ as foundation stone of the Church. As the sinful city of Babylon will be redeemed in the heavenly Jerusalem, so God is born into the sinful world of human flesh. The creator is present in the creation, for its redemption. So, he writes, "as the Godhead is in every place, from every place symbols may be taken for it; and not being any of these things in external properties, it can be everything in figure." So it is that sacred scripture can describe Christ as door, gate, sheepfold, or shepherd, without indicating that he absolutely is any of these things; but all these things do, as it were, symbolize, and so "name" God in their various capacities. The created universe is replete with significance, revealing the unknowable God. And so, the Psalmist concludes, since all things dwell in God, vivified by the wellspring of his presence, all rejoice and praise.

Dionysius is perhaps best known for his apophatic or negative theology, which is to say that God as unknowable can be "known" only through unknowing. Yet for all that one cannot know what God is, Dionysius does devote an entire treatise to the *Divine Names*. This describes creation as a unified, harmonic hymn of praise. We cannot, he writes in the first chapter, either "express or conceive what the One, the Unknown, the beyond-being self-existing Good is,"[2] but as this sentence betrays, we can at least know *that* there is One, unknown, beyond-being and Good. These are not meaningless designations or arbitrary terms. They are names discerned,

---

2 *Divine Names* 1.6.

not given, harmonies in which to join, not new tunes to invent. Even if the Devil really did have the best tunes, it would only be because he had stolen them from God.

The primary name of God for Dionysius, as for Proclus, is the Good, because it is out of nothing but goodness that being is generated. Being therefore is a name secondary to the Good. These are Platonic derivations, but in Divine Names 2.1, Dionysius offers the authority of scripture to bolster both. This is not some veil of biblical respectability applied as an afterthought to cover an otherwise naked Platonism. Dionysius maintains that only the "divine oracles," as he calls the Scriptures, should be used to name God. All names, he insists, apply to the three persons of the Godhead indivisibly. God reveals himself to Moses in the burning bush as "I am he, who is" (Exodus 3:14), and again in Revelation as "He who is, who was, and who is to come" (Revelation 1:8). Dionysius identifies these three tenses as the persons of the triune Godhead. The first two refer to the Father and the Son, who said "I and the Father are One" (John 10:30); the last, to the Holy Spirit. Yet the highest name for God remains not being, but the Good. The Divine Word, Christ, says that "none is good except God alone" (Mark 10:18), and yet refers to himself as good (Matthew 20:15). The Spirit is referred to as good in the revelation to the prophet Nehemiah (9:20). That God alone is good signifies the transcendence of divine goodness, its excellence beyond even the highest goodness in creation. Thus goodness, rather than being, expresses the "essential nature" of God insofar as due reverence permits.

In the Good and all the subsequent names that flow from it, Dionysius continues, consists the entirety of reality. All beings share in the goodness, truth, beauty, and oneness of God; and because of this, one can discern and so name something of God truly from absolutely every being. As Dionysius writes in the Divine Names, "the Good . . . is not entirely uncommunicated to any single created being, but benignly sheds forth its superessential ray."[3] All things communicate God's being to some extent; that is to say, all things "name" God by what they are.

Yet here we reach the limits of what cataphatic or positive speech can say about God and finally discover him as unnamable and unknowable. It is not so much a paradox that God can be named by all names and yet by none of them; rather, it is precisely because God can be named by all names that he excels them all, and so cannot be limited to any of them, not even to the highest name of the Good.

---

3   Divine Names 1.2.

This is not merely some Platonic fancy. The four-letter name of God in Hebrew tradition, as revealed to Moses in the burning bush, is never spoken by observant Jews. It is written in the Bible, but never read aloud, the reader substituting Adonai, the Hebrew word for "Lord," in its place. The Divine Name is referred to reverentially as the *shem ha shem,* "Name of Names." Dionysius no doubt picks up on this in the reference his master St Paul makes in the ancient, pre-Pauline Christological hymn of Philippians 2:9 to the "Name above every Name" at which every knee should bow, identified there as the Holy Name of Jesus. Not for nothing have the churches of the East developed so highly the meditation upon the Holy Name in the famous Jesus Prayer, or the Western Church devoted a feast to it; for the Name "Jesus," *Yeshua* in Hebrew, means "God saves."

In one simple word, the import of the Divine Word, second person of the Trinity, is revealed. The nature of God is to save. Indeed, he becomes incarnate not to condemn the world but to save the world. This, insofar as we can perceive it, is the ultimate meaning of being, the ultimate "Name" of which all beings are lesser reflections: the gift of salvation.

HYMNING

OW CAN ONE EXPRESS THE INCOMPREHENSI-
ble? Even as any name pertaining to God is revealed, it must
at the same instant be covered up, a paradox St Augustine
struggles with in the opening of his book *De Doctrina Christiana*. After
discussing the nature of God, he asks:

> Have I said anything, solemnly uttered anything that is worthy of
> God? On the contrary, all I feel I have done is to wish to say some-
> thing . . . because God is inexpressible; and if what has been said
> by me were inexpressible, it would not have been said. And from
> this it follows that God is not to be called inexpressible, because
> when even this is said about him, something is being expressed.[1]

Ever the Platonist, Augustine elsewhere advises that "if you understand
something, it is not God."[2] Rather, one must go beyond understanding,
beyond language, and into the experience of divine silence if one is to
know the unknowable God, and by that knowing become one with him.

Before his baptism, St Augustine had been reading the Platonists: particularly, it seems, those of Plotinus's school. Back in 386 in Milan, he had
tried by himself to achieve the mystical heights expressed by Plotinus, who
wrote of "the flight of the alone to the alone,"[3] wherein one seeks by inward
meditation the grounds of one's own soul beyond being, and passes to the
formlessness of the One beyond all concepts and thinking. Augustine did
enjoy some fleeting success, a glimpse of eternity, through these Platonic
spiritual exercises in which he engaged alone. Yet it was the Christian ser-
mons of the Bishop of Milan, Ambrose, that brought those Platonic spiritual
insights to full fruition. Ultimately, Augustine experienced his deepest vision
of God not in solitary meditation but in the shared religious experience
of the Church, the community of the saints into which he was baptized.

1 *De Doctrina Christiana* 1.5 in Augustine and Hill, *Teaching Christianity: De Doctrina Christiana*.
2 Sermon 117.5, on John 1.
3 *Ennead* 6.9.11.

The most momentous of these, which marks the real turning point of his *Confessions*, is the experience of divine silence he received through meditation with his mother, Monica, shortly after his baptism in AD 387 and before her death.[4] They were alone in a villa in Ostia, the port town of Rome near the mouth of the Tiber, looking out onto the garden. They had been discussing spiritual matters, and came to muse on what the eternal life of the saints would be like, "which eye has not seen nor ear heard, nor has risen into the human heart." From there, together, they embarked upon an extraordinary *itinerarium mentis*:

> We wandered through all bodily things, and to the heaven itself, where the sun and moon and stars shed light over the earth. Still we kept soaring, deeper in thought and speech and wonder at your works. We came into our minds and transcended them, close enough to touch on the realm of unfailing plenty from which you feed Israel forever with the food of truth. There, life is Wisdom, through whom are made all things which ever were or ever shall be; yet she herself is not made, but is just as she was and ever shall be — or to put it better, "was" and "shall be" are not in her, but only Being itself, because she is eternal (for "to have been" and "to come to be" is not to be eternal). And while we were speaking and straining after her, with heart at bursting point, we just about made contact with her — and we breathed, and left the first fruits of the Spirit bound there, and returned to the noise of our own mouth, where a word both begins and finishes. But what is like your Word, our Lord, which endures in itself without aging and makes all things new?[5]

At first reading, this may seem a rather talkative, even loquacious, way of expressing what I want to maintain is wordless union. It is in conversation that Augustine makes his spiritual ascent, not through fostering a Zen-like indifference to verbal and visual images in silent meditation: in conversation, further, not with great philosophers or sages, but with his unlettered mother of ostensibly simple faith. Together, they soar into the heavens by digging further down into their minds, in thought and speech. Paradoxical as it may seem, this is the practical expression of Augustine's earlier intuition of God as "higher than my highest height and deeper than my innermost being."[6] And in this there is really no paradox at all: it is

---

4   *Confessions* 9.10 (my translation).
5   *Confessions* 9.10.24.
6   *Deus interior intimo meo et superior summo*, Augustine *Confessions* 3.6.11.

perfectly consistent with Plotinus's Platonic logic of all things unfolding from the One. To follow the Delphic maxim and to know oneself truly is to know one's source and origin. Plotinus would surely sympathize, too, with Augustine's flight to Wisdom, the pursuit of philosophy, here in her Jewish literary personification. He would also recognize Augustine's conviction that it is at the point where language begins to fail that one begins to touch upon Wisdom. It happens at that liminal juncture where the usual terms of being and time, "bodily things" and verbal tenses of past and futurity, unravel in the face of Being itself and eternity. For the One beyond being is thereby beyond understanding.

Augustine speaks — and it is worth remembering that ancient texts were written to be read aloud — to express what can be expressed of that which is beyond comprehension. Yet he contrasts two very different kinds of expression. After their experience, he and Monica return to the ordinary everyday speech of the day-to-day world, to the "words of their own mouth" and their clear beginnings and endings, their grammatical containment and ordering of reality in sentences and syntax. Yet what they experienced, albeit tentatively, was the endless Word without origin, the Word who was made flesh, and whom Augustine identifies here with the creative Wisdom of God: the simple Word from which all words derive.

Where Augustine differs from Plotinus is in his discovery that we do this, not alone, but in communion with one another. Plotinus tries to avoid reducing this material realm to an unfortunate evil of debatable necessity. But at times he does stray in that direction, making the realm of beings — which means, among things, one another — something best escaped. L'infer, c'est les autres. If any mere converse with fellow human beings could lead one to the heights of philosophy, it would surely be with elite philosophers, urbane sages of Alexandria or the Academy. One can hardly imagine Plotinus reaching the One in the company of an elderly Christian woman of nomadic Berber stock. Such an ordinary soul might be capable of accidentally stumbling onto true opinion and leading others there, but not of expounding the true foundations necessary for firm philosophical knowledge. For Augustine, though, even the simple have recourse to a fount of guaranteed truth – the Scriptures, which are the closest mediation of that unspeakable, unifying Word to which human words can attain. It is in the discussion of these many words that human beings, not despite their multiplicity but through communion with one another, can touch upon divinity.

Yet the meeting point of words and the Word is itself non-verbal. The cardinal point of the experience Augustine relates, it seems to me, is when they finish speaking, and after the eternal instant of a single, pounding heart-beat, they "breathe." The word might also be translated "sigh," though this perhaps bears unwanted connotations of medieval courtly love or Byronic romanticism. I imagine it more as a breath that has been held some time, perhaps without realizing it, and is finally let out with relief. Before they returned to the world of physical words, articulated by lips, this wordless exhalation united him and his mother with the voiceless Word in a deeper intimacy than either had experienced before. In case I seem to be making too much of a single verb here, the sense is borne out by Augustine's reference to the "first fruits of the Spirit," a quotation from St Paul's Epistle to the Romans (8:23). A few verses later in the same letter Paul writes of the Spirit helping "us in our weakness; for we do not know how to pray as we ought, but the Spirit himself intercedes for us *with sighs too deep for words*" (Romans 8:26). It is not by our verbosity, the heaping up of endless phrases, but in the wordless language of the Divine Spirit, the breath of God which carries his silent Word, that we are lifted together into the knowledge that passes all understanding, that exceeds all merely human words, and so brings us into contact with divine Wisdom. In the silence after words, the incomprehensible Word finds perfect expression.

Augustine attempts to exposit the incomprehensible silence of God primarily by reference to speech. About song, and music more generally, he is ambivalent. He did write an entire treatise on music under the straightforward title of De Musica, in which he treats music, and in particular the inborn human sense of rhythm, as a mediation of divine order in the cosmos. Yet when it comes to actual music he is torn between taking it as an aid to godliness, particularly in the beautiful chant settings of the Psalms, or as a luxurious distraction.[7] This is perhaps indicative of the legacy of Plotinus upon him, that element of distrust towards the sensory and sensual building on Augustine's suspicion of the flesh, which still lingered from his Manichean past.

Given the higher place given to the sensible realm by Dionysius's Eastern strand of Platonism, it is perhaps unsurprising that he is far less reserved about the goodness of music: so much so that he grounds his theory of language not so much in speech as in song. While all things bear the name of God in their own degree, even all those names together fail to describe God. This is because God is beyond being, and so beyond intellection and beyond articulation in anything like normal speech. Yet this does not mean we cannot articulate anything of God at all. What we say about God will

---

7 *Confessions* 10.33.

ultimately always be untrue; or rather, incapable of attaining to the fullness of truth. We must simultaneously affirm all names of God, and deny them.

We may not speak truly about God. We may nonetheless speak truly to God. We may join in the cosmic choir that names and un-names God for all time. The purpose of language is not to describe God so much as to praise God, and this act of praise, properly speaking, is to join in God's own self-expression. As in Augustine's experience, the reversion to silence via language orients us and lifts us towards the silent One from whom all names derive. The difference is that Dionysius finds in music a closer analogue than speech alone to the silent, divine Word.

Dionysius calls this proper use of language "hymning." Yet it is not restricted to creatures with larynxes. In a short passage replete with Platonic terminology, he explains how hymning constitutes the work of everything that lives:

> For the beyond-living and life-springing Life is both Cause of all life, and is generative, and completive, and dividing of life; it is to be celebrated from every life . . . and contemplated, and sung by every life; . . . [it is] without need of but rather beyond-full of life, life-causing yet beyond-living, or however one might praise the Life which is unutterable by human speech. [8]

Here Dionysius follows Plotinus in designating God as the Good who is beyond being. This is a necessary consequence of Parmenides' principle, expressed in Plato's dialogue of the same name and repeated in the Phaedrus and Timaeus, that intelligibility is the very meaning of being.[9] As the rays of the sun give beings both growth and nourishment to life and the possibility of seeing one another, so the rays of divine goodness give both being and intelligibility to all things. These are inseparable: there can be no unintelligible being or non-existent intelligible.

This leads to the fundamental division between Platonic and materialist thought: while materialists see physical things as the only realities, for the Platonist, thoughts too are real. In fact, thoughts are more real than material things because they are more intelligible. I can conceive of a perfect circle, but I could never draw or make one, or even perceive one with my senses, for there is no perfect circle in the material realm: the idea of the circle is more truly a circle than any instantiation. So, too, with universals such as love or goodness: they are conceptually more perfect than their

---

8   Divine Names 6.3.
9   Phaedrus 247c.7–8, Timaeus 27d6–28a3.

instantiations in any person, however loving or good, since our love and goodness can only ever be a flawed approximation of the ideal. The truly real is the truly intelligible.

Think for a moment of the mathematical laws that govern the universe. We cannot maintain that they are mere signs we have mapped onto the terrain, as it were: they would be true whether or not humans were able to measure and perceive them. Indeed, the universe could not exist without them. Yet the laws of number and geometry would be true whether the universe existed or not. Their language is not an external addition to reality, but part of its very fabric.

In the passage above, Dionysius connects generation with division. Abstract ideas give unity to beings, but also distinction. If we go to the zoo, we can pick out the monkeys from the antelopes because we have the ideas of monkey and antelope that identify like with like, but simultaneously differentiate unlike from unlike. We can say then that without exception all beings share both in unity and in differentiation, in sameness and multiplicity. Putting that into Platonic terms, every being participates in both the idea or form of the One and the form of the many. To be is to be in some respects the same as other beings, and in other respects different; and in the very act of asserting this we admit that to be is a matter of *intelligibility* as one and many.

Oneness and multiplicity are both intelligible concepts, and are therefore real, unless we want to maintain that thoughts have no reality. Yet one is more necessary than the other. It is impossible to conceive of multiplicity without the concept of oneness, since multiplicity is basically the idea of lots of "ones." Oneness precedes multiplicity; multiplicity results from the idea of "one" repeated in sequence. Oneness is the prerequisite of multiplicity; or, to return to Dionysian language, the One *generates* the many.

All beings share in oneness and multiplicity, and as such are themselves divisible. This is obviously true of a person, who is physically divisible into a vast array of fleshy parts, but also conceptually differentiable as, say, European, Italian, woman, wife, mother, depressive, libertarian, and optometrist, among any other categories in which she may exist. It is true even of atoms, not only because they can (despite the literal meaning of their name) be split, but because they themselves are many and different from one another.

The only "thing" of which divisibility is not true is the idea of the One itself. It is the only form in which all beings share, from grains of sand to the form of the monkey or the idea of happiness, each of which comprise multiple component parts. So, the One is the measure of all things.[10] All

---

10   *Ennead* 6.8.18.3.

beings are dependent on it: there must be oneness for anything to exist. It is the principle by which differentiation, and hence existence, are possible.

The materialist answer to this is that there is no such thing as sameness: sameness is a category imposed by the mind for the sake of convenience, but really, no two things share in any single, same universal property. There is no such thing, say, as "man" or "woman," except for a mental construct shared or imposed by humans as a social construct. No two men or two women actually have any real, universal sameness between them, because universals are not material and therefore are not real. "Man" and "woman" do not exist. Only particular beings exist, whom we happen to categorize as men and women. To be consistent, the materialist would have to accept that "human" is similarly just a social construct. Who is or is not, in particular, a human is then up for grabs. One could quite legitimately reprogram society — which does not, of course, really exist save as a conglomerate of individuals — to recognize some beings we once considered human no longer to be so. Certain societies have of course already achieved this dubious accolade.

In contrast to such nominalism, the Platonic commitment to the reality of sameness, and so the reality of difference, gives rise to two vital and complementary principles. While there must be oneness for anything to exist, there must also be multiplicity. So, because the idea of the one admits no divisibility or differentiation, *the One is not a being*. And because the One is not a being, and being is defined by intelligibility, *the One is not intelligible*.

The Platonic One is certainly not a "Supreme Being." Rather, the One is the condition by which all beings exist, while remaining itself beyond the categories of being and non-being. The One generates by dividing, but is itself the sole undivided, ungenerated, unintelligible beyond-being. Plotinus goes so far as to describe the One as "nothing," "not anything," and "not existing."[11] Hence, Dionysius will describe God as "being" only insofar as he is "beyond-being."

Nor is the One a "First Cause." Plotinus is reluctant even to describe the One as a "cause" at all in any conventional sense,[12] but only insofar as all being is dependent on the One. He wants to avoid the causal sense that the One is acting as some "other" upon its dependents, since in the One, there can be no otherness.[13] To return to the metaphor of the sun, the One is not an object giving light but is the light itself.[14]

---

11 *Ennead* 6.9.3.41, 6.9.3.38 – 41.
12 *Ennead* 6.9.3.49 – 52.
13 *Ennead* 6.9.8.24.
14 *Ennead* 5.5.7.13 – 23.

This is the technical sense of the causality Dionysius ascribes to God. Like Plotinus, he resists the sense of one "thing" acting upon another. We are not talking here about a domino rally. Rather, causality in this Platonic sense means the participation of "effects" in the unifying ideas they embody. Since they cannot come from nowhere, these effects, says Dionysius, "pre-exist in their causes."[15] For a thing to be is for it to unfold out of the "cause" in which is pre-exists; we might think of beings unraveling from potential into becoming, as long as we do not confuse what is a trans-temporal, metaphysical principle with actions governed by time and space. We are speaking, tentatively, about the relationship between form and matter.

God is the *generative* cause of all beings insofar as they pre-exist in him in undivided unity. The *division* of beings is our participation, to varying degrees, in the indivisibility of the One who is beyond being. Hence, while Dionysius will say that God is "the life of living things and the being of beings,"[16] he is neither life nor being when considered in abstraction from the beings he generates: "the Being of all things is the divinity beyond Being."[17]

In the same breath as describing God as generative, Dionysius also calls him completive. All being are generated by God by an unfolding into multiplicity from his sublime and undivided unity; and yet, the Platonists opined, even as beings unfold from him, they are being refolded back into him and restored to perfection. God gives us existence but does not abandon us to fractured multiplicity, to drift apart as atoms. Our existence is defined by both procession from our source and return to it, in an ongoing tension that sustains being between unity and multiplicity.

Because God gives us existence, "the One" is not the highest name Dionysius or his Platonic predecessors discern in him. We have seen, too, that they will certainly not describe him as "being" without substantial qualification. As giver of being, the highest Platonic name for the One who is "not being, but excels beyond being"[18] is "the Good."

We have a name for the source of being derived not from the evidence of our senses, not mapped by us onto an external object, but discerned and unveiled by reason as the unquantifiable, ineffable One and Good. Even so, we can easily be led into error if we think the Platonists were speaking of the Good in primarily moral terms. Goodness is the source of being. So to be good in the technical use of the term is *to be most fully what*

---

15   *Divine Names* 2.8, 645D.
16   *Divine Names* 1.3, 589C.
17   *Celestial Hierarchy* 1.4, 177D.
18   *Republic* 508e.1–3.

one is.[19] Given that what a being is pre-exists in its "cause," the good for any being is unity with its cause; and ultimately the good of all beings is unity with the One, in which all beings are "enfolded." The One, then, is ultimate Good insofar as it generates beings and gives them the possibility to become what they truly are. We can now make out the circuitous loop of the Platonic universe, in which, as Plotinus put it, "for all things, the origin is their end."[20] To be is simultaneously to receive being passively from the One, via the variegated forms unfolding from it, and then, by those same forms in which each being participates, to return to unity. This Name, the highest Dionysius thinks we can properly utter, praises God for giving us both existence and salvation: in this, it is none other than that Name given above all other Names of Jesus, "God saves."

What we have not explored is how beings return to their source. While our generation as beings is passive on our part, the Platonists saw the motion of return as more active. It is a Platonic dictum that all things inherently desire what is good. Even when a desire is for something evil, that desire is predicated by the deeper desire to continue to exist, which in itself is good because existence is good. All things, the Platonists thought, possess an inherent yearning to continue to exist. Even stones do not suddenly collapse into dust. There is a certain tension holding them in place that keeps them in being, and hence keeps them intelligible as stones. All beings yearn for their continued being, which is to say for the Good.

Plotinus maintained that God has absolutely no need of anything, a sentiment with which Christian theologians would have to agree; but concomitantly, he argued, God also has no desire for anything.[21] The erotic pull is all one-way: from beings to the Good, via the collective Intellect. For him, Beauty was an effect of the Good rather than a proper name for the One and the Good, which he regarded as beyond beauty. Proclus refined this doctrine by arguing that the Good and Beautiful are indistinguishable in beings, and so beauty is not merely an effect but the manifestation of God's transcendent, beyond-being oneness within the created order of beings. We yearn therefore not only for an effect of God, but directly for God himself. Proclus portrayed this yearning as *eros*: love, in the burning, active sense of desire. He saw all things as erotically yearning for the Good according to their various measures: inanimate matter simply by being, living things by life, and intelligent beings by knowledge. Every being desires to be fully

---

19 See Proclus *Elements of Theology*, prop. 13.
20 *Ennead* 3.8.7.17.
21 *Ennead* 3.8.11.

itself in the harmonious order of existence that unfolds from the One and the Good. Hence, Proclus said, the Good can properly be called the Beautiful, because it is beauty that awakens desire. "In a sense," Douglas Hedley notes, "beauty is a bait — it lures the mind toward the intelligible."[22]

This makes the outfolding of existence from the One as much a participation in his beauty as in his goodness. Our yearning to return to him is not unrequited, as though we were gazing from afar at an aloof beauty. Rather, our yearning is drawn by the gravity of his erotic, enfolding pull, an active participation in the divine beauty. Following Proclus's lead, Dionysius took his thought to its conclusion and identified the entire Platonic circuit of procession and return with St John's proclamation that God is love: and so the Good and the Beautiful, we find, is synonymous not only with the gift of being and salvation but also with love. Love is the Divine presence in all things through generation, completion, and the maintaining of the tension between the two, which yields that differentiation without which love could not be. There can be no love without another. Beings exist, in short, to make love possible.

When we find our true love, we celebrate with gifts and songs. So, for Dionysius, celebratory song is the rightful response to the divine love that unites all things. Yet it is also, in a sense, God's own song. The Old Testament describes God as creating beings through speech, and in the New, John particularly identifies Christ himself as the creative Word of God. Dionysius combines these Semitic sensibilities with the Platonic identification of being and intelligibility. And so he portrays the whole of existence as the beautiful, yearning song of God. Playing on words, he said that God as the Beautiful (in Greek, *to kallos*), "calls" (*kalei*) all things back to him. He both generates beings and calls us back, like a lover, to himself. *Eros* does not just constitute "half" the circuit of being, our response to the Good: it defines the entire circuit. God is love, and beings' desire for him is the part each plays, according to capacity, in the cosmic harmony by which that love is manifested.

Dionysius's emphasis on song is a development of the theurgic Platonic tradition of Proclus, from whom he borrows the term "hymning" to explain familiar Platonic doctrines: for example, he describes effects as "hymning" their causes.[23] This no doubt reflects the grounding of his Christian religious life in the sung psalmody of the daily offices and the chanting of the Eucharist. Yet I do not think his use of "hymning" is merely dressing up

---

22   *The Iconic Imagination*, 74.

23   *Divine Names* 1.5.

Platonism in the garb of Christian cultus. Rather, hymning is what allows praise otherwise "unutterable by human speech."

While Proclus does speak of hymning, the pagan Platonic tradition had been predominantly visual in its metaphors for intellection. Plato's allegory of the Good as the all-illumining rays of a life-giving super-existent sun connects true being with true seeing. Plotinus maintained that all things are a "byproduct of contemplation" and indeed that all engage in "contemplation" of the Good themselves according to their proper measure. [24] Plotinus's word for "contemplation" is *theōria*, which literally means "vision." Images, he says, are of a higher order than verbal propositions, approvingly citing the Egyptian use of hieroglyphs over the blunt tool of an alphabet [25] (a position with which, as a speaker of Japanese, I have some sympathy). His great treatise on contemplation in *Ennead* 3.8 is framed largely in the language of images and reflections.

By recapitulating Platonic doctrine in musical rather than visual terms, Dionysius applies Judeo-Christian experience of God to deepen Plotinus's apophatic emphasis on the unknowability of the One. Because the One is beyond being, and so unintelligible, Plotinus wrote, "if you want to grasp the isolated and alone, you will not think." [26] If a picture paints a thousand words, music takes us to conceptions and intuitions transcending description in language. Nietzsche recognized this in his *Birth of Tragedy*, arguing (against Plato) that poetry is the most profoundly expressive form of language because it leaves space for meanings eluding prosaic description, and that music in its wordless expression communicates at a deeper level still.

To be is to be sung and to join in the song of our making. The Divine Word is beyond words, and so is better expressed as song: even the wordless song of the days and nights in the nineteenth Psalm, or the seas and whales in the *Benedicite*. It is a song in which even the stones can join; and so, without voice or vision, they join in the divine contemplation that is both their generative origin and their loving end. Ultimately then it is a song sung in that silence, the still, small voice of calm, which is revealed as the ultimate language of God. By joining it, we may touch *agnosia*: the unknowing of God beyond reason, beyond naming, and beyond being.

We are left with the nameless name of God, which we cannot speak but only sing in praise — and that only in silent response to love's gift of being and the experience of orientation towards unity. In this we will find some

---

24 *Ennead* 3.8.1; 3.8.8.26.
25 *Ennead* 5.5–6.
26 *Ennead* 5.3.13.

likeness with the inconceivable Name of Amida, in which Shinran tentatively discerns transcendent wisdom speaking praise in thanksgiving for the gift of the Vow. We have here two modes of "being as contemplation" in which one exists most fully by participating in ineffable Wisdom's contemplation of itself. The initiative in both cases begins with the transcendent and unchanging source, of which sentient beings, or intelligent souls, become thanks-giving instruments. There is undoubtedly a distinction to be made, in that Shin Buddhists would not claim to worship Amida as Christians are called to worship God. But even this distinction may not present as wide a gulf as it first seems. For while it is true that Christians worship God as one essentially other from ourselves, it is equally true that this worship is, in a profound sense, the work of God himself, by the power of his utterly immanent Spirit, breathing through us like the breath of a flute-player through his instrument. Liturgy, the work of the people, is at its core theurgy, the work of God. Both hymning and the *nembutsu* reveal reality as a harmonious song of self-emptying love, thanksgiving, and praise.

THE SAVING NAME

Ama no hara
furisake mirebu
Kasuga naru
Mikata no yama ni
ideshi tsuki kamo.

"If I look out over the plain of heaven,
    above the mountain of Mikasa in Kasuga
    has emerged the moon."
    —Abe no Nakamaru (AD 701–770),
            Kokin Wakashū 406

O N THE EVE OF LEAVING CHINA, ABE NO NAKA-
maru marveled that the moon illumining his present shore
was the very same shining on those he loved at home in Japan,
where he would soon return. This would become such a conventional motif
in Japanese poetry that its religious symbolism could easily be missed. The
moon traditionally represents enlightenment, and Kasuga, written in the
Chinese characters for the sun and the spring season, substitutes for the
Pure Land.

One might speculate here on the parallel use of springtime to represent
birth in the Pure Land and the rebirth of the Resurrection. This should not
prove too much of a surprise to the Catholic Christian, at least, for since
its earliest days, the Church adopted and shared cosmological and natural
signs with its pagan contemporaries. The sun for Plato represented, but was
quite clearly distinguished from, God as the unitary source of both life itself
and the light that gives us perception and knowledge of life.

The most famous portrayal of this comes in the Myth of the Cave in
the *Republic*, where those tethered in the gloom of a fire's lesser glow are
finally liberated into the full sunlight of day, where they can both see and be
with clarity. This motif was an obvious candidate for adoption by the early
Christians, whose savior rose in Spring and on "Sun-day," called himself the

Light of the World, and was himself God incarnate, Life, and Truth. Hence the orientation of churches eastwards, to face not Jerusalem as some might suppose but specifically to face the sun; and hence the growing conviction of Emperor Constantine that the god he worshipped as Sol Invictus, the Unconquered Sun, was for all his light a mere refraction of the one true God's Conquering Son.

In his poem, Abe no Nakamaru envisages the rays of Amida, the Buddha of boundless compassion and light, shining on all existence, everywhere: whether in China or Japan, whether shining from the sun or the moon. These terrestrial signs are celestially illuminated by the saving light of the reality both utterly beyond and intimately within them.

The nominalism that secular modernity has inherited from William of Ockham insists that there is no fundamental meaning to being, and that names are simply convenient mental constructs more or less shared between different, individual minds. In contrast, Shinran and Dionysius alike see the cosmos as itself radiant with a glory beyond all comprehension and that yet mysteriously self-manifests not as an impersonal force but with a specific and real *character*: that is to say a true "name" beyond names, in which all names share some vague but nonetheless real part.

We need to get away again from the textbook simplification that Buddhists see the world as entirely an illusion, especially if it leads us to think Buddhism is basically nominalist. For Shinran, the Pure Land, the *nembutsu*, and the Name of Amida are not merely "fingers pointing at a moon," life rafts to be thrown back into the sea when we safely reach the shore. Rather, they are names expressing true reality insofar as it can be expressed. Reality consists in the Name, rather than the name constituting nothing more than a convention imposed by, or even for the sake of, human minds. This is the opposite of nominalism, which assumes names are more or less arbitrarily imposed by conscious entities as a sort of map on an external reality.

For Shinran, Amida is not a merely human concept or myth to be grown out of. Rather, the very Name of Amida Buddha is the expression of his salvific power. The word "salvific" may seem like an all-too-Christian interpolation, but the verb *tasukeru*, "to save," is one Shinran himself uses. It is the other traditions of Buddhism — the "Path of Sages," as he puts it — that are *upāyas* (expedient or saving "means") like the proverbial moonlit finger. They are to be respected as such. Nonetheless, Shinran deliberately turned away from them to take refuge in the real truth to which they only pointed. That truth was the Name of Amida, its recitation in the *nembutsu* with the *shinjin* of deep entrusting in his Vow, and rebirth in the Pure Land.

We have already explored the oneness of the Name and Vow of Amida. The Name of Amida in itself means "unbounded light," but when Shin Buddhists speak of the Name they are referring specifically to the formulation of the *nembutsu* in which the name is recited: *Namu Amida Butsu*. *Namu* is both the Buddha's call to take refuge in him and our very act of taking refuge in response to this call. The Name cannot be isolated from its invocation. This is because the Name makes the Vow known to us, which in turn elicits *shinjin*, that is, our trust, refuge, or "faith" in that Vow.

In chapter 11 of the *Tannishō*, Yuien-bo confronts the heresy that the Name and Vow can be considered separately, as though one might take refuge in the Vow without the recitation of the Name in the *nembutsu*, or conversely might receive enlightenment through saying the Name without taking refuge in the Vow. The nominalist would say the name for anything is arbitrary and can be separated from what it refers to. Shinran expressly rejects this view. *Shinjin* cannot be separated from the Name of Amida. The Vow is effected, or perhaps better said realized, through the *shinjin* expressed in the *nembutsu* — which is to keep the Buddha (*butsu*) in mind (*nen*) while saying his Name.

I am being deliberately very wary in my language about the *nembutsu*. In a Shin Buddhist temple one will find people saying the *nembutsu* over and over again. And even in general conversation Shin Buddhists might from time to time interject "Namu Amida Butsu" or its abbreviated form of "Namandabu" to express thanksgiving or wonder in the way an Evangelical Christian might proclaim *extempore* a "praise be" or "amen." From a phenomenological or anthropological perspective, we might be tempted to say these Buddhists are engaging in religious practice — chanting, reciting, or even praying the Name just like their Christian counterparts.

This is where the "religious studies" mentality of supposed objectivity shows its weakness, obliging us to turn to philosophy and theology proper. From the perspective of Shin Buddhism the "practice" of "saying" the *nembutsu* is neither *our* practice nor just a declaration of faith. In fact Shinran explicitly calls it "no-practice" because it doesn't have its genesis in us but in the working of Amida. So we find ourselves straining against the conventional use of words, as one might expect of this no-practice that is supposed to bring us to a realization beyond rational cognition. At best, we might say that when it is said in true *shinjin*, the *nembutsu* is the inconceivable working of the Vow, such that the Name of true reality *speaks itself* through the invoker.

The Name, then, breaks the alterity between Buddha and sentient beings through its own self-saying, yet without dissolving their difference. Professor

Kemmyo Taira Sato, head priest of the Three Wheels Temple in London, offers an analogy of this truth in a conversation he had with Professor Kō Hirasawa, former Provost of Kyoto University. Hirosawa had lived with the great D. T. Suzuki for the last three years of his life. He himself was now 95 years old and sick in hospital. Clearly he had been rather sprightly when still a youthful 94:

> Last autumn I climbed the Higashiyama Mountains in Kyoto and came upon a pine tree and a maple tree standing side by side. It was a beautiful sight. Had I chanced on it previously, what I would probably have found beautiful was the contrast between the green of the pine and the red of the maple. But I did not feel that way now. Instead I was struck by the beauty I saw in the way the green of the pine and the red of the maple melted into one another without either one being lost. [1]

This led Professor Sato to recall the definition of enlightenment in the *Avatamsaka Sūtra* as "the true world in which different individual entities fuse into oneness without any obstruction, all being interrelated and none losing that which integrally makes them what they are." [2]

The Name in Shin Buddhism, then, does not "just" represent but actually is the true "unbounded light" which reveals and effects the diversity that constitutes being and its intelligibility — and through and in that diversity, the indivisible unity which is beyond being and so beyond reason, and which can therefore be realized only through unknowing. Yuien-bo concludes, then, that the Name and Vow are one because Shinran describes both as *acintya*, "inconceivable," beyond knowing. This is not to say that the Name is a conceptual vacuum, a placeholder for an unintelligible "nothingness" like the emptiness of Western nihilism. For Dionysius, God beyond being is manifested in the person of Christ, about whom we can know a good deal, and the Name of Amida is no more dispensable for Shinran than is the name of Christ for the Areopagite. To give some sense of what Amida's Name might mean, we will have to journey to his Pure Land.

---

1   Kemmyo Taira Sato, *Great Living: In the Pure Encounter Between Master and Disciple* (NY: American Buddhist Study Center Press, 2010), 68.
2   Ibid.

THE PURE LAND
AND THEOSIS

> The Buddha and land are the fulfilled Buddha and fulfilled land.
> All of this is none other than the ocean of true reality or suchness,
> the inconceivable Vow. This is the central purport of the Larger
> sutra of Immeasurable Life, the genuine significance of the true
> essence of Other Power.[1]

T HE VICE-ABBOT OF SHUNKOIN, A ZEN MONASTERY
in Kyoto, is well-known for his ministry to foreigners through
English-language Zazen and teaching sessions. The temple itself is
also known for its rock garden. Painstakingly raked patterns of pebbles seem
to flow around its black boulders. I had read that such gardens were visual
representations of the impermanence of things, and had always assumed
that they were so carefully raked for the sake of the viewer's meditative
practice; discerning the sea in stones and thus transcending dualism to see
things as they really are. Maybe this is so. But what I found out from one
of the Vice-Abbot's dharma talks was that the deeper significance of the rock
garden is not so much in the serene beauty admirers so enjoy as in the act
of raking itself. If the gardener focuses on the lines he has already made,
what is behind his rake, as it were, the line he is making at that moment
will wobble, will not be smooth. To make the lines smooth he must leave
behind what has passed and rest his attention solely in the present moment.
Attachment to the past is a delusion, for the past no longer exists. There is
only ever the intersection of past and future.

Zen Buddhism is largely skeptical of metaphysics. This is a considerable
pitfall for any comparison with ontologically-grounded Western thought.
Many Buddhist and Christian scholars would aver that our philosophical
basis is so radically different that any such comparison is liable to prove
fruitless or misleading,[2] and it is a charge to which we must be sensitive.

---

1   Kyōgyōshinshō 2.101 in Shinran, *The Collected Works of Shinran*, 68.
2   For a summary and rebuttal of such views see Gordon D. Kaufman, "Some Buddhist

We may think we are comparing apples with pears when really we are comparing them with snails. To speak of comparative Christian and Buddhist "metaphysics" could be a category mistake as blatant as comparing arboreal fruits with mollusks.

Yet Shin Buddhists have not unanimously shared the general Buddhist opposition to metaphysical speculation. The mid-twentieth-century Kyoto School of philosophers, while not all Shin Buddhists themselves, were strongly influenced by the thought of Shinran and his successors, which they read in conjunction with their German contemporary, Heidegger. Earlier still, in 1893 the Shin cleric Kiyozawa Manshi published his controversial *A Skeleton of Philosophy of Religion*, which treats explicitly of metaphysics and is influential in the Ōtani school of Shin Buddhist thought to this day.

Nor is Buddhism per se necessarily so averse to metaphysics as some might profess. The contemporary Australian Shin Buddhist scholar and cleric John Paraskevopoulos, who has written several short and readily available books on the Shin tradition, argues that Shinran's own thought represents the culmination of a certain metaphysical strand of Mahāyāna thought. In Nāgārjuna's non-dualistic identification of samsara with nirvana as *śūnyatā* ("emptiness"), Paraskevopoulos discerns a "complex ontology which sought to integrate existence in its entirety, and at all its levels, with Suchness."[3] He finds in the Pure Land path the most developed understanding of *śūnyatā* not as mere "Void," but as a womb-like emptiness of "fullness and plenitude," "the inexhaustible font of all merits, virtues, wisdom, and compassion," and as such "a true and existing reality which both transcends and suffuses all things."[4] Whether we regard this language as strictly ontological or not, and whatever status we accord the term "metaphysics," it should be clear that there is at least some basis for comparison even with the more ontologically driven species of Western theistic thought.

That said, even if we remain heedful of more general Buddhist skepticism towards metaphysics and ontology, the Pure Land Shinran describes should certainly not be understood as a straightforwardly ontologically "other" realm. It need be taken no more literally than Isaiah's depictions of the child playing on the asps' den or the lion lying with the lamb. In a sense redolent to the Christian of Christ's teaching that the Kingdom is

---

Presuppositions: Metaphysical A Response to Ryusei Takeda's Paper, 'Pure Land Buddhist View of Duhkha,'" *Buddhist-Christian Studies* 5 (1985): 25–48.

3 John Paraskevopoulos, "Conceptions of the Absolute in Mahayana Buddhism and Shinran," *Sacred Web*, no. 3 (1998): 128.

4 Paraskevopoulos, 137.

already "within you," Shinran teaches that the Pure Land (Jōdō) is, ultimately, neither identical to nor other than the Impure Land (edō) of samsara. One the one hand, Shinran does explicitly assert their difference, to the extent that he even speaks of a purgatorial "borderland" (henji) around the Pure Land where non-Shin Buddhists who have practiced other paths will achieve rebirth, where they can learn and prepare to be born again. Even there, they will find "happiness beyond knowing"[5] — that same word, fukashigi or in Sanskrit, acintya, again. This implies that for rebirth in the Pure Land one must transcend even the difference between knowing and unknowing. True knowing is unknowing. It could hardly get more Socratic. Yet where Shinran's Pure Land resonates more closely with the later Platonic tradition, is in its understanding that however wonderful any temporal realm or heaven may be (and without doubt, Shinran thinks such realms exist), they are still infinitely incomparable to the realization of oneness with the self-emptying reality that transcends all distinction.

For Shinran, the Pure Land is the compassionate embodiment of the Name, the Vow, and nirvana itself. This is comparable to how, for Dionysius, "heaven" indicates not a created realm but oneness with God. Descriptions of the purple clouds and bejeweled flowers of the Pure Land might bear comparison to biblical passages in Revelation or Isaiah about heaven, but even within Christian tradition there is no unanimous consensus on the metaphysical status of such motifs. Few would contend that the gold-paved streets of the heavenly city should be read as a literal description of a place. While the doctrine of the resurrection of the body persuades biblical scholars of a more voluntaristic mold that heaven will indeed be a literal reworking of the material earth because God has told us so, this is not the only possible reading. Jesus's own resurrection body displayed both physical and spiritual aspects: in some episodes he eats or breaks bread, while in others he can appear and vanish suddenly in a locked room. St Paul, too, writes that the "physical body" that is "sown in dishonor will be raised in glory" and as a "spiritual body" (1 Cor 15:44).

A comprehensive evaluation of biblical teaching on heaven has to take into account both physical and spiritual accounts of the resurrection, as the more Proclean strand of Christian Platonist tradition has done. Plato's Theaetetus (176b1) described the aim of human life as achieving "as far as possible likeness (homoiōsis) to (a) God." Plotinus and Proclus had described the aim of their philosophy as henosis, "becoming one" or "unification." Christian Platonists adopted the concept but adapted the terminology: Sts Clement of Alexandria

---

5 Lamp of the Latter Ages in Shinran, The Collected Works of Shinran, 527.

and Athanasius spoke of "being made God," applying for the first time in extant literature, respectively, the verb *theopoieō* and the noun *theopoiēsis*. The Cappadocian Fathers Gregory of Nazianzus and Gregory of Nyssa were more daring, adapting *henōsis* to their neologism of *theōsis*: "becoming God." Dionysius used these words as synonyms and added *koinōnia*, or "communion," as we have seen. For him, the descriptions of heaven and the resurrection point towards a union or "communion" with God that is ultimately beyond words or concepts and transcends the dichotomy of material versus spiritual, so that whether visible or invisible, "all things may be all in Christ."

Both Shinran and Dionysius are attempting to articulate a foundational reality which of itself is not a "being," but nonetheless permeates all dimensions of being, visible and invisible, with its radiance and invites us to realize union with itself. Far from a contentless "emptiness," Amida Buddha *as* Pure Land signifies the "emptying" of reality into an infinite plenitude of potential reality. As such, Amida constitutes a Name beyond names which is not a merely human marker of an external reality, but encompasses, effects and even *is* all reality.

Shinran does not treat the Pure Land as a mere symbol, any more than he does the Name of Amida or its recitation in the *nembutsu*. He does portray the Pure Land as an *upāya* pointing to nirvana, certainly, but only insofar as it really *is* nirvana. *Upāya* here is not a synonym for falsehood nor even for transience; rather, it is what the Shin scholar Bandō Shōjun (1932–2004) calls "the dynamic aspect of truth."[6] There is something of the iconic or sacramental about it from a Christian perspective. It is not a bare symbol that might arbitrarily be replaced with another in a nominalist sense. Rather it signifies and bequeaths meaning.

Like the divine Logos, Amida's Name is conceived of as a word beyond words that both expresses and constitutes true reality. The Pure Land is rooted in Amida's transcendent wisdom (in the form of act and motion), both grounding and sustaining all beings and working for their salvation. Things are given meaning not by the external imposition of names by will, whether mortal or divine, but by the Name that confers the gift of reality as spiritual liberation.

*   *   *

To return to the present question, then: how do we ascertain the meaning of our lives and that of the world around us?

---

6   Shojun Bando, "Shinran's Indebtedness to T'an-Luan," *Pacific World* 3, no. 2 (2000): 17–31.

Dionysius and Shinran do not offer the same answer. But their speculation on the relationship between naming and being reveals what we might tentatively call a close metaphysical overlap. They are certainly far closer to one another than to modern Western nominalism. I do not wish to suggest that these are identical doctrines, but they are at least analogous. They are closer too than the cosmetic similarities between Shin and Protestant thought.

In each case they see meaning as gift rather than something we make for ourselves. Neither sees this world and our identity in opposition to some greater, other reality. Neither views our everyday world as illusory or ultimately unnecessary, still less as fundamentally evil. Rather, they see all things as expressive of, and participating in, one ultimate and good truth. The everyday world of things is necessary for us to perceive that truth, and yet its totality does not exhaust that truth because, while the true and the good is in all things, it is none of them.

Neither Amida nor God is a being, not even the supreme being. Both are characterized by emptiness, yet not the nothingness of modernity but rather an infinite plenitude constantly outpouring. In each case true reality is in a sense the activity of emptying. Our own true selves, then, are likewise to be found in the emptying of the self that is false. There is an overlap here between Christ's teaching of taking up the Cross, reinforced by St Paul's notion of dying that Christ might live within,[7] and the Mahāyāna no-self doctrine. By such self-emptying we discover our shared identity in a Name that speaks itself from silence and is, by its very speaking, a gift of the "Other."

Shinran calls Buddhists to let the Name of Amida speak through them; Dionysius calls Christians to join in the cosmic praise of the One whose name means "God saves." Yet how can we presume to speak the incomprehensible and unspeakable? How can we hymn that which is beyond name and being?

In the next chapter, we will see how our guides see this being put into practice: through theurgy and *nembutsu*.

---

7 Galatians 2.20.

CHRIST, REVOLUTIONARY?

I do not understand my own actions. For I do not do what I want, but I do the very thing I hate. For I do not do the good I want, but the evil I do not want is what I do. — Romans 7:15, 19

THE ETHEREAL GYGES' RING OF THE INTERNET offers unparalleled opportunities for doing what we hate and getting addicted to it. We can click ourselves into well-stocked supermarkets of illicit lovers, people offering themselves up as commodities to be swiped up or swiped away; we can find ourselves sucked into porn vortices which drain away the days, and refine our sexual palette so specifically that we become sexually crippled by newfound and unwanted fetishes; we can start to find the screen more enticing than our wife or husband, who cannot live up to the voracity of the highly particular desires that the market has inculcated into us unawares. The same caveat can be applied to any number of other addictions, but the sexual is the most powerful, the most devastating, and the most easily manipulated of all. If the Church is obsessed with sex, it is so only as a mirror of the wider human society in which this most basic and most powerful drive is used to intensify even the most mundane transaction. Advertisers know this best of all, but whatever our daily business and whatever our marital status, we strive to look sexually attractive, which translates as "young."

This has always been so. It is new only in its scale, its sheer ubiquity. St Augustine had a notoriously heady sex life in his earlier years, and even when he became Christian he pleaded with God, "Give me chastity: but not yet!" He accounted for the strength of the sex drive by his theology of the Fall, maintaining that until the fateful fruit was tasted, Adam and Eve had complete and rational control over all their bodily functions. That sex was something shameful and secret, he thought obvious: why would brothels be hidden in the back streets except that nobody wants to be seen going in? Were it otherwise they would at the forefront of the busy public square, and like certain of the Cynics, we would mate unselfconsciously on the streets.

Yet Augustine could not have foreseen an age where photographs of beautiful and barely dressed young men and women peer down from billboards all around, or pop up on glowing screens to advertise the latest perfume, chocolate, motorbike, toothpaste, or electricity provider; still less, an age where one could watch and even join in with a whole range of sexual spectacles from behind a screen in one's own bedroom. Only twenty years ago, if you wanted to access pornography, prostitutes and swingers' clubs, you would have to do as Augustine did, and make the effort to find secret places. Now, on our smartphones, we hold a vast pornographic catalog in our hands throughout the day. We even give these things to our children.

There are libertines who think this is all really rather wonderful, the sort of people who are already, rather predictably, talking about introducing "porn literacy" to schools. They are, I suspect, the minority, and a childless (they might prefer "child-free") minority at that. But then, modernity itself seems to have little place for children. Their innocence is an inconvenience to the life of sexual liberation promised by the billboards and the screens. The consumer ideal perpetuated by advertisers is of youth, an eternity spent in one's early twenties, "unencumbered" by children and so perfectly placed to devote one's life to the consumption of luxury "experiences." Ironically, the desire for the appearance of youth confected by the market conspires against the very act of reproduction that would generate genuine youth, which is to say, children.

Again, Michel Houellebecq captures this well. His protagonists are almost always, as he describes himself in The Map and the Territory,[1] types of the "irresponsible bachelor." In the rare instances they are mentioned at all, children appear in only two contexts: either as unnamed nuisances, or as people you are not yet allowed to have sex with. Children are pretty much the last to remain in that category. Homosexuality is now viewed not only with tolerance and compassion, but as something in which to take pride, an ethical lifestyle choice that avoids contributing to the environmental evil of overpopulation. Advocates for consensual adult incest quietly gather muster. Despite the advocacy of pederasty and "cross-generational sexual encounters" by certain gender critical theorists, such as Gayle Rubin,[2] children remain the last untouchables. With their demanding dependence, lack of disposable income, and stubborn sexual unavailability, Houellebecq portrays children as the final obstacle to the atomized life of the ideal Western consumer.

---

1 Michel Houellebecq, The Map and the Territory (London: Vintage, 2012).
2 Gayle S. Rubin, "Thinking Sex: Notes for a Radical Theory of the Politics of Sexuality," in R. G. Parker & P. Aggleton (eds.), Culture, Society and Sexuality: A Reader (London: Psychology Press, 1999).

It does not take much theology to see that there is a contest within our desires between our nature and our will. Like the charioteer of Plato's *Phaedrus*, our reason pulls us to and fro between our appetites and emotions. I do not want to get fat, so I do not eat the second donut. I do not want to lose my wife and children, so I do not go home with the girl I met at the bar. Yet as long as nobody finds out, I might just slip on that ring of Gyges, turn invisible, lock the bathroom door: after all, nobody's getting hurt. It's only play between consenting adults.

It can be hard to know what we really want, and so what we should really do. Do we act morally only because we fear getting caught, by our parents, our spouse, or the all-seeing eye of God as Great Policeman in the Sky? Or perhaps to avoid the feeling of shame, which turns our stomachs but in the end is "only" something society has induced in us from an early age? How, in the end, do we distinguish between these and our natural desires? And if a desire is indeed natural, does that mean it should be gratified? Is desire itself fundamentally good, or bad?

Ask a non-believer, and many a believer too, and they will suppose that Christians behave because they think God is watching them, like the sinister Santa Claus who is "coming to town." You'd better watch out. A vague popular awareness of psychoanalytic and anthropological perspectives then starts to cast doubts. Might this God not be some sort of Freudian projection, an idealized father-figure as punisher and judge? A Catholic I knew at university used to turn the image of Mary he had in his bedroom to face away whenever he brought a girl home. Had this anything to do with reverence for that chief among saints, or was it really just a deep-seated shame at his absent mother's imagined disapproval?

"If you consider Christianity exclusively in its dogmatic or institutional expressions, one can obtain a deeply misleading view of European culture as one of radical disenchantment."[3] The reason God has fallen out of credibility in so much of Western society is the either-or mentality to which we have fallen captive. We live in a world of dualisms. The binaries of reason versus desire and of culture versus nature are born of the fundamental binary of God versus creature. If we cannot conceive that our desires may be simultaneously instinctive *and* rational, it is because we have lost sight of the intimacy between mind and matter. Consequently, when we distinguish cultural influences on our desires from natural instincts, and worse, widen the gap further to distinguish the human from the animal and the rest of the world, we have forgotten that our culture is part of our nature as very

---

3   Hedley, *The Iconic Imagination*, 78.

much *social* animals. And all this comes back to that differentiation of God, as being, from other beings, which makes it impossible for us to see that God might be working not in opposition to but precisely *through* our desires, our fears — and even perhaps through our shame. God is relegated to one of two places in the dualistic universe we have created: either as an unreal projection of our minds or a real and dominant mind in his own right. In either case, he is externalized and made either an approver of or obstacle to our desires.

All modern questions about our will, desires, and moral action are inescapably theological. This is so even if those questions presuppose the non existence of God, because the kind of God they are rejecting can only ever be the God of specific theological content. To reject "gods" *tout court* implies a certain polytheistic theology grounded in the univocity of being — the idea of gods as beings greater than us but of the same essence nevertheless. If such divinities exist, they are not what Christians would call God.

Early Christians were accused by the pagan Roman powers of atheism on the grounds that they rejected just these kinds of gods, or at least denied that such entities were gods. The accusation was fair. Whatever God was like, he was nothing like these gods. Angels and demons would be the closest parallel in the Christian mythos. For a Christian, the answer to the question of what God is like could only be answered comprehensively by reference to his self-revelation in Christ. All Christian theology is Christology. There is nothing un-Christlike in God. For this reason we should expect that in purely historical terms the development of Western thought, which was nurtured for centuries in Christian soil, would have Christological roots.

Echoing the earlier tale of two Islams, we can shed some light on modernity by telling a tale of two Christs. The modern Christ is the rebel and bachelor, the angry revolutionary who overthrows the tables in the Temple, and by his miracles and resurrection from the dead turns the natural order upside down, revealing the omnipotence of the divine will and calling the faithful to emulate his ways. The older Christ is the iconic figure who reveals the world as divine self-emptying, and the divine will as one with God's nature as love and the Good. One exhorts revolution, the other harmony.

Dionysius's Christ certainly tends more towards the latter. For him, the Incarnation is like an icon, signifying how God's work and God's will are active within the whole realm of nature. We will see that the sacramental rituals Dionysius develops from Platonic theurgic magic become the channel of God's salvific will, which is one with his nature, through the material world — working through the hands and hearts of humans and the spiritual intelligences of saints and angels. We will see too the resonances between Dionysius's Christian theurgy and Shinran's Buddhist practice of the *nembutsu*. Understood through his doctrine of other-power, the recitation of the Name of Amida is not something a "practitioner" does, but is the Name speaking itself through sentient beings. As such, it is consonant with the broader Mahāyāna emphasis on no-self. With parallels to St Paul's articulation of Christian kenosis and entering the mind of the self-emptying Christ, Shinran speaks of becoming truly who one is by losing one's self. Shinran's world of self-emptying plenitude is far closer to the sacramental world of Dionysius than to the bare materialism of Western modernity. Together, our two sages show how Buddhists, Christians, and Platonic theists more broadly share a similar vision of an enchanted cosmos, replete with salvific intent. This sacramental worldview commends a communitarian, ecologically-oriented morality that takes human desire seriously as an aspect of the supernaturalized realm of nature, rather than in opposition to it.

The other, revolutionary, Christ is often framed as a prophet of social justice. That the Church should advocate for justice is uncontroversial, but the precise meaning of the epithet "social" preceding it is open to a variety of interpretations. Since its advent in South America halfway through the last century, Liberation Theology has so thoroughly penetrated our institutions of formation, our liturgy, and our homilies that inevitably it has also penetrated our thought. After all, *lex orandi, lex credendi*: what we pray is what we believe. To the earlier Liberation Theologians, social justice meant the prioritization of the Church's resources to the material improvement of the living conditions of the poor. If necessary — and sometimes it really was — Christians, they said, should join revolutionaries to overthrow corrupt and oppressive regimes. But more than that, capitalism itself was seen as a structure embedding sinfulness which needs to be overthrown before any attention is paid to sin as the spiritual condition of individuals.

In baptismal homilies, I have sometimes tried to sweeten the pill of Original Sin by translating it into Liberationist terms, such as "structural" or "social." I have made excuses for myself or others in Confession, saying, never mind: we were bound to do this or that, all things considered, under the circumstances. As I watched the 2020 American race riots on Japanese TV, I wondered how much this had primed my mind to accept the burning of cars on streets and the assault of police officers as ineluctable and excusable excess born not of individual ill-will or irresponsibility but wholly of an oppressive social system.

As an Englishman I have considerable sympathy for disarming civilians and most of the Police — only a small number of our officers are trained to carry firearms. But when we blame "society" for a violent shooting instead of the indiscipline or iniquity of certain policemen (or even certain groups of policemen), or blame "society" for violent riots rather than their individual propagators, we erode both agency and responsibility. We do not thereby just excuse other people's faults, but also our own. My mobile phone may have components made by child slaves in Africa, but I can't help it because I am stuck without agency in the deterministic realm of structural sin and, besides, think of all the good I can do by using it to post photos of the latest protest or demonstration on Instagram. It is as though I can offset the sin of the bitten Apple in the same way I offset my carbon emissions — another unfortunate side-effect of structural sin which, as a mere cog in the great machine of society, I cannot realistically be expected to avoid. It's all the big corporations' fault, or my parents' generation's fault — just as long as it isn't my fault, it doesn't matter whose it is.

But in the end, Christ will not judge society and find it wanting. He will judge me. Anything that dilutes the pressing need for individual contrition, repentance, and reform is in danger of perpetuating a literally damning contradiction of the Gospel. God may achieve the salvation of societies through the salvation of individuals, but it is presumptuous to suppose the Church can achieve the salvation of individuals through the salvation of society. Liberation theology teaches us that solving the problem of poverty and inequality, which frankly is as insoluble as the problem of human nature, will lead to a great upsurge in devotion to God and a renewal of personal morality; remove the need to sin, and you will remove sin itself. Ironically, this plays into the hands of those who want to say that problems like domestic violence, drunkenness, or theft are poor people's problems, or that gang violence is a black community problem. There are violent, criminal people among the white middle and upper classes too. Those with the least need — or excuse — to sin are just as prone to do so. They are just less likely to get caught. No matter what inducements to sin one removes, it remains part of our fallen nature.

Make no mistake, this theology of discontinuity has had some impressive results. We can see its bold effects in the social works of great Christians both Catholic and Protestant, from medieval Franciscans in their love of the poor to the post-Enlightenment Quakers, or the modern American black Baptists who have fought righteously against racism and oppression. Through protest against the natural human propensity to war and control, swords and guns have been beaten into ploughshares, old orders have fallen, the hungry have been fed, and the rich sent away empty. The tale of the revolutionary Christ is utopian and attractive. It makes sense of the Church as the continuation of the Incarnation of Christ, and the embryonic perfect society of the Kingdom. It is theology that originated from the lived experience of poverty rather than from prestigious universities in the Northern hemisphere, however much the latter may have appropriated it for their own ends more recently. It precludes the laziness of merely trying to pray problems away, and makes the Church take action, do something, to address injustice and inequality. This is surely good. So, is the Liberationist Christ after all the real one? Jesus did overturn the tables in the temple. He did speak of setting mother against daughter and father against son, and said that he had come not to bring peace, but the sword. In this light, the Cross does look like Karl Barth's "crisis point" where the natural order of death is completely overturned — the culmination of a series of miracles, from calming storms to healing lepers, showing the domination of the supernatural will of God over the natural order, and rejecting any sense of harmony between the two: hence his famous "Nein!" to natural theology. There is, it would seem, nothing divine about nature. Christ reveals God as the agent of radical change. His miracles signify the overthrowing of the natural order and the limitations of the human intellect in comprehending the sovereign will of God. Salvation is about overthrowing a natural order too corrupt and fallen for sublimation.

Yet, for all its appeal, the picture of Christ as a proto-Che Guevara does not represent the majority historical view of Christian theology. In the West, theurgic Platonism had been confined to the sidelines of Western theology for some centuries, obscured by the new lights of deism and rationalism. Among other influences, the late-nineteenth-century revival of patristic studies in the Church of England brought it back to light. Interest burgeoned in the theology of the Orthodox churches of the East, and so in the writings of the Early Church Fathers. This renewed interest was shared in the Roman Catholic Church, particularly in France, and would eventually nurture such great thinkers as Henri de Lubac and Hans Urs von Balthasar. Anglicans and Roman Catholics alike began to reassess their more recent tradition in light of the writings of the Fathers. The former became far more aware of the Catholic and Platonic inheritance of their cherished Book of Common Prayer, the normative source for Anglican theology; the latter, of the way in which their theology had been channeled into an overly narrow reading of St Thomas Aquinas. English clergy were sanctioned by ecclesial authority, and even imprisoned by the state, as they began to put into practice the liturgical ramifications of their findings. Anglican priests were imprisoned for placing crosses and candles on the altar, and riots started over the wearing of surplices. Henri de Lubac was for some years debarred from writing Catholic theology by the Society of Jesus for his reinterpretation of Aquinas and advocacy of a return to patristic sources. He responded to the ban by writing two volumes on Shin Buddhism instead. [4] De Lubac and the nineteenth-century Anglicans alike were criticized for exposing how the theological focus of the Western Church, whether Catholic or Reformed, had narrowed since the time of Ockham to its contemporary myopia.

More recently, the definition of God in terms of sheer power has led to human attempts to emulate him on such terms and supplant him. The arbitrariness of such a divine will has led many to question whether what God wants is really good at all. Given the evils that beset the world, if God is really "in charge," he is at best fickle. If God could not be resisted, then he needed to be retired. If God is best defined by revolution, how better to emulate him than to revolt against his Church? Theologians of the late twentieth century, such as Don Cupitt, have gone so far as to claim that atheistic secularism is the apogee of the Christian faith.

The rebel Christ of the Liberationist mythos represents a limited range of perception. It is not false, but rather a half-truth which, on its own, becomes a lie. The story is consonant with a very broad overview of the story of the Bible as a whole, but as read through a lens tinted with the hues of Marxist and, now, postmodernist preoccupations. In these readings the Old Testament is to be taken as the story of God's people in their struggle for freedom; from the Egyptians, from the Babylonians, and from their own corrupt rulers and traditions. The New Testament provides Jesus as the ultimate liberator, who is not so much a key to the Old as someone who kicks the door in. There is a rather Protestant disdain for tradition here that verges at times on the anti-Semitic: if only the Jews had listened to their prophets they would have abandoned their life-denying traditions, so Jesus came to set them free. And they still didn't listen! Such a reading of the Bible in fact seems rather unjust to the Jews, and it is instructive to note what is focused on and what has been omitted. Supernatural agency, and in particular miracles, can be taken or left: whether or not they really took place is irrelevant to the narrative, so we can afford to be agnostic about them. We can apply the same agnosticism to supposedly historical accounts of events, especially those of the Old Testament, including the accounts of direct divine revelation to Moses through things like talking fires or stone tablets on mountaintops. Perhaps most importantly, we do not need to pay much attention to ritual texts relating to temple worship

---

4   Henri de Lubac, *Aspects of Buddhism*, trans. George Lamb (London: Sheed and Ward, 1953).

in the Old Testament and its continuity with Christ's own institution of the Church and Sacraments, because on this reading, ritual and tradition are things from which Christ comes to liberate us, rather than to perpetuate.

These omissions come from seeing the Bible through a lens of discontinuity and disruption gleaned from the selective reading of Jesus's life and teachings in the Gospels. The method betrays modern discomfort with the miraculous, but also with tradition. In particular, it betrays the modern desire to maintain a sharp division between the spiritual and physical orders, the latter including the political. Overall, it is a narrative of discontinuity and as such, despite its Catholic roots in South America, is comparable to more Lutheran and Calvinist thought. Barth shouted his famous "Nein!" to natural theology because the Nazis had deified Darwinism, which constituted a scientific orthodoxy of the day, into a wicked racialist and eugenic polity. He and his Lutheran contemporary Dietrich Bonhoeffer believed that only the radical, disruptive *difference* of the Gospel could break such idolatry. Their fire was directed against the whole notion of religion as something continuous with natural order. Barth described all religion as "unbelief," and Bonhoeffer called for a "religionless" Christianity. Religion as a concept was all too natural, too pagan, too human. Any continuity of God with nature was a taming of God, an idolatrous restriction of his disruptive will.

Barth and Bonhoeffer, as a Calvinist and Lutheran respectively, were deeply influenced by St Paul's Epistle to the Romans, which nourished their theology as much as it had nourished that of their founding Reformation fathers. So, their reading of Paul is understandably colored by Reformation preoccupations: the overthrow of corrupt tradition, the opposition of law to grace, and so on. Yet the Paul whose work they marshalled in the fight against religion, tradition, and continuity is the same Paul who the pseudonymous Dionysius the Areopagite believed embraced the natural theology of the pagan Greeks and the divine liturgy of the Jewish temple rites. If he has engendered such radically divergent readings as those of the sacramental Platonists and voluntarist Protestants, we might reasonably look to him to arbitrate on the tale of two Christs.

St Paul's works are the earliest expressly Christian writings, earlier than the Gospels. They are written in Greek and make use of Greek philosophical terminology. Yet they are no less the work of a deeply *religious* Jew. Paul's understanding of Christ is replete with references to Jewish religious tradition, including those liturgical and ritual elements to which the Reformers were largely hostile. The Catholic liberation theologians who followed them likewise tended to downplay the role of both the priesthood and the sacraments in their ecclesial communities, gathering laypeople primarily around the study of the Scriptures.

Under the influence of Liberation Theology, many liberal Christians nowadays tend to read St Paul much as they read the Old Testament: selectively and somewhat sniffily. They discern in Paul exactly what they despise in the Jewish scriptures: a God with a masculine preferred pronoun, jealous and prone to anger, who reinforces social and gender hierarchies and is decidedly heteronormative. That is, a God embroiled in just the sort of "purely social" constructs from which the liberationists believe Christ came to set us free. In contrast to the bachelor Christ, for instance, Paul has quite a lot to say about marriage. Where Christ called his disciples friends and spent time scandalously unchaperoned with women, Paul rails against breaches of Eucharistic hospitality and hierarchy. Christ said not a word about homosexuality and (some add with a nudge and a wink) was once found with a naked man running from his tent, while Paul is firm on Old Testament sexual proprieties. In short, Paul is just too Jewish, too bound up with the cultural conventions and traditions of his age. The old patriarch embraced unfortunate contemporary — and entirely human — conventions and so corrupted Jesus's original message of freedom. That the Church gave his writings a canonical place in Scripture only shows how quickly the Pauline "rot" set in.

Today's culture wars in the West are analogous to two radically different understandings of God, dependent in turn on two radically different understandings of Christ: that is to say on theological, and thus Christological differences. The God proclaimed as one supremely powerful being among other lesser entities occluded the older sense of God as the source of Being itself, who spoke of himself as such from the burning bush, and whose words Our Lord echoes throughout John's Gospel every time he said, "I am." Instead of the God of the Trinity and the Incarnation, of Word and Spirit both transcending being and yet immanently present within it as its origin, principle of order, and end, we were left with merely a "great big god" who exists, and as such is delimited from the existing things he has made. This god would ultimately prove unbelievable not only to philosophers such as Heidegger, with his grand critique of ontotheology, but apparently also to the educated majority of what had once been Western Christendom. Understandably unsatisfied with what Dreher calls "moral therapeutic deism," many Westerners who retain any sense of spiritual agency at work in the world have turned to Buddhism or Islam, where they find spirituality and tradition undefiled, intact, and presented in intellectually credible terms.

For these Westerners, all that remains of their latent Christian tradition is the discarded appendix sliced from the side of the dying god of power: materialism. Having defined God in opposition to creation and eliminated him from it, we have come to see ourselves as little gods in his misconstrued image, free to use and abuse the fruits of a now despiritualized, externalized world to whatever end we please. Hence utilitarianism, deforestation, slavery, and the reduction of all things (even human) to resources, are the products of a theology of radical discontinuity between God, us, and nature — and of the mutual exclusion that we imagine persists between these three. Seeing creation as wholly discontinuous with God, we end up with a fractured view of the Incarnation, in which Christ enters matter — not to perfect the good nature that inheres in it already by the grace of God — but rather to destroy that nature and replace it entirely. This implies a likewise fractured view of the human, whose soul is at war with the body; and of the created order, since matter is devoid of goodness until subjected to use by the mind; and between the individual and society, since the latter is merely part of the same unhallowed realm of nature that the willing agent must overcome. We are left with a kind of antichristology, in which Christ reveals God as in rebellion against his creation.

Perhaps because they know that such a god is incredible, many liberal Christians have largely abandoned theology to shift the public focus away from him and his worship towards the more tangible possibilities of social justice and service. Liberal clergy tend instead to deflect or trivialize theological problems, thinking it enough to replace them with good deeds and social activism, and then amend or design completely new "liturgies" around their latest political convictions. Many of these are good: soup kitchens, homeless shelters, campaigns against exploitation and the illicit use of arms, for example. However, a theology of discontinuity and disruption is not necessary for such endeavors and will not ultimately sustain them, because it is not grounded in the reality of God, but in the exercise of human power. Hence it leads to distortions in the realms of human sexuality and identity, which can be effected only by the selfsame technological domination of nature which, in avenues such as warfare and farming, the liberal professes to despise. Women's bodies in particular are seen as "problems" to be solved by medical and technological intervention, whether by will in the West or by State coercion in Communist China. A strong body-self dualism is at play in the way our reproductive organs and functions are seen as an impediment to liberty and prosperity. The body, like the rest of the material world, must be tamed so that the immaterial will may flourish unimpeded. Biology is an obstacle to be overcome. Rather than the Divine Word of fulfillment, who assumes matter and elevates it to the communion with the Father which he himself enjoys, we are left with a merely human, revolutionary Word of condemnation, who comes to liberate us not through but *from* our bodily existence.

The implications of this revolutionary Christology for justice have moved on from the modern rivalry between Marxism and capitalism, and are now reverberating in today's culture wars. "Intersectionality" is a watchword of critical theory's social justice advocates. By this is meant a hierarchy of power based not on individuals and their actions, but their membership of social groups categorized on a bipolar scale of oppressors versus oppressed. In essence this is a diffusion of the relatively simple Marxist analysis of history by class division into far more numerous social groupings, including race, sex, sexuality, and disability. The "intersection" of intersectionality is where various of these social identities overlap. First proposed by Kimberlé Crenshaw in 1996, intersectionality can be a valuable tool for discerning where a person is falling foul of multiple layers of injustice: for example, while a woman is more vulnerable to exploitation and abuse than a man, a black woman in the US is more so, and a disabled black woman even more still. Greater attention should therefore be paid to those at greater risk, and those whose voices are least likely to be heard need louder advocacy. The danger of this approach however is that it can be used to advocate a hierarchy of victimhood and oppression. The fewer intersectional overlaps of oppressed identities one can claim, the higher one is in the hierarchy of oppression; the more one's identities intersect, the stronger one's claim to number among the victimized oppressed. Nor is this in any sense assumed to be a neutral analytical tool. The express purpose of analyzing the hierarchy is to destabilize oppressive identities, deprive them of normative status, and so equalize society: to put down the mighty from their seat and exalt the humble and meek; to replace the Alpha with the Omega here and now. Justice is a noble pursuit and essential to the Church, no doubt. However it is not for the Church here and now to judge the standing of entire segments of society — based on ethnicity, skin color, sex or sexuality — and to pronounce judgment.

Still less does it belong to the Church to stimulate and perpetuate division based on those identities, or to deny the individual agency of the people who comprise them. The social justice movement is hardly explicable as a development of Western mores without reference to Christ. The Christ to which it refers, however, is the revolutionary Christ whose Kingdom is very much of this world. He comes, not to reconcile the world and sublimate it in the Kingdom of Heaven, but to abolish and cancel all that stands in the way. Forgiveness is not a revolutionary sentiment, and there is little forgiveness to be seen among those calling on others for constant "checks of privilege" on other people; not because of who they are, but because of the categories that have been imposed on them. Intersectionality is being used by some to try to force the eschaton (but in an entirely "immanent" manner and without reference to the sacred). Certain of its advocates presume to mete out divine justice without divine forgiveness and — by means of bloc punishments — without divine knowledge of or care for particular souls. This kind of social justice can become a warped idol of the divine justice, lacking that divine compassion and divine forgiveness to which we as mortals cannot attain in this life.

Combine all this with a hyper-Calvinist dualism of the saved and the damned, and you end up with the modern mindset of the social justice puritan, which is ultimately antisocial and unjust. The binary of the elect few and the damned masses are transposed to the identities of oppressed and oppressor, powerless and empowered. The myth of the undeserving poor is reversed by the new myth of the undeserving rich. Yet this is a Calvinistic dualism through the lens of Rousseau. What is lost is Calvin's quite proper Augustinian sense that in fact, none of us is deserving. Our very existence is a gift freely given, not a right earned, and all the more so our eternal life. The equality the Cross establishes is that of our shared and absolute need for divine grace, which is yielded by the divine compassion expressed in Christ's atoning sacrifice for the forgiveness of sin. When some classes of people are rendered more deserving of that grace than others, and when individual Christians lose the ability either to repent of their own sins or to forgive the sins of others, the Gospel is lost.

What is needed is a return to the God of the Fathers, who is at once beyond and within his creation, higher than our greatest heights and deeper than our inmost depths, in whom we live and move and have our being, and so who knows each one of us with utter intimacy; the God whose image is expressed in every being, and so to be honored and praised both in every instantiation and in the ordering of the whole; the God whose creation is a song in which we join in polyphony, rather than strike against in cacophonic discord. The means Dionysius offers to join in this song is the Divine Liturgy, which he portrays in terms of Eastern Platonic theurgy. In the liturgy we perceive a very different kind of Christ from that of the revolutionary set on dividing the world. The sword he brings is not for dividing us from our fellow beings, or cutting loose our minds from our bodies. It is rather for the surgery of the soul by which we are liberated from the spiritual evils that beset us and that thwart our pursuit of the harmonious way.

GETTING DRUNK WITH GOD

> Out of his senses . . . inebriated, [God] has projected everything
> that is good, while staying over-full of all of them, an excess of
> all infinitude, and yet again dwelling outside and transcendently
> above all things.
>
> — Dionysius, *Epistle* 9.5, 1112C

DIONYSIUS IS NOT ALWAYS AS SERIOUS AS HE
is made out to be, but his play here is in earnest. The image of
God as drunken giant is taken from the 78th Psalm and so, for
Dionysius, it constitutes a revelation of Sacred Scripture; and he insists that
the least appropriate images we find of God in the Bible are in fact the best.
The less appropriate the image, the lower the risk of idolatry: we are in
no danger of really thinking that God is a giant who gets drunk. Yet here
Dionysius takes the metaphor further, finding in the "drunkenness" of God
an insight into the creativity of the divine nature.

The relationship between divine goodness and the divine will has caused
problems not only between Christians and Buddhists, but between Christians
and Platonists too. To recap from the chapter on Being — from a Buddhist
perspective one of the main barriers to belief in a creator God is the sense
that he might not have created, because he did so only as an act of will.
This leaves an unacceptable dualism between the creature and the creator,
placing them in opposition rather than harmony. Instead, Buddhists taught
the principle of mutual, interdependent arising, with no single prevalent
will dictating the course of things.

Christians have indeed always maintained that God might not have created, and this caused a problem when they tried to express their teachings
in the Platonic language the educated world spoke for most of the first
millennium of the Church's existence. Platonists insisted in various ways
that the created order was a natural overflowing of the divine nature, and
not a matter of the exercise of God's will. God creates because God is good
by nature. The opposite path, which Ockham would eventually pursue, is

to say that creation is good because God wills it. Yet this path, as we have seen, sunders goodness from both the divine nature and the created order. Not wanting to walk that way, Platonists were therefore faced with assimilating the divine will with the divine nature. Plotinus treats of the matter systematically in *Ennead* VI.8, but Dionysius approaches it more playfully here. The problem, basically, is whether God as good by nature is therefore necessarily generative of being, or whether God creates by sheer will. Monotheists have been keen to preserve the freedom of God's creative act, but this comes at the potential cost of making the divine will arbitrary, calling into serious question the idea that God is in any meaningful sense just.

Plotinus's solution is that since there can be no "external" law beyond the One to compel it, its goodness is its own law, and so the divine will essentially is the divine nature. Dionysius's image nuances this. God, he says, is "out of his senses" or, more literally, in *ecstasy* from them, as though his head were reeling. Creation is God projecting all the good things inside him — and yet they somehow remain within him while he is at the same time "ecstatically" outside and beyond them all. If the metaphor were stripped away, we would be left with the standard Platonic conviction that the divine creative will is straightforwardly one with the goodness of the divine nature: God's will and God's nature cannot be dissected. Yet the metaphor adds a new layer of meaning. This divine inebriation falls somewhere between sheer will and emotional excess; God, says Dionysius elsewhere, is drawn out of himself as though "bewitched" with love for his creatures.[1]

Dionysius's image paints a picture of a certain suddenness, an improvisatory spontaneity: a playfulness redolent of Plato, but also of Plotinus's *Ennead* III.8. This tract, explicitly framed as a kind of play, relates how contemplation underlies the generation and existence of all beings. All things depend for their existence on principles which in themselves are abstract and intelligible. Those abstract, intelligible principles are therefore logically and causally prior to any physical existing things. Plotinus applies this line of reasoning to nature itself. Nature generates physical things spontaneously, without reasoned intent, but nonetheless following abstract, intelligible principles or laws (Plotinus calls them *logoi*). Nature itself is therefore engaging in a kind of contemplation, or *theoria*, of those *logoi*, albeit in a passive way that Plotinus likens to the uncontrolled and freely flowing thoughts of a dream. Yet nature itself is the product of the contemplation of the divine Soul, which in turn gives existence to the "forms" or ideas of God that pre-exist in the divine Mind. Those forms

---

1   Greek *thelgetai*, DN 4.13, 712B.

are themselves generated by the Mind's contemplation of the One, or the Good. The One alone does not contemplate, because it is entirely simple, and so beyond the distinctions of self and other that knowing and being necessarily entail: for to know, there must be a distinct "knower" and a distinct object known; and "to be" is to the share the category of "being" with everything else that "is." For Plotinus, the One can therefore, formally speaking, know nothing in the conventional sense — for discursive reasoning would imply multiplicity. Rather, all things are enfolded within the One as their ultimate cause and origin. In a fashion beyond our comprehension, on this model God knows all things intuitively and simply by contemplation of himself, since all things are enfolded in him. To put it in more obviously Christian terms, since it is God in whom we live, and move, and have our being, God knows us simply by knowing himself — and this self-knowledge is not a matter of discursive reason, but rather is the necessary precondition for any discursive reason to take place. God contemplatively, intuitively "knows" all beings into existence. Not only we but even inanimate things are aspects of God's self-contemplation, and participants in it. The stars and planets, even lumps of rock, are produced by and depend for their existence on non-physical, intelligible principles; but more, they communicate those principles in shape, color, weight, and so on, even to creatures like plants and animals that have no spoken language.

Seeing the world in this way considerably widens the semantic range of words like "knowledge," "intelligence," and even "sentience." It is thus that Plotinus can speak of all things not only existing as the result of divine contemplation, but as contemplating entities in their own right. All things depend for both their generation and continued existence on their communication with the rest of the universe. This has implications for the way we tend nowadays to divide mind and matter, and to subordinate the supposedly unreasoning realm of nature; and also, surely, it calls into question atomized understandings of the human self as an "individual" set apart from others and the rest of creation. To be godlike is not to be, as closely we can, an all-powerful, tyrannical being. It is rather to enter fully into the dreamlike, contemplative play by which God spontaneously creates. It is to be like an inspired artist rather than a wilful technocrat. It is, in short, to harness the will to the imagination. It is to be at rest in the dreamlike contemplation of the divine Logos that gives us an all-things shape, and the divine Spirit that animates us.

Like the crucifixes Japan's hidden Christians carved onto the back of Buddhist statues in times of persecution, this is where I think we find hidden Dionysius's theology of the Cross. For what Proclus calls *ecstasy*, Dionysius baptizes with the Pauline, biblical image of *kenōsis*: the self-emptying of God proclaimed in the Christological hymn of Philippians 2:5–11, wherein Christ divests himself of divine glory and equality with God to take the form of a servant. Because all things inhere in the One, God is simultaneously "standing outside" himself in creation and yet, at the same time, completely unmoved and contained. I have already suggested that kenosis, the self-emptying of God revealed most profoundly in the Incarnation of Christ, is vital to Dionysius's theology. Kenosis has some conceptual overlap with Proclus's term, *ekstasis* or ecstasy — the word I translated as the "outside" of "outside his senses," which Dionysius used to introduce the metaphor of the drunken God above. Proclus used the word to indicate how causes inhere in the One, so that God is simultaneously "standing outside" himself in creation while remaining completely unmoved and contained. In *Divine Names* 13.3, Dionysius speaks of ecstasy as the "non-path" by which intelligent beings may aspire to communion with the transcendent "Name beyond every name." In that very Pauline sense of losing the self to find the self, we are called to join in the self-emptying of God by self-emptying ourselves, all things finding their true stability by standing outside themselves. In short, Dionysius is telling us to let go and get drunk with God. Then, with renewed and emptied minds, we will see that the divine will is none other than the divine goodness. As St Paul himself puts it:

> Be not conformed to this age, but be transformed by the renewing
> of the mind, so that you may prove what is the will of God, good,
> well-pleasing and perfect. (Romans 12:2)

Dionysius's boozy metaphor is a way of trying to express a truth about the divine will and divine nature that goes beyond rational cognition. This is very much in tune with Buddhist sensibilities. Just as Shinran speaks of the *nembutsu* as "practice which is not practice," and even as the "way which is not a way," so Dionysius here invokes the "non-way" that takes us beyond intellection and naming into communion. The closest he can come to explaining it is as the interaction between lovers, which breaks down the identity and differentiation between nature and will, leading to action at once natural and yet no less involuntary. As he writes elsewhere: "divine Eros is ecstatic, in that it does not permit the lovers to belong to themselves, but only to the beloved."[2] That, after all, is the grammar of

---

2   *Divine Names* 4.13, 712A.

love: the mutual abandonment of the will between the beloved generates the truer, better will.

So how do we get drunk with God? How do we not merely subdue our will to his, as Ockham and his descendants would have it, but rather lose our will precisely to find the freedom of God's own loving, playful, creative self-abandonment? We are left in a quandary. We are saying that our participation in God is really a matter of abandoning self and will. Yet any action we take towards abandoning the self and will is itself an act of self and will. It is a similar quandary to the controversy between Shinran and Hōnen about the status of the *nembutsu* as other-power or self-power practice. There seems to be no way out of this voluntarist loop, short of the Calvinist double predestination: some are born to sweet delight, some to endless night, and there is nothing we can do about it either way. At the end of his life, much of which he had spent struggling with the British monk Pelagius, who taught that humans could earn their own salvation, even St Augustine had to admit that he could not solve the conflict between human freedom and God's will.

I certainly cannot claim to navigate us out of those Pelagian waters that left the greatest father of the Western Church stranded, but Dionysius and Shinran do offer some light to guide us. The Eastern Church as a whole did not face the threat of Pelagius's teachings, and so was never pushed into articulating such a strong doctrine of Original Sin as the Western Church, by which Augustine contrasted our fallen nature starkly against the goodness of divine grace. While Augustine was himself a Platonist, the Eastern Platonic strand — more prevalent among the Eastern fathers, Dionysius among them — articulates a greater sense of continuity between grace and nature, the divine goodness and the created order. We will see that Shinran's world, too, is grounded in a fundamental shared goodness, despite the great polarity he opposes between the wretched human being and the perfect compassion of Amida Buddha.

The key concept Dionysius and Shinran share in this regard is *participation*, whereas dualistic systems can only ever attain to *emulation*. Emulation is the relationship of one being to another. The Christian who believes that God is a fundamentally alien being will try to obey his will by emulating Christ or the saints. To be Christlike means to copy Christ as an external model. This leads to moralism of "Christian values" often promoted in now more-or-less secular schools on the basis that one can follow Jesus's teachings and take him as a role model regardless whether or not one thinks he is God, or even whether or not he existed. Faith, on this nominalist model, is separable from good living, and means only the intellectual assent to a set of beliefs.

Neither Shinran's *shinjin* nor Dionysius's approach to unity with God can be called "faith" in this sense of the word. Both demand, rather, a kind of entrusting in the salvific goodness that is behind, within, and the end of all reality — like the drunkenness metaphor, a sort of active passivity or willed unwillfulness that leads to oneness with that which is beyond intellection and even will. Their solutions to the quandary of relationship between the human will and the good brought both Dionysius and Shinran into conflict with their own traditions: in Dionysius's case with both Christianity and Platonism, and in Shinran's with Mahāyāna Buddhism.

THEURGY, REENCHANTMENT,
AND THE MUSIC OF PURITY

But th' holy men of God such vessels are,
As serve him up, who all the word commands:
When God vouchsafed to become our fare,
Their hands convey him, who conveys their hands.
O what pure things, most pure must those things be,
Who bring my God to me!
— George Herbert, *The Priesthood*

RDAINED DEACON IN THE CHURCH OF
England in 1624, George Herbert spent four years in prayerful deliberation before he accepted the gift of priestly orders.
The responsibilities of the priest were awesome: to bind or remit sins, to preach and expound the Holy Scriptures and, above all, to administer the sacraments. As a priest, he could not dare defile those hands which would "serve up" God under the species of bread and wine. They must become vehicles as fit for the purpose as the pure and spotless host itself. Even so, Herbert was under no illusion that the gifts of Holy Communion could be impeded by the dirt of his hands or, for that matter, augmented by their cleanliness. True to Augustinian theology, as long as the minister was validly ordained, his personal unworthiness could not hinder the effect of the sacraments which, as the Church of England's 26th Article of Religion has it, "be effectual, because of Christ's institution and promise, although they be ministered by evil men." Here, then, is the root of Herbert's paradoxical verse: even as the priest's hands "convey" God, it is God himself who "conveys their hands."

Herbert's poem beautifully expresses the tenor of Dionysian theurgy, a development in the late Platonism of the pagan Syrian philosopher-priest Iamblichus. For Dionysius, if theosis — oneness or, as he sometimes expresses it, "Communion" with God — is the salvific purpose of all reality, then theurgy is the vehicle for its realization. Vitally, while this theurgy is the work of human hands, it is as its name suggests no less *Theou ergon*, the "work of God."

Dionysius's ten *Letters* are among the least studied of his works, which is a shame because they above all connect his Platonic teaching on theurgy most directly with the Eucharist and so with the work of Christ. Coming back to the ninth letter, in which we read of the "divine drunkenness" above, Dionysius describes Wisdom mixing her bowl with solid food and sacred drink.[1] The sacred drink represents the flowing of God's providence as overflowing source of all existence, and the solid food stands for the stable nourishment that gives strength and goodness to beings. He extends the metaphor to apply it to what he calls the "tradition of the theologians," making the drink stand for cataphatic exposition of the divine revelation, and the solid food stand for theurgic elements (*sunthēmata*) used for apophatic, sacramental union with God in his hiddenness. Taking the figure of Christ as Wisdom Incarnate, Dionysius then makes the "drink" the teaching of Jesus, including his parables, and the "solid food" becomes the Eucharist. The divine revelation in Scripture — and in the material elements of the cosmos by which God lifts us into theurgic union with himself — are united in what Dionysius calls in Epistle 4 the "theandric" or divine-human work of Christ. It is through Christ that theurgy becomes the consummation of theology,[2] and when bishops and their priests celebrate the Eucharist they are not doing so merely in imitation of Jesus as an historic figure, but are participating in the work of the living Word and Wisdom of God, by which he offers the entire cosmos to the Father through his sacrifice on the Cross.

Theurgy had been controversial even among pagan Platonists. Porphyry wrote to Iamblichus asking how he could believe his magical incantations might affect the will of the gods. Iamblichus replied with a letter of his own, now known as the *De Mysteriis*, in which he makes it very clear that in no way does theurgy involve mortals manipulating the divine. On the contrary, the divine goodness expresses itself in myriad ways as "symbols" in the physical matter of things, and theurgy is the practical means of participating in the higher realities they represent. In Platonic terms, theurgy is the vehicle by which the higher spiritual causes have their effect in the material realm. Ritual practice is not a bending of those causes to the will, but a surrendering of the will to them, as it were opening the latent channel of their grace. Without theurgy, Iamblichus argues, we risk leaving the

---

1   *Epistle* 9.5, 1105D.
2   *Ecclesiastical Hierarchy* 3.5, 432A – B.

material realm as a "desert, without gods," a disenchanted realm. We risk, in short, denying the goodness and therefore the reality of creation.

In the West, St Augustine firmly resisted this development of Eastern Platonism. In *The City of God* (Book X. 9 – 10), he equates theurgy to necromancy and reviles it as a discourse with demons. Augustine builds his argument against theurgy by citing the letter of Porphyry to Iamblichus, written on Plotinus's behalf. So, Augustine reveals himself as the inheritor of that more intellectualizing strand of Platonism, in which the divine is experienced through an intellectual ascent towards the unknowable One; not so much through things as through words. We saw this in the mutual religious experience he enjoyed with his mother as they looked out on the garden in Ostia, an experience that resulted from conversation; and elsewhere in the *Confessions* we read of how his conversion to the Christian faith was provoked by a voice like a child's telling him to pick up the Bible and read. Conversation, voices, and reading are Augustine's primary vehicles of salvation — words and images guiding spiritual progress to the Word beyond words and the invisible image. It is not hard to see how Augustine's very verbal strand of Platonism would later inspire the Protestant Reformers, especially Calvin, and give strength to their call for a Church guided by "scripture alone."

Augustine's Eastern coreligionist Dionysius, on the other hand, keenly adopted the theurgical thought of his fellow Syrian Iamblichus. He used it as the basis for a sacramental theology of participation in a divinely-graced world that was both more thoroughly Platonic and more thoroughly Christian. More thoroughly Platonic, because it resolved the tension in Plotinus's thought between the spiritual and material realms; more thoroughly Christian, because it treated the material realm with the due dignity that the Incarnation of Christ in matter necessitated. Augustine is one of the greatest and most influential theologians, pastors, biblical commentators, homilists, and Platonic philosophers of Western Christendom, and Dionysius's output is negligible in comparison with the sheer volume of his work. Nonetheless, we can see in Augustine a hangover of the soul-body dualism that sometimes appears in Plotinus, and that Augustine had once found attractive in the Manichean sect with which he flirted before his conversion to Christianity. It would be unfair to pin all the Western problems of disparagement of the body and its urges on Augustine (as some do), but without doubt the division he maintained between the physical and the spiritual has had harmful repercussions that persist in the West to this day. It also led Calvin to declare more or less what Iamblichus had feared: that the world, in the end, is of itself evil, utterly reprobate and fallen, incapable of communicating the divine nature save by the addition of God's grace, which is added arbitrarily and almost as an afterthought. Dionysius's theurgy, conversely, sees the physical as participating in the spiritual, and as the vehicle of salvation rather than an impediment to it. As such it offers a valuable corrective.

Nonetheless, Dionysius faces the same charges even to this day from his fellow Christians: that his sacramental adoption of theurgy is a kind of magical manipulation of God's will. This is to misunderstand the Platonic makeup of his thought and subject his world to the unfortunate divisions of the modern Western mindset. I am in fact not averse to describing sacraments as a kind of magic: a specifically chosen and inducted individual wears special clothes to speak inherited words over sacred objects in order to effect an objective change. That sounds a lot like magic to me. However, the source of that "magic," which Christians would better name "grace," is not the will of the priest, for Dionysius any more than for Iamblichus. Rather, it is God's work — the literal meaning of "theurgy" — being effected *through* the priest, the people, and the material objects of the ritual. Coming back to Herbert, their hands convey him, who conveys their hands. Take any element away, and the sacrament is incomplete: one cannot baptize without water, marry without a betrothed, consecrate the Eucharist without bread and wine, or without a validly ordained priest. Nor, Canon Law rightly insists, can one substitute any of the elements: say, cola for the wine or rice for the bread of the Eucharist, or a webcam for the physical presence of the priest. Whatever chagrin avant garde pioneer ministers may harbor, this is not a matter of tedious Church legalism, nor a bigoted disregard for "inculturation," but a longstanding resistance to the nominalist instinct that says, like Humpty Dumpty to Alice, that things mean only what I decide they mean. The ancient law of the Church, rather, shows a latent if sometimes forgotten commitment to the realist, more Platonic view, that things symbolize a greater reality in which they participate, and that they do so objectively, not merely as a matter of human custom.

We saw earlier that critics of Dionysius accuse him of a solipsistic mysticism, as though he taught that one could achieve salvation by meditating all the names of God away. A proper focus on the roots of his theurgic teaching conclusively discredits that view. There is nothing individualistic about theurgy. A contemporary scholar of Iamblichus, Gregory Shaw, describes theurgy as "divine activity communally shared,"[3] and quotes

---

3   Shaw, *Theurgy and the Soul*, xx.

Iamblichus himself saying that "it is impossible to participate individually in the universal orders, but only in communion with the divine choir of those lifted up together, united in mind." Oneness with God, *theosis*, comes only through full engagement with the multiplicity of the spiritual and physical realms of existence. Surprisingly, if anything, Augustine's Platonism is the more individualistic and intellectualizing. In theurgy, God conveys his salvific nature not through words to individuals but through matter in communal actions.

Nor can salvation be achieved by one's own meditative power. On the contrary, writes Iamblichus, we do not "draw down the gods" with our rituals; rather, the "felicitous accomplishment of divine works is imparted by the gods alone."[4] Western readers may be concerned that theurgy smacks of Pelagianism, yet even the pagan Iamblichus robustly rejects any sense of salvation by works: neither right knowledge nor bodily purity, he writes, can attain to salvation. Proponents of "synergy," the doctrine of the Eastern Church that makes us "co-workers" with God — a phrase which despite its Pauline scriptural authority, thanks to Augustine raises hackles in the West — will find little support for it in Iamblichus, who insists that nothing "which is human cooperates [sic] anything to the end of divine actions."[5] Even when someone speaks wisely, he says, "this is not a human, but a divine work."[6] Indeed, it is "the awareness of our own nothingness, when we compare ourselves to the Gods," that "makes us turn spontaneously to prayer."[7] You could not ask for a more robustly non-dualistic identification between the divine work of salvation and its ritual realization by created agents. The interrelationship between the divine salvific will and its human agents, especially the priests appointed as vehicles of the theurgic mysteries, is neither one of simple obedience to an external will nor one of mindless absorption into an undifferentiated divine morass. Rather, Iamblichus construes it as one of "possession" or "mania," a sort of divine madness: and so we are brought back to Dionysius's metaphor of getting drunk with God. Through participating in the sacraments we come to realize that the exercise of our will in responding to the divine call is in fact none other than the divine call itself, echoing through creation. Like drunks in some midnight choir, we hit harmony despite ourselves, neither quite willing nor entirely out of control. Theurgy is the opium of the mass.

---

4   *De Mysteriis* 3.20.
5   *De Mysteriis* 2.11.
6   *De Mysteriis* 3.17.
7   *De Mysteriis* 47, cited in Shaw, 126.

Enchanted with a drunken ecstasy, God pours out being for the sake of its return to him. Dionysian theurgy is the ritual outworking of that return, which assumes the fundamental goodness of created things thanks to their participation in God and their orientation towards reunion with Him. This could not be any further removed from the privatized meditative approach to salvation of which he is sometimes accused: it is so communal that it embraces not just the Church, not even just the whole of humanity, but the entire cosmos. Through the sacraments, and especially in Baptism and the Eucharist, the human will loses itself in drunken play with the divine goodness, bringing it into harmony with the entire graced order of Being-as-salvation.

Theurgy is the practical outworking of the idea that the whole universe is enchanted with the divine goodness, and every aspect of it calls us into communion with the One in whom it lives and moves and has its being. Through it, our will is conformed to God's goodness, our work to his work. In this we find an analog to Shinran's refinement of the doctrine behind the *nembutsu*.

> In other-power, no-working is true working.
> (Shinran, quoting Hōnen, *Lamp of the Latter Ages*, 2)

Recent decades have seen the growth of something called "Applied" or "Engaged Buddhism," particularly under the aegis of the Vietnamese monk Thich Nhat Hanh, whose 1963 book bears the latter title. In the Francophone realm of pre-War Indochina, *engagé* was a Marxist and revolutionary term used by those who resisted the imperial regime. In this it shares common roots with the Christian Liberation Theology of South America. Yet like Liberation Theology, Engaged Buddhism's Marxist historical and cultural analysis has enjoyed considerable influence outside its homeland among the "progressive" elites of the West, and especially in the academy. Engaged Buddhism tends to focus on ethical concerns, issues of social justice and human rights, and the beneficial psychological effects of meditation.

Engaged Buddhist academics point out that this is nothing new. Marxist influences on Shin Buddhism arrived in Japan with Christianity in the late nineteenth century. We find examples of contemporary Shin Buddhist clergy like Kiyozawa Manshi (1863 – 1903) embracing socialist thought, and of Japanese socialists and communists discovering in Shinran a proto-Marxist liberator within their own cultural and historic milieu. Hayashida Shigeo, for instance, was imprisoned as a communist by the military state during the Second World War and, as some prisoners in the West find Christ in jail,

Hayashida came out in praise of the *nembutsu*. Psychiatrists synthesized the work of Freud and Jung with Shin Buddhist teaching, replacing the Greek and biblical mythical types with analogues from Buddhist tradition, in one case to the extent of forming an entire Shin Buddhist psychotherapeutic movement called Naikan therapy. The Buddhist Japanese have innovated on Western developments in sociology and psychology as much as they have, more famously, in technology.

For all its fruits, such an emphasis on Buddhism's ethical and meditative elements raises the question whether, really, Buddhism needs to continue to exist at all. We have seen the same problem with demythologized Christianity. If in the end Buddhism and Christianity can be reduced to ethical systems identical to those of social democracy and their spiritual elements pared down to mindfulness meditation with no metaphysical strings attached, then we should not be surprised to see adherence to them diminish. In the West this is obviously what is happening to liberal Christianity, which appears to be on the verge of extinction. Yet it is also happening with Buddhism in Japan, where adherence nowadays means little more than paying very expensive funeral fees to whatever sect one's family happens to belong to when someone dies. Many Japanese do not know what school of Buddhism they belong to until they have to organize a funeral. The younger Japanese are increasingly moving away even from this minimal participation, as new all-in-one funeral venues offer a similar service to temples at a fraction of the price. Buddhism seems to have little future as a funeral provider or advocate of liberal social mores. The Japanese people have little need of Buddhism to answer their social needs, let alone their ethical or spiritual questions. There are more people in Japan practicing yoga and Flamenco than Zen meditation.

Shin Buddhist priest John Paraskevopoulos is wary of this tendency to reduce Buddhism to a system of ethics and meditation. He argues in his book *Call of the Infinite*[8] that Shinran's thought undercuts any such analysis. Shinran is utterly dismissive of human ethical efforts for the same reason he eschews meditation. This often surprises Westerners, who assume that all Buddhists meditate. Yet we can see in Shinran's controversial approach to the *nembutsu* that Shin Buddhism is not about meditation at all.

Shinran so firmly resisted the salvific power of meditation that he disavowed even the recitation of the *nembutsu* as a saving act. His master Hōnen had taught that self-power, *jiriki*, could not effect Birth in the Pure Land. One had to rely on the other-power (*tariki*) of saying the *nembutsu*, taking

8   John Paraskevopoulos, *Call of the Infinite* (Brooklyn, NY: Angelico Press, 2017).

refuge in the inconceivable working of Amida's Name. Repeating the Name should become one's sole practice. But, argued Shinran, does the recitation of the *nembutsu* not then become just another act of self-power? His solution to this problem was the doctrine of "Once-Saying." One could not be "saved" by repeating the Name meditatively. All that was needed was to say it once with absolute *shinjin*, deep trust in the other-power of Amida Buddha, and that would suffice. One would not necessarily know when that efficacious Once Saying had occurred, and so continue to say it. In outward form, then, there was nothing to distinguish the practice of the *nembutsu* as between Hōnen's followers and Shinran's new True Pure Land daughter sect. Philosophically speaking, though, Shinran's stress on other-power was unprecedented. Hōnen had understood the saying of the *nembutsu* as the practitioner's own work, but Shinran denied this to the point of calling the *nembutsu* a "non-practice." Rather, Shinran taught, when it is said with *shinjin*, the *nembutsu* is Amida's Name speaking itself *through* sentient beings. Ironically, it is the very *otherness* of Amida's power that makes Shinran's *nembutsu* the pinnacle of the Mahāyāna teaching of no-self. It is by losing one's self that one truly finds it, so that one's own work is none other than the Buddha's. Only by our ceasing to work does Amida's Vow work within us to effect salvation, which is none other than truly seeing reality as what it is: the outworking of the Vow. Like Dionysius's theurgic model of reality, we have here a ritual act that is properly understood as a participation in the salvifically-oriented goodness in which reality subsists, and that is simultaneously the consummation of human existence.

Nor should Shinran's *nembutsu* be seen, any more than theurgy, as an individualistic act of mystical union. For while one may seem to be saying the *nembutsu* alone, metaphysically speaking, it is the Buddha, which is to say the infinite realm of reality, that speaks through the *nembutsu*. When you stop saying the *nembutsu* and, as it were, the *nembutsu* speaks through you, the Buddha's "mind of great love and compassion" (*daiji-daihi shin*) enables one freely to benefit all other sentient beings. Your voice becomes one with what Shinran calls the "Music of Purity" which reverberates from the Pure Land:

> The delicate, wondrous sounds of jewel-trees in the jewel-forests
> Are a naturally pure and harmonious music,
> Unexcelled in subtlety and elegance,
> So take refuge in Amida, the Music of Purity.
>
> (Shinran, *Hymn of the Pure Land*, 39)

Shinran's claims are metaphysical rather than meditative or moralistic. Shin Buddhism is grounded not in the meditative practice of self-power, but, like Dionysian theurgy, in participation in reality. That reality, Paraskevopoulos insists, is subject to metaphysical claims. When Shinran says that Amida Buddha's infinite light and wisdom permeates all things, when he uses metaphors such as the "ocean of compassion" and writes of the glory of the Pure Land, when he speaks of a Vow which unfolds in "Music of Purity" and speaks through all sentient beings, he is saying that all this is true, good, and beautiful. Paraskevopoulos cites the Buddha himself telling his disciple Ananda that "communion with the beautiful . . . is the whole of the holy life."[9] Dionysius would surely have concurred.

Shinran's participatory metaphysics differs from Dionysius's in that the *nembutsu* is the saying of a word rather than the offering of a material thing. In this a difference is exposed between Christianity on the one hand and Shin Buddhism and Iamblichean theurgy on the other: in Christian thought, the Incarnation happened historically in the Lord Jesus Christ and is extended in history through the physical bodies of Church and Sacrament; whereas for Iamblichean theurgists one might say that everything — as an incarnation of one divine soul — bears sacramental significance. Shin Buddhism is perhaps more readily analogous to the latter sense.

This is not to say that Dionysius rejects the divine presence in all things: far from it, he understands all things as expressions of the divine theophany, with Christ as their culmination. And so, Christians might see the *nembutsu* as participating in that theophany, without compromising on our insistence that Christ and the sacraments he has ordained remain its normative and ultimate means of fulfilment. Without presuming to speak for Shin Buddhists, I submit that they too may recognize a far closer kinship to Christianity than the dualistic metaphysics for which we are sometime impugned, and may even see our religion as an outworking of Amida's Vow, even if they reject the specificity of the Incarnation in Christ, his sacraments, and the Church he established to perpetuate them.

Despite our considerable and irreconcilable differences, there is enough conceptual overlap in our ways of seeing reality as the salvific, self-emptying unfolding of goodness in truth and beauty to help us articulate a common resistance to the disenchanted realm of modernity. At present, the masters of that realm mine our spiritual traditions, Christian and Buddhist, for

---

9 Paraskevopoulos, 75.

elements they find useful. They demolish the metaphysical struts that held the cave mouth open and try to replace them with the scaffolding of disenchanted materialism, whether of the Marxist or capitalist brand. In the former case, they try to extract tales of conflict and rebellion to foster new and perpetual revolutions; in the latter, ethical systems and meditative methods, "lifestyle choices" that will help workers and consumers cope with and perpetuate the profitable status quo. They will take Christian "values" or Buddhist "mindfulness," but do not see that without God or Buddha neither can stand.

Much of my pastoral work, whether among non-Christians or lifelong believers, starts with dispelling the notion that Christianity is a moral system. This is particularly difficult work for a chaplain in historic church establishments, such as schools, hospitals, and universities, which have recently become more or less secular. Such institutions are cautious of appearing partisan and do not want non-Christians, who are most likely the majority of their clients, to feel excluded by their ethos; yet they are either bound by their statutes, or simply historically-minded enough, to pay some homage to the intentions of their founders. This usually emerges in a commitment, hidden somewhere in a mission statement on a subpage of their website, to "Christian values" along with a hasty disclaimer that all are welcome, regardless of their religion.

It is hard to tell the leaders of such institutions that "Christian values" do not exist. Any values extracted from the Christian religion are no longer Christian. Christianity is not a value system. The import of Christ in the Christian mythos is not that he was a great moral teacher who gave us a code to follow, or even an example to copy. What makes Christianity Christian is the recognition that Christ is God Incarnate. This is a theological and metaphysical claim, and simultaneously a soteriological one. Christ saves, not because of his teachings, but because of who and what he is. We are saved not by copying him, not by following any rules, but by his free gift of himself. This gift outworks itself in the Sacrament of the Eucharist, for which Baptism is a prerequisite. To put it Platonically, we are made good by our participation in God; and theurgically our participation in God is effected by God himself, who draws us into his divine work of the Crucifixion and Resurrection by the gift of himself in the matter of bread and wine. Outside this economy of salvation, it is not just that we cannot properly understand God, or that we cannot act morally. Rather, outside it, there is no truth, goodness, or beauty. The Eucharist does not show us reality: it is Reality. It does not show us how to be good: it is the Good, working through us. It is not a sign accessible to voyeurs, but an act that has to be experienced as "truth beyond wisdom."[10] No "values" can be discerned from it, because the true value of the Good cannot be discerned and cannot be emulated: it can only be participated. Christianity is a way of salvation, not an ethical system.

Shin Buddhism has historically not seen itself as an ethical system either. According to Shinran, Amida's other-power expressed in the Vow is the sole true reality, inconceivable in its goodness:

> The directing of virtue embodied in Namu-Amida-butsu
>   (the *nembutsu*)
> Is, in its benevolent working, vast and inconceivable.
>   (Shinran, Hymns of the Dharma Ages, 51)

Amida's goodness is so absolute that it renders any merely human ethical efforts null and void. Shinran insisting that we *bonbu*, foolish creatures afflicted by "blind passions," can achieve no good whatsoever by our own merit. We are not even in the position to judge between good and evil. "To abandon the mind of self-power," he wrote, is "to abandon the conviction that one is good . . . and further, to abandon the judging of people as good and bad." He went so far as to say that even the recitation of the *nembutsu* should not be understood as a "good" act. Rather, it brings us into the mind of compassion, which alone is good and enables goodness. That goodness does not emerge, directly, in the elimination of material poverty and impediments, but in the compassionate gift of bringing fellow sentient beings to awareness of their oneness with the true and lasting reality of the Vow, whatever their material circumstances.

Are we left then with two irreducible alternative realities, the reality of the Eucharist versus the reality of Amida's Vow? It might seem so from a Shin perspective as much as a Christian one. One can take refuge in the reality of the Vow, writes Shinran, only if one avoids the worship of gods:

> The Nirvana Sutra states: If one has taken refuge in the Buddha,
> one must not further take refuge in various gods.[11]

This should no longer present Christian readers with any problem. As we have seen, Dionysius's God is no god, and has more in common with the Nameless Name of Amida Buddha than many contemporary Buddhists might like to allow. Neither Dionysius's God nor Shinran's Amida Buddha

---

10 Epistle 7.3.
11 Kyōgyōshinshō 6 – 2.82.

is defined primarily in terms of being, but of goodness. To live truly is not to emulate that goodness as something external but to participate in it and realize one's latent oneness with it and all other things.

Does the doctrine of creation get in the way of this irenic view? We have discussed the problems it raises in relation to the divine will and the disparity between God and creation. For Dionysius however this is a secondary concern. According to his teaching there is being only because God is primarily good, and the purpose of being is its own salvation, namely its return to the Good in which it always and already inheres. Dionysius's drunken God is utterly spontaneous and yet acts always in accord with his good nature. This brings him closer to Shinran, who in his *Notes of Essentials of Faith Alone*[12] explicitly, but more cautiously, refers to the working of Amida's Vow as the "good." God's creative spontaneity finds an analogue in Shinran's teaching of *jinen honi*, the "dharmic state of nature." The word for nature, *jinen*, usually read as *shizen* in modern Japanese, is made up of two ideographs which Shinran explains as meaning "self" and "being made so." In other words, "nature" is things as they are in and of themselves. *Honi*, or "dharmicness," means that this nature of things is effected through the "dharma," which means law or teaching. Shinran understands the dharma as Amida's salvific Vow. So, the nature of things (*jinen/shizen*) is inseparable from their dharmic ordering towards salvation in the Vow (*honi*). Amida's Vow is to rescue sentient beings from their otherwise inevitable suffering in this samsaric realm of change, decay, and death; yet salvation is woven into reality and the *nembutsu* is the means by which we recognize this truth and participate in it. There is a marked ontological difference between Dionysius and Shinran here, in that for Dionysius, God is unambiguously the source and origin of existence as well as its redeemer, whereas for Shinran things have arisen as they are without a creator. To be born in this world is, for Buddhists, the result of negative karmic ties to past lives, which would make for an interesting comparison with certain pagan Platonists, but for the Dionysius this cannot be the case: both as a Christian and as an heir to Proclus he sees creation as fundamentally good, however corrupt it may have become. Even so, the fact that this kind of inter-traditional discussion is even possible shows that Christians and Buddhists are engaged in a common endeavor to pursue the truth about reality, and can frame that endeavor in mutually intelligible terms of a universe metaphysically ordered towards salvation.

The *nembutsu* links the naturalness and spontaneity of *jinen*, things simply being what they are, with *shinjin* and *tariki*, other-power. The attempt to

---

12 Shinran, *The Collected Works of Shinran*, 453.

exercise *jiriki*, self-power, only gets in the way. Any attempt to define good and evil by our own calculation will lead only to error. It is only by utter trust, *shinjin*, in the other-power of Amida's salvific Vow that things can be seen as they truly are, for thereby the unreality of so much that we consider reality is exposed to our view. The *nembutsu* is the direct opposite of calculation, to the extent that the *Tannishō* describes it as *higyō-hizen*, "not-action, not-good" (that is, not *our* good but that of Amida).[13] It is only after all such calculation is abandoned (Shinran writes in a surprisingly Platonic turn of phrase) that our karmic ties to the impure land are transformed into the good.[14]

The *nembutsu*, properly understood as Amida's speaking his own name through the practitioner possessed of *shinjin*, is the non-calculative means by which sentient beings can "see" and so share in the spontaneous naturalness of things as they really are. Compare this with the theurgy of the Eucharist, an action carried out by Christ through the community of believers in a way that lifts them beyond intellection into the creative self-emptying of God. The *nembutsu* is no more a mere recollection of Amida's Vow than the Eucharist is a mere memorial of Christ's New Covenant by his sacrifice on the Cross. Rather, the *nembutsu* is the Vow making itself known, analogous to how Dionysius's theurgic Eucharist is the enacting of divine goodness. In neither case does evil and suffering emerge from the work of God or the Vow of Amida; rather, the evil we perceive in the world is provisional and ultimately unreal, a lack of true reality rather than an instantiation of it. Both the Vow of Amida and the New Covenant of Christ reveal a fundamental goodness from which all that is truly real flows, from which all derives true meaning, and towards which all is oriented.

Theurgy and the *nembutsu* are analogous means by which ritual action unites sentient beings with transcendent goodness beyond name and comprehension. Together, both speak of an enchanted world the meaning of which is inexpressible through anything other than a love beyond words. There are differences, to be sure, and there is a greater gap in Shinran's thought between the metaphysical origins of things and their salvific goal than there is in Dionysius's. Even so, with their analogous senses of participation in a transcendent, salvific goodness that bestows both the fullness of life and intelligibility despite coming from radically different philosophical and spiritual traditions, Dionysius and Shinran are in far greater agreement with one another than with the Western materialist philosophies and the

---

13 Shinran, 665.

14 *Notes on Essentials of Faith Alone* 1, in Shinran, 453.

value-based, emulative ethical systems that emerge from them. Both Amida's Vow and Christ's sacrifice are expressed in terms of a will to save. However, that will is identical, respectively, to the *nature* of Amida or to God as good. Goodness is not imposed by any will, whether of man or god. It is not discerned from afar and emulated by the power of human wills. Rather, it is imbibed by participation in the transcendent love that eternally empties itself for the sake of beings.

The truly liberating message in both Dionysian Christianity and Shin Buddhism is that we become good, and start to do good, not by exhausting, frenetic acts of will, not by emulating a revolutionary Jesus or activist Shinran, but by letting the Good beyond Being work in and through us. As Shinran says, this is the easiest way, but also the hardest: again, a bit like getting the camel through the eye of the needle. If we can achieve this — or rather, if we can allow this to be achieved in us — then finally we will find that what we want and what we do are perfectly aligned in spontaneous, natural, graced freedom.

As Westerners enter the Agora and see the empty plinths of Islam, Taoism, or Buddhism, we need also to look within and rediscover the self-emptying One at the heart of reality whom our own Christian tradition proclaims. We need to re-establish the lost way that grants us communion with the wider world and with our common origin and end, the Alpha and Omega of all things, the self-giving One who has revealed himself in the person of Jesus Christ. The West will rediscover its identity and its tradition only in him, but will rediscover him only by walking the road we used to share with the East. We will not find him in isolation — so bitterly divided is our own house. But together with Jews, Muslims, Buddhists, and surely others besides, we can uproot the overgrowth, carve out the old path, and make straight the way to the Good.

CONCLUSION

PERHAPS LIKE YOU, I HAVE BEEN SPENDING TIME in enforced isolation, seeing much more of my immediate family and catching up with old friends online. I hear of their fears for their own friends, relatives, spouses, those who are vulnerable to the Coronavirus, those who are dying or have died alone because of it, those who are risking getting infected themselves to work in the wards and so putting their own lives on the line. This has led me to realize how much time until now I have spent in unreality, how much time I have spent insulated by my work, my busyness, my media consumption, from the pleasure and the pain, the little joys and overwhelming sadness, the risk and reward of real life. The kind of real life that the majority of the world experiences all the time, but to which the busy life of the affluent inoculates us. The irony is that, in a way, I was more quarantined before the isolation: quarantined by the relentless, driving unreality of modern life.

I should probably point out that by "reality" I mean something quite different from the common-sense use of the word in the West. I don't primarily mean the things we can touch and smell and see and weigh and measure. These things can and do and will change and pass. The world, even the universe, will one day come to an end. The majority of its people, who are poor and face death every day, know this far better than those of us with access to the technologies and medicines that can protect and prolong our lives. It takes a time of trial like this to make us realize that however great our technical skill, we are not in fact masters of the universe, not even of the world; and worse, that our technological prowess is at least as much the cause of all this death and devastation as their remedy, as much the poison as the cure. It is through rapidity of transport by air and sea that the virus could spread so rapidly; through our desire to create even greater wealth that we were slow in halting its spread. As people die in ever vaster numbers, and even we and those we love come under threat, the seas and sky recover from the damage we have done. And so, we are brought face-to-face with a truth that is not relative, is not arbitrary, is not something we have made up or can change: death is real, and we have played a part in a culture that promotes it.

But this is precisely why the things we consider real are not in the end the most real after all. The reality of existence is limited because all things change and die. What would be more real, in fact what would constitute true reality, would only be that which cannot change and cannot die — realities that humans do not invent but discern in hidden places; truer, permanent realities that underlie the passing realm we mistakenly think is real because it is all we can touch and see. Proportion, harmony, law: these are real, because they cannot change and die. They are not just "in the eye of the beholder." They are absolutely true, whatever we think of them. In the harmony of their order they constitute an absolute beauty that does not need us to recognize it. And through participating in this harmony rather than seeking to control and overthrow it, to impose our human-made "map" onto what we think reality should be, we can find an absolute goodness: absolute because it is not just for us, nor only for the greatest number or the most powerful, but for everything that is — the environment, animals, and all the natural order of which we are only one part.

The great philosophies of the entire world have all recognized the impermanence of the limited sphere by which moderns designate "reality." The ancient thinkers of Greece, Persia, India, Africa, Arabia, and China all understood that this passing world could not be what is most real. Christians were not unique in this regard. Many in the West assume that the new way of thinking is the norm, that people have always just assumed that this world is reality, and any ideas about a reality beyond it are only matters of individual, maybe even idle, speculation. This is wrong, an historically falsifiable assertion. Even so, with exactly the same pride and superiority with which we once forced Christianity on other parts of the world by war and empire, we now force our modern secular way of thinking on the world by commerce and technology; or we enforce postmodern relativism by the soft power of educational establishments, charitable organizations, protest groups, and churches. In our arrogance we fail to see that this way of thinking has only ever been a minority way of seeing the world. And worse, we try to force our map of reality. Sometimes literally, drawing up boundaries that still cause conflict between nations to this day; sometimes metaphorically, creating the weapons and means or the social opprobrium to impose our will on one another.

At the empirical level the Coronavirus is a disease that needs treatment, and Western medicine certainly seems the surest way to stop it. Yet it is also a mask for an ideological virus of modern Western thought, which has spread throughout the world. By the end of the nineteenth century, we in the West thought we could redefine reality and do a better job. We fell for the myth of progress, blindly believing that our mastery of the world would lead to prosperity and peace for all. At the beginning of the next century, that technology gave us the means for the unprecedented devastation of the First World War and the ideological backing for both Nazism and Communism. A hundred years later, following upon a century of greater death by human technology than ever before, we again risk destroying the world and one another. Capitalist democracy is arguably the least bad political option for the world, since it does ascribe value to the material realm, encourages personal responsibility for the use of goods, and commits people as owners of land and homes to a particular place and community rather than delegating agency and responsibility to such a vast, impersonal, and ultimately unaccountable body as the nation state. The considerable trouble with this rosy picture is that the majority of people cannot afford land and homes, and are increasingly forced by international market dynamics to relocate not only to other cities but even other continents just to make enough money to survive. The Western ideology of capitalism, sundered from any concern for the reflection of the transcendent good in the familial and parochial communities of old, has in this way contributed to the spread of the virus. Meanwhile, the equally Western ideology of Communism exported into China seems to have led to the silencing of voices that could have warned us of the virus early on. The Western ideology of utilitarianism that drives both these political systems encourages us to think the world has no real goodness in itself but is there to be used for what is good for us humans. The Western ideology of postmodernism, strange hybrid of Marxist and individual-ist concerns that it is, categorizes us into identity groups and sets them against each another in a struggle for power and dominion. It encourages us to see all fathers as fundamentally abusive or absent, all colonists as fundamentally exploitative, all men as fundamentally rapists, all employers as fundamentally slave owners, all white people as fundamentally racists. The West has reached a peak of skepticism and self-hatred unparalleled in its history. Cui bono? One might well ask who exactly benefits from the promotion of the fissiparous ideologies of race and gender criticism. One way to address the question might be to look at which foreign powers are investing heavily in American and European universities. One way or another, the West seems hoisted upon a petard of its own rather recent